Employment and Work Relations in Context Series

Series Editors

Tony Elger and Peter Fairbrother

Centre for Comparative Labour Studies

Department of Sociology

University of Warwick

The aim of the *Employment and Work Relations in Context Series* is to address questions relating to the evolving patterns and politics of work, employment, management and industrial relations. There is a concern to trace out the ways in which wider policy-making, especially by national governments and transnational corporations, impinges upon specific workplaces, occupations, labour markets, localities and regions. This invites attention to developments at an international level, tracing out patterns of globalization, state policy and practice in this context, and the impact of these processes on labour. A particular feature of the series is the consideration of forms of worker and citizen organization and mobilization in these circumstances. Thus the studies address major analytical and policy issues through case study and comparative research.

State Regulation and the Politics of Public Service

The Case of the Water Industry

Graham Taylor

MANSELL

London and New York

First published 1999 by
Mansell Publishing Limited, *A Cassell imprint*
Wellington House, 125 Strand, London WC2R 0BB
370 Lexington Avenue, New York, NY 10017-6550

British Library Cataloguing-in-Publication Data
A catalogue record for this book is available from the British Library.

ISBN 0–7201–2312–7

Library of Congress Cataloging-in-Publication Data
Taylor, Graham (Graham John)
State regulation and the politics of public service : the case of the water industry / Graham Taylor.
p. cm. — (Employment and work relations in context)
Includes bibliographical references and index.
ISBN 0-7201-2312-7
1. Water utilities—Government policy—Great Britain. I. Title.
II. Series.
HD4465.G7T39 1998
363.6'1'0941—DC21 97-33504
CIP

Typeset by York House Typographic, London
Printed and bound by The Cromwell Press Ltd., Trowbridge, Wiltshire

Contents

PREFACE

In recent years there has been an increasing interest in the way in which the privatization and restructuring of public services have impacted on the delivery of services and the conditions of employment for workers within public service organizations. There have been fundamental changes in the organization and delivery of public services associated with the commercialization and privatization policies of the 1980s and 1990s. But what is public service? How did it develop? Why has its meaning changed over time? Why do industries and services which purport to serve the common interests of the 'public' evoke such unpopularity and opposition on the one hand yet command widespread public support and loyalty on the other? Between 1978 and 1986 I lived this contradiction and asked these questions in my capacity as a waterworker employed by the Yorkshire Water Authority. I worked in the organization for seven years in a post which was primarily concerned with dealing with consumer complaints and problems. For seven years I lived the central problem of public service of how to balance the 'public interest' with the 'particular' interests of individual consumers.

There were also other contradictions which became increasingly apparent during my employment as a waterworker. I felt that I was a public servant committed to the ideals of public service. I was, however, employed by a state-sector organization that was ineffective and conspicuously failing to deliver the services demanded by the public with whom I was in contact on a daily basis. I was also a waged worker and a trade unionist prepared to damage the service provided to the public through industrial action – for example, in 1982 I went on strike for four weeks in an attempt to increase my salary. My colleagues simultaneously espoused the ideal of 'public service' and undermined it by acting in a self-interested and obstructive way which minimized the effectiveness of the organization. Many of my older colleagues reflected back to the halcyon days when water came under the control of Sheffield City Corporation and when the ethic of 'public service' really did underlie the objectives of the water service. For these workers, this municipal utopia had been destroyed by the centralization, rationalization and commercialization of the post-war period.

During the early 1980s the restructuring and commercialization of the water industry was intensified as part of the Thatcherite project of monetarism. The Yorkshire Water Authority was streamlined through the shedding of half the workforce. Cost centres replaced departments and, perhaps most telling of all, consumers were replaced by customers. To me, living through the commercialization and restructuring of the water industry, it became increasingly clear that, while these reforms were being carried out in the name of the 'public' as ratepayers, they diverged markedly from what the 'real' public wanted as consumers of water services. What had been thought of as essential maintenance was suddenly redefined as an expensive luxury. Presentation increasingly became more important than substance. Accountants replaced engineers. Contractors replaced direct labour. The organization was moving inexorably towards privatization. The movement was resisted by consumers, workers and managers – just about everyone directly connected with the industry. Before the water industry entered this final stage of transformation I left the industry in order to enter higher education, but the concerns and contradictions experienced during my time as a waterworker have been carried forward into my subsequent academic experience and research.

Thus, a number of biographical factors intensified my increasing concern with exploring the apparent contradictions of public service. Probably of most importance was my employment as a state worker. However, this was galvanized by the events of 1984/5 when, as a result of the miners' strike, the region in which I lived fast appeared transformed into a 'police state'. Under the 'rule of law' police officers terrorized the community by setting up roadblocks, undermining the industrial action of the NUM and physically abusing mineworkers, their families and anyone with the nerve to defend mining communities against the ravages of monetarism. I experienced the state as brutal, violent and far from impartial. But I had been a part of the state apparatus and had believed that I was serving the 'common good'. I quickly discovered that this *real* contradiction does not fit easily with the models of the state espoused by many of the disinterested and dispassionate *cognoscenti* that inhabit higher education. To quote Toni Negri, 'it is obvious that with such people we are talking about different things – it is as if we were both talking of the Great Bear, but for them it means a distant constellation of stars, while for us it means the present reality of a ferocious animal' (Negri, 1978/9: p. 116). In this book I approach the problem of the capitalist state and the contradictions of 'public service' as a worker and from the perspective of labour in an attempt to uncover both the ferocity of the state and how the state can overcome this diabolical form in order to appear as the embodiment of the 'common good'. I hope this will highlight the scope for a reinvigorated politics of public service 'in and against' the 'neo-liberal' state.

This book, itself the product of a social process and the identification and exploration of the crises and contradictions outlined above, would not have been possible without the advice, encouragement, assistance and criticism of many people. In this regard I am particularly grateful to Simon Clarke for his excellent supervision of the doctoral thesis from which this book developed, to Tony Elger for his helpful and positive encouragement and advice in regard to the final drafting of this book and among others, to Peter Fairbrother and Theo Nichols. Finally, I am grateful to the many water company managers and trade union officers who kindly gave me their time in order for me to collect the empirical data on which this book is based.

Abbreviations

AScW	Association of Scientific Workers
CAWC	Central Advisory Water Committee
CCC	Consumer Consultative Committee
CSC	Customer Service Committee
DoE	Department of the Environment
DWI	Drinking Water Inspectorate
EFLs	External Finance Limits
FoE	Friends of the Earth
FUMPO	Federation of Unions of Managerial and Professional Officers
GMBATU	General, Municipal, Boilermakers' and Allied Trades Union
GWGU	Gasworkers and General Workers Union
HRM	Human Resource Management
HSE	Health and Safety Executive
ILP	Independent Labour Party
KWS	Keynesian Welfare State
LCC	London County Council
MBW	Metropolitan Board of Works
MEA	Municipal Employees Association
MHLG	Ministry for Housing and Local Government
MMC	Monopoly and Mergers Commission
MWWD	Municipal Waste Water Directive
NALGO	National and Local Government Officers' Association
NCC	National Consumer Council
NRA	National Rivers Authority
NUM	National Union of Mineworkers

NUPE	National Union of Public Employees
NVQ	National Vocational Qualification
NWC	National Water Council
OCC	Organic Composition of Capital
OFWAT	Office of Water Services
PSBR	Public Sector Borrowing Requirement
RPI	Retail Price Index
RWA	Regional Water Authority
SDF	Social Democratic Federation
SWC	Statutory Water Company
TQM	Total Quality Management
TRPF	Tendency for the Rate of Profit to Fall
VEU	Vestry Employees' Union
WRB	Water Resources Board
WSPLCs	Water Supply PLCs

1 The Problem of Public Service

The privatization and restructuring of state industries and agencies in recent years has resulted in the notion of 'public service', as it has been understood throughout most of the present century, entering a sustained if not irreversible crisis. The last two decades have seen a fundamental transformation of the way in which public services are organized and delivered. The transformation has been part of a wider process of social change associated with the crisis of social democracy and Keynesian state regulation and the restructuring of state and society according to the 'neo-liberal' principles of the New Right. Traditional models of public service have been increasingly challenged by 'neo-liberal' forms of state regulation and service management which are premised on the commercialization of social relations both within service organizations and between public services and their consumers.

Traditional models of public service were premised on the idea that essential public services should be provided by the state, as only the state could be trusted to deliver services in an impartial way that contributed to the 'common good'. The limited ability of the state to represent the 'common good', however, is evident from the examples of conflict, crisis and contradiction which mark the historical development of public service. I want to begin my analysis by outlining a series of alternative approaches which have been developed in an attempt to explore the development and crisis of the modern state and which can be used to explore the development of and crisis in state-administered public services. The debate over the form and function of the modern state is extremely complex, and so, rather than present a comprehensive résumé of this debate, I have focused on approaches which allow a degree of analytical leverage to be applied to the analysis of the forms of state regulation and administration associated with public service. The resulting paradigms provide both a conceptual map of the terrain covered by this book and a comparative framework in which to assess the insights and limitations provided by these diverse approaches. Later I will develop the argument that each of these approaches is able to provide a valuable, although partial and mystified, perspective on the development and crisis of public service which can be combined to provide a fuller and richer analysis.

Pluralist Perspectives on Public Service

According to the pluralist model of the state the 'common good' is something that emerges from the struggles and competition between diverse interest groups, political parties and state actors. The pluralist paradigm is important as it has been developed as a principal locus of support for the existence of public service as an ideology and practice. Throughout the history of the welfare state, progressive liberals and social democrats have used the argument that the state is a neutral embodiment of the 'common good' to support the regulation, municipalization and nationalization of public services. Indeed, the Fabian Socialism that has dominated the discourse of public service in Britain is premised firmly on a pluralist perspective of the modern state. However, as the welfare state has developed, and as it has become more apparent that the state does not unproblematically represent the 'public good', the focus of the pluralist perspective has shifted towards a concern to minimize the influence of powerful groups and interests on the development and execution of state policy. The pluralist perspective, and its manifestation in state ideologies such as Fabian Socialism, provide therefore a useful starting point for an analysis of the development and crisis of public service.

The early development of both pluralism and Fabianism were marked by a concern to demonstrate that no one interest or party is able to dominate the policy-making process within state institutions (see Dahl, 1956, 1961 for a statement of 'classical pluralism' and Chapter 2 below for discussion of the early Fabian position). According to this 'classical' pluralist position the state is constituted by the existence of countervailing powers and there is a constant flux in the dominant coalition of interests within the state apparatus and between national, regional and local levels of government (Galbraith, 1953). The growth in public service administration by governmental organizations and the corresponding growth in state employment and state expenditure would thus be presented as a direct result of democracy. The state provides a device through which the democratic demands of citizens for improved public services could be directly translated into policy programmes (Rose, 1984; Rose *et al.* 1985). Indeed, for other pluralists, the state developed public services as part of a positive strategy for the development of policies which reflected the 'public interest' and which fostered social consensus (Birch, 1964). This was the position of the early Fabians such as George Bernard Shaw and Sidney and Beatrice Webb who, as I will show in Chapter 2, directly equated the development of democratically established public services with the development of socialism.

As the state has developed there has been an increasing recognition among pluralists that the pursuit of the 'common interest' could be deflected by the self-seeking behaviour of important pressure groups both within and outside the state apparatus (Halperin, 1974). Indeed, this was the position taken by Fabian socialists such as Richard Crossman and Anthony Crosland who, as I will show in Chapter 3, analysed the crisis and contradictions of 'public service' in the immediate post-war period in terms of the unrepresentative and self-seeking behaviour of organized interest groups; Crossman highlighting business and state managers while Crosland focused on the labour movement. For the Fabians, the democratic accountability of the state was always constrained by the necessary domination of public service provision and regulation by 'experts'. In this sense there is an important parallel between Fabian Socialism and Weberian sociology. Writers within the Weberian tradition have been concerned with the way in which the development of a complex administrative apparatus in response to democratic pressure results in hierarchical forms of state bureaucracy dominated by 'instrumental' rationality (Weber, 1968). An important counter-measure against bureaucratic domination is the vision and leadership provided by political élites (Schumpeter, 1944). Indeed, political élites may exclude certain interest groups in order to construct the 'public interest' through the corporate concertation of the dominant political and economic élites in society. More recently, pluralist writers have been concerned with the important role of administrative élites in determining the inclusion or exclusion of interest group agendas (Simon, 1957), and this has led many Weberian commentators to highlight the way in which public services are necessarily dominated by corporate and bureaucratic élites which mediate and deflect the pressures of representative democracy (see Saunders, 1984, 1985a, for a discussion of this approach in the context of the UK water industry).

The pluralist perspective offers a number of important insights into the development and form of public services. Clearly, on a political level public services have been used to secure public consent and have become manifest in forms which perpetuate the interests of powerful élite groups. The approach demonstrates, therefore, the gap between the rhetoric and reality of public service and the limits to the democratic determination and control of public services in the 'public interest'. The pluralist perspective has also explored a series of crisis tendencies which allow an insight into the crisis and restructuring of public services in recent years. A rather different approach is taken by 'conservative' and more 'radical' pluralist writers. Among the former, an important approach is to focus on 'government over-load'. Conservatives have argued that the growth in state services has undermined the entrepreneurial orientation of individuals thereby contributing to economic decline (Bell, 1976), and that the increasing complexity of social problems and interest group politics has made modern societies increasingly 'ungovernable' (Crozier *et al.*, 1975; Douglas, 1976; King, 1975). According to this 'conservative' approach the resolution of the crisis is through political leaders reducing the expectations of the electorate. While the political programmes of both the Conservative and Labour parties in recent decades may be seen to present evidence of a lowering of political expectations in regard to the delivery of public services, these approaches fail to consider either the contradictions underlying the democratic control and provision of public services or the dynamics which resulted in public expectations needing to be reduced in the first place.

The more left-leaning pluralists have analysed the crisis of the state in terms of the over-centralized and over-bureaucratized nature of the state and a lack of democratic participation by ordinary citizens in the development of state policy (Dahl, 1982, 1985). A particular problem that is highlighted is the way in which the corporatist structures of the Keynesian Welfare State (KWS) excluded unorganized interests and allowed 'particular' groups such as trade unions to equate their own interests with the 'public interest', thereby undermining the 'civil consciousness' on which successful liberal democracies depend. These pluralist analyses argue that the crisis of public service can be addressed through a combination of market socialism, industrial democracy, decentralization and new forms of social ownership (Hodgson, 1984; Nove, 1983). This has been the approach of the Fabian left in the UK to the contemporary crisis of public service (Callaghan *et al.*, 1990; Labour Party, 1989; Pfeffer and Coote, 1991; Smith, 1986). Again, these writers usefully highlight the undemocratic and contradictory nature of public service. However, this approach fails to consider why there is a tension between citizenship rights in the spheres of production and consumption and why the strengthening of consumer rights by the state is necessarily premised on the control and partial demobilization of organized producer groups. The importance of public service workers to the development and crisis of public service has, however, been the concern of writers who develop an essentially pluralist conception of the state to explore the specificity of public service industrial relations.

The industrial relations approach: the decline of a 'model employer'?

The pluralist model of the state has also been developed by writers interested in industrial relations and the relationship between public service industrial relations and changing forms of public service management and regulation. It was particularly influential in regard to theorists interested in the corporatist arrangements which developed in the post-war period. The development and crisis of public service have been explored by writers with an interest in the way in which the organizational specificity of public sector organizations has facilitated the development of particular ideologies and practices of public service management and trade unionism. As I will show in Chapter 3, for Fabian socialists such as G. D. H. Cole the organizational arrangements of the public sector allowed men and women to realize their intrinsic propensity to 'serve' their fellow human beings. This reflected the ethical basis of British socialism as espoused by writers such as R. H. Tawney and R. M. Titmuss, but, more importantly, it became an important ideological legitimation for the development and expansion of public service. Associated with this was the widely accepted idea that the working and bargaining arrangements associated with public services resulted in the state acting as a 'model employer' (Fredman and Morris, 1989). It is, therefore, the shielding of public services from the pressures of the market which has resulted in a particular form of public service management based on bureaucratic proceduralism, consensual industrial relations strategies and an essentially 'political' orientation marked by a commitment to clients and customers (Pendleton and Winterton, 1993). Similarly, a particular form of public service trade unionism developed, marked by bureaucratic centralism and a similar commitment to clients and consumers. This 'public service' orientation is thus seen as externally generated and maintained by the institutional protection of public services from the market.

The analysis of crisis in these forms of theorizing is usually quite straightforward. A crisis in the 'economy' precipitates a 'political' crisis of the state and the state applies financial pressure on state institutions and agencies. In response to this pressure, public services are restructured through progressively rigorous forms of commercialization and privatization. In their analysis of the commercialization of the Post Office, for example, Batstone *et al.* (1984: 30–2) argued that the strategy of commercialization undertaken by managers in the state sector was determined by external 'political' constraints. Similarly, Ferner (1985, 1987) explored the commercialization of British Railways, and the public sector more generally (Ferner, 1989), through the impact of government imposed 'external finance limits' on public service organizations. This tightening of the regulatory framework and subsequent privatization has resulted in the intensification of labour within public services (O'Connell Davidson, 1993) and the apparent transformation in the role of the state as 'model employer', as the state has become an exemplar of 'flexible' employment practices and adversarial industrial relations (Pollert, 1988: 56). As I will show in Chapter 8, these approaches have been useful in highlighting the way in which institutional changes within public services have impacted on public service managers and workers. Public services have been resubordinated to the rigours of the market either directly through privatization or indirectly through deregulation and commercialization, and the public services have been at the forefront of management attempts to increase the flexibility of labour and to introduce 'unitaristic' HRM strategies (Walsh, 1995).

There are, however, limitations with this type of analysis. The first problem is that the industrial relations approach is unable effectively to theorize the crisis and decomposition of Fabian modes of public service. There is a tendency to see the crisis as emanating from the 'outside' of the public services, which creates a 'fiscal crisis' and which then forces the restructuring of the state and state employment. This ignores the contradictions which emanate from within state institutions. It glosses over the way in which a crisis of the state may be created by the political autonomy of state actors and the contradictions of state employment (Fairbrother, 1989, 1994). The contradictory form of the state restricts its ability to act as 'model' for either capital or labour (Thornley, 1995), and this is likely to be intensified in a context of globalization and the increasing domination of societies by transnational corporations. This is related to the more general point that the industrial relations approach fails to theorize adequately the institutional linkages between the state and the 'political regime' within the workplace (Burawoy, 1986; Hyman, 1989b: 202–23). There is also a neglect of consumption and the extent to which workers as consumers may have been alienated by the centralized and bureaucratic form of public services. Clearly, a fuller analysis of the crisis of public service requires a more developed analysis of the links between the state, the politics of production and the politics of consumption, and a central objective of this book is to synthesize these disparate areas of analysis. The dysfunctions of public service for consumers, however, have been the concern of 'neo-liberal' writers interested in the contradictions underlying the direct administration of services by the state.

The neo-liberal approach: back to the future?

This neo-liberal approach is important, since the public service state initially developed in a period dominated by *laissez-faire* liberalism. Indeed, the limitations and reformulation of classical liberalism provided a major impetus to the growing importance of state provision during the nineteenth century. As I will show in Chapter 4, the concepts and categories of neo-liberal thought have been incorporated into the institutional restructuring of the state following the deregulation and privatization of state industries and services. Neo-liberal writers usefully highlight the contradictions of state administration and employment and the way these can be addressed by subordinating the allocation of goods and services to the market decisions of impersonal consumers. As we shall see, however, the neo-liberals seriously overestimate the extent to which it is possible to 'depoliticize' the provision of goods and services either through the state or the market and thus the possibility of solving the 'problem' of public service.

In Britain, the 'neo-liberal' approach reflects the increasing influence of 'public choice theory' and the 'Austrian School' of economic thought as intellectual paradigms (Dunleavy and O'Leary, 1987: 73–86). These paradigms lead to a particular and distinctive view of the 'public interest'. The most important neo-liberal writers to develop a 'public choice' approach are those drawn from the so-called 'Virginia School' (Buchanan and Tullock, 1962; Niskanen, 1971, 1973; Olson, 1965, 1982). The primary concern of these writers has been to apply micro-economic and mathematical models to the analysis of the state and 'political' behaviour in order to demonstrate the impossibility of the state and its political and administrative personnel behaving in the 'public interest'. The general proposition developed by the public choice approach is that politicians, voters and bureaucrats behave in self-interested ways to maximize their own individual welfare rather than pursuing the welfare of society. While the 'Austrian School' rejects the positivism of the 'Virginia School', writers such as Hayek (1944, 1960) also stress the impossibility of the state representing the 'public interest'. According to Hayek the complexity of modern society means that it is impossible for the state to possess the information which would enable it satisfactorily to regulate either the state or the economy according to the 'public interest' (or indeed determine what the 'public interest' is or should be). The only 'public interest' that exists is constituted by the state maintaining the spontaneity which emerges through the operation of economic and political markets.

The role of the state in neo-liberal theory is thus minimal and negative. The self-seeking behaviour of voters and politicians results in 'Wagner's Law'. This law posits that state expenditure will grow over time as citizens in modern societies progressively demand better standards of existing public services, the extension of existing public services over ever wider spatial areas and qualitatively new forms of public service (Wagner, 1962). This is compounded by the 'institutional entropy' which results from the high 'information costs' required to maintain the means of surveillance that are required to ensure the state functions in an efficient and effective way (Auster and Silver, 1979). Public choice theorists highlight the intrinsic weakness of democratic mechanisms of party competition for maintaining the efficiency of the state, as party leaders constantly raise voter expectations in their quest for votes. Indeed, state bureaucrats have a rational self-seeking motivation to expand their budgets, create waste and over-supply public services. The state is able to obscure inefficiency through its ability to increase state debt, thereby increasing inflation and 'crowding out' more efficient private sector investment (Friedman, 1968, 1982). According to the neo-liberal approach, therefore, the legitimate role of the state is to preserve or to reinstate market mechanisms.

The work of neo-liberal writers is useful in highlighting the way in which the political/administrative involvement of the state in the provision of public services has undermined the economic efficiency of the capitalist economy, and the way in which economic recovery is dependent on the reseparation of the 'political' and 'economic' spheres of society and the depoliticization of public service provision and regulation. The immediate problem with the neo-liberal approach is that focusing on the formal rationality of capitalism allows no consideration of the way in which the substantive irrationality of capitalist social relations contributes to the crises and contradictions of public service. There is also a problem with the neat differentiation that is made by neo-liberals between the 'economic' and 'political' spheres of society. Other commentators who fit into a broadly-defined pluralist tradition have, by contrast, stressed the essentially political nature of markets and a recent tendency towards the increasing alignment of the state and capitalist enterprises in the context of the globalization of production.

The new institutionalism: markets as politics

An important attempt to overcome the problem outlined above, but one which retains an essentially pluralist conception of the state, is provided by writers concerned with the institutional linkages between the state and markets. The so-called 'new institutionalists' highlight the way in which markets deviate from the models of neo-classical economics, which present market relations as comprising the action of self-seeking anonymous actors (Baker, 1984, 1989; Flegstein, 1987; White, 1981). Rather, there is a concern to demonstrate the way markets are made up of 'networks' of action and meaning that are created by the 'political' behaviour of actors within both 'economic' institutions and the state. An important example of this approach is that which has developed the notion of the 'extended state'. The increasing domination of state and society by large transnational corporations has resulted in institutional linkages between corporations and the state which have developed to service the needs of an increasingly globalized economy. There has been a concern to break down the rigid dichotomy between the 'economic' behaviour of firms and other organizations and the 'political' behaviour of state institutions, and to identify the increasing convergence between economic and political modes of organization and the emergence of a unified 'planning system'.

According to this approach, the professionalization of the state is held to have resulted in the development of a 'public service' ethos among state workers which has increasingly reduced the need for the democratic control of state administration. In this context 'knowledge élites' have come to play an increasingly important role in state policy development and implementation (Dunleavy, 1981, 1982), and within corporations, corporate policy is increasingly dominated by a 'technostructure' of expert professionals (Galbraith, 1969). The professionals in both corporations and the state are working in a context of increasing complexity and risk which emanates from the institutional differentiation which is inherent in the intensification of modernity (Giddens, 1990). The response has been an attempt to reduce complexity through the development of internal mechanisms of social and organizational control based on organized systems of power and money (Luhmann, 1979). This has been manifested in corporations through the 'internalization' of market transactions and the development of new institutional forms designed to manage uncertainty or exploit the opportunities of monopoly through a reduction in 'transaction costs' (Williamson, 1975, 1985, 1994). There has also been an attempt to reduce 'information costs' through the development of more sophisticated financial and information control systems which allow systematic policy and managerial judgements to be made on the basis of routinized performance indices. There have also been important changes to frameworks of control within both corporations and the 'extended' state as policy decisions are increasingly determined by 'networks' of decentralized committees pulling together diverse specialisms and sources of information and producing agreed decisions. In this context the 'public interest' is determined at the interface between the commercial imperatives of large corporations and the public service ethos of public and private sector professionals.

This approach suggests a number of key insights into the recent restructuring of public services. Most notably, there has been an apparent convergence between the state and capital across many areas of economic and political life. As I will show in Chapter 4, the privatization of the water industry has been accompanied by the creation of a regulatory agency which is designed to act as 'quasi-markets' in an attempt to depoliticize issues of service provision and delivery. As the above approach demonstrates, this market is politically constructed and operates through the application of political processes. It is therefore difficult to see how the neo-liberal state agencies that accompany privatization can depoliticize public service to any marked degree. These regulatory institutions have, moreover, attempted to reduce the complexity of both the regulation of public services by the state and the provision of public services by private companies, through the use of sophisticated information and financial control systems based on routinized performance indices. This has been encouraged by an ethos of 'customer care' in which 'empowered' professional managers within both state institutions and utility companies have reinterpreted 'public service' in ways which attempt to minimize information and transaction costs.

There are, however, important limitations to this approach. The focus on the institutional level ignores wider patterns of power and inequality and the way in which increasing efficiency involves the exercise of power in order to maximize the production of surplus value (O'Connell Davidson, 1993: 67–99). Moreover, the notion of 'markets as politics' (Flegstein, 1995) conflates state and capital in a way which fails to consider the possibility that the political discretion available to state actors and managers in both the public and private sectors may undermine the accumulation of capital. Furthermore, the approach is ahistorical as it fails to consider adequately either the dynamic behind the present convergence between state and capital or the contradictions behind their implied separation at earlier stages of development. The important institutional changes need to be placed in a wider context which takes account of the dynamics and contradictions of capitalist development. I will now consider what contribution a Marxist approach makes to this project.

Marxism and Public Service

In most Marxist approaches the ability of the state to transcend the narrow 'economic' interests of the capitalist system is clearly transcribed and the 'public services' provided by the state serve, either directly or indirectly, the long-term interests of the capitalist system. Clearly, however, systems of welfare and utility provision have developed which appear to have threatened the long-term stability of the capitalist system. Indeed, the intensity of public service restructuring in recent years would seem to underline the extent to which traditional patterns of utility provision became increasingly dysfunctional for capital accumulation. The response of Marxists to the development and crisis of the public service state has been complicated by fundamental disagreements over the issue of the form and function of the state. This reflects the ambiguous and fragmentary nature of Marx's own writings on the subject. Marx planned but never completed a full exposition of his analysis of the state (Rosdolsky, 1977: 12), and as a result later Marxists have tended to build models of the state premised on Marx's fragmented and inconsistent allusions to the state. The main problem is that the dominant paradigms of state analysis within the Marxist tradition have failed to consider adequately the contradictions inherent in the capitalist state and in the services and utilities administered and regulated by the state.

This is apparent in the so-called 'instrumentalist' approach to the analysis of the state which develops the notion that the state is a straightforward 'instrument' of the capitalist class (Marx and Engels, 1965: 35). In the post-war period this approach has resulted in 'essentialist' and 'economistic' analyses of the capitalist state in which the state is seen as a political superstructure 'determined' by the dynamics of the economic base. The state unproblematically represents the interests of the dominant class and is the central site of class struggle and conflict (Miliband, 1969, 1970). In analyses of the welfare state which develop this paradigm (see for example Gough, 1975, 1979) there is no assessment of the structural limits or contradictions of state policies. While other writers have attempted to explore the impact of welfare spending on the crisis of the state, this has been focused on the 'unproductive' nature of state expenditure (Bullock and Yaffe, 1975) and has not explored the contradictions inherent to the capitalist state form. In other words, writers in the 'instrumentalist' or 'fundamentalist' approach have systematically failed to consider how the state is able to appear as a representative of the 'public interest' and the contradictions underlying the appearance of the state in this form. This is a vital precondition for an effective analysis of public service.

The 'structuralist' strand of Marxist theorizing on the state has been premised on the notion that the state had a degree of 'relative autonomy' from the capitalist class and that this relative autonomy was a vital pre-condition for the state serving the 'average' interests of the capitalist class as a whole. The autonomy of the state is limited by the material dependence of the state on the resources of civil society for its own reproduction (Marx and Engels, 1970: 79–81). In other words, while the 'general interest' pursued by the state can diverge from the interests of particular branches of capital, the activities of the state are likely to serve the totality of capitalist interests in the long run. The notion of the 'relative autonomy' of the state from civil society has been used by later Marxists to argue that this also implies the relative autonomy of the 'political', 'ideological' and 'economic' spheres of society. The work of Antonio Gramsci has been particularly important and influential in developing the argument that at any particular moment both the leading or 'hegemonic' ideas and political ideologies and practices have a degree of autonomy from the 'economic' dynamics of capitalist development. The most developed recent example of this approach is to be found in the work of Nicos Poulantzas (Poulantzas, 1973, 1978), who suggests that the state has its own dynamics and crises and that the analysis of these dynamics and crises requires concepts and categories derived from political science and sociology (see Clarke, 1991a for a critique of Poulantzas). This has allowed theorists influenced by Poulantzas to analyse the breakdown of the welfare state as either a political (Jessop *et al.*, 1988) or an ideological (Hall, 1983, 1988) crisis. Again, the particular form of the state and the relationship between this form and the dynamic of capital accumulation is not explored or developed. In other words, while this approach allows an exploration of the political and ideological specificity of the state and the contradictions underlying the appearance of the state as an agency of the 'common good', these are not related to the crises and contradictions of capitalist development in any systematic way.

An attempt to overcome this problem was provided by the so-called 'capital logic' approach which first emerged in the 1970s and which sought to overcome the weaknesses of the 'instrumentalist' and 'structuralist' analyses of the state through an attempt to 'derive' the logical form of the capitalist state using the materialist categories developed by Marx in *Capital.* The so-called 'state derivation approach' (see Holloway and Picciotto, 1978 or Jessop, 1990: 35–41 for review) attempted to develop a 'form theoretical' analysis of the capitalist state by deriving the form and function of the state from the logic of capital. According to this approach the separation of state and civil society and the appearance of the former as an embodiment of the 'common good' can be logically derived from the generalization of commodity production. The separation of state and civil society is both possible and necessary in a society of generalized commodity production. It is possible because surplus value is extracted from the direct producers on the basis of formally free exchange in the market rather than through extra-economic compulsion. It is necessary because an institution is required that is not immediately subordinate to market forces in order to ensure the reproduction of wider patterns of commodity production and exchange.

In the 'capital logic' approach the state thus acts as an 'ideal collective capitalist' (Altvarter, 1973) and from this form it is possible to derive the main functions of the state. The state provides a stable legal and monetary framework to enable uninterrupted commodity exchange. The state also functions to ensure the reproduction of labour when it is threatened by the market through the introduction of labour legislation or through the direct provision of use-values through the nationalization of basic services (Blanke *et al.*, 1974; Müller and Neusüss, 1978). The state also played an important role in counteracting the crisis tendencies of capital accumulation as manifested in the tendency for the rate of profit to fall (TRPF). The state, therefore, has a central role in the restructuring of capital and the reorganization of the labour process. The capital logic approach has been extremely useful in demonstrating the way in which the state is an essential component of capitalism and the impossibility of the state functioning in a 'class neutral' way. Second, this approach highlights the importance of *money* and the *law* as the abstract forms through which the state attempts to regulate the contradictions of capital accumulation. The 'political' form of the state implies that the state is not immediately subordinate to capital and that this regulation can never be total. The state is, therefore, both determined by the crises and contradictions of capital accumulation and cannot escape these crises and contradictions. Public services are both necessary to the reproduction of labour and also riven by the crisis tendencies of capitalist development.

There have been a number of objections raised against the 'capital logic' approach from within the Marxist tradition. Methodologically, the approach is ahistorical and functionalist and is thus incapable of exploring the historical origins and development of particular state forms (Gerstenberger, 1990, 1992). While the capital logic approach usefully highlights the logical necessity for the development of public services, it is incapable of analysing either comparative or historical variations in the form taken by public services. The lack of historicity also means that this approach is incapable of adequately analysing the crisis tendencies of the state and its administrative forms. As these weaknesses became apparent two routes were taken from the state derivation approach (Bonefeld and Holloway, 1991: 4). On the one hand writers such as Hirsch (1991a) and Jessop (1991) attempted to 'reformulate' state theory in order to trace the historical development of the articulation between different forms of capital accumulation and the state. On the other, theorists such as Holloway and Picciotto (1991) were concerned to break with the functionalism and essentialism of the capital logic approach in order to move away from the notion that capitalism develops according to predetermined objective laws and to highlight the way in which the laws of capitalist development are the forms through which class struggle exists. As I will argue later in this chapter, the latter approach has much to offer as it allows a synthesis between logical and historical analyses and an effective link between structure and agency or struggle in the development of state administration. Before developing this argument I want to show how the work of the regulationists, and more recent strands of post-Marxism and post-structuralism, have contributed to the analysis of public service labour and administration, yet fail satisfactorily to address the relationship between structure and struggle in analyses of the development and crisis of the state and state-administered public services.

The Regulation Approach

Regulation theory developed out of a concern to trace the 'articulation' between the dynamics and crises of capital accumulation and the changing form and function of the state (Aglietta, 1979; Hirsch, 1991a,

1991b; Lipietz, 1982, 1987; Mazier, 1982). The central crisis explored by regulationists is the TRPF, which results from the way in which the level of capital investment in the means of production constantly outstrips levels of consumer demand. This contradiction cannot be resolved by the hidden hand of the market, and the social and economic reproduction of capitalism is thus dependent on a regulatory framework of political and cultural institutions and practices. Capitalism is seen as developing in a series of 'long-waves' in which a particular 'regime of accumulation' is supported and reproduced by a historically specific 'mode of regulation'. In this way a detailed meta-history of capitalist development is produced alongside a detailed typology of a series of politico-cultural regulatory configurations which have supported the capital accumulation process.

In *A Theory of Capitalist Regulation: The US Experience*, Aglietta developed the argument that the central function of the state is to regulate the crises which result from the 'disproportionality' between the capital and consumer goods sectors of the economy (Departments I and II). In the nineteenth century and the twentieth century prior to the crisis of 1929 there was, according to Aglietta (1979: 65–110), an 'extensive' regime of accumulation supported by a 'competitive' mode of regulation in which the principal crisis tendency is the limited consumption power of the mass of the population. In this phase of development the proportionality of Departments I and II was maintained through the stable expansion of capital through imperialism, the expansion of the working day and the cyclical destruction of capital through the cutting of wages and prices and the destruction of productive capacity. The 'competitive' mode of regulation was ruptured by the development of more 'intensive' forms of production based on Fordism and Taylorism. The development of Taylorism and Fordism as methods of mass production destroyed the equilibrium between Departments I and II and resulted in the development of new modes of 'Fordist' regulation appropriate to the new forms of intensive accumulation, and between 1929 and the early 1970s capitalist development was marked by a 'Fordist' regime of accumulation and mode of regulation (Harvey, 1990: 123–40).

The core feature of the Fordist mode of regulation was the way in which Keynesian demand management techniques allowed the rising wages and welfare expectations of the working class to reconcile workers to the intensification of labour associated with Taylorism and

Fordism and provided the market for the rising mass of consumer goods. According to Aglietta, Fordism did not overcome the disproportionality between Departments I and II but transformed the way in which the crisis became manifest. The existence of monopoly capital allowed the depreciation of capital in Department I to be socialized by the state through the expansion of credit. The resulting inflation was the mechanism through which proportionality was maintained but which also provided the long-run crisis tendency of this regime of accumulation. Inflation intensified class struggle, destabilized economic calculations and drove down profits. The response of the state was to expand credit further in the form of welfare and unemployment benefits in order to maintain demand. The expansion of credit was not enough to relieve the over-accumulation of capital in Department I and the result was stagflation. The limits of Fordist accumulation were thus set by the limited ability of capital to increase productivity to absorb the costs of rising consumption norms and capital depreciation. In the 1970s the Fordist regime of accumulation began to break down and capital attempted to develop new accumulation strategies to increase the production and realization of relative surplus value. A principal mechanism of achieving this aim was the recomposition of the state and the development of a neo-Fordist mode of regulation which has encouraged the introduction of new strategies of flexible accumulation in both the public and private sectors.

The regulation approach has been extremely influential in the analysis of the crisis and restructuring of the welfare state. Clearly, the regulation approach could provide a historical model of the development of public service. As I will show in Chapters 2 and 3, the development of the UK water industry was, until the post-war period, grossly ineffective owing to the *ad hoc* and decentralized way in which it had developed. This could be seen as resulting from limited consumer demand and the limited ability of the state to raise the credit for large-scale capital investment projects. The centralization and rationalization of the water industry in the post-war period could then be analysed as part of a Fordist state project to 'plan' the expansion of public services both in response to the rising consumption norms of the working class and in order to use up the expanding product of Department I. In the generalized crisis of Fordism during the 1970s capital developed new 'flexible accumulation' strategies in order to overcome the crises of Fordism (Harvey, 1990: 141–72). In this process, public services such as the water industry could be seen as the key sites of neo-Fordist restructuring which have been subjected to the pressures of restructuring and commercialization in an attempt to increase the production of relative surplus value. To use a recent regulationist conceptualization of the recent restructuring, the Keynesian welfare state could be seen as having been transformed into a 'Schumpeterian workfare state' (Jessop, 1994), and public service bureaucracies into decentralized and flexible networks of autonomous administrative agencies (Murray, 1989; Sanderson, 1992; Stoker, 1989).

It would therefore be possible to analyse the commercialization and restructuring of the water industry over the past two decades as part of a 'post-Fordist' state project to resolve the crisis of Fordism and to establish the norms and institutions necessary for a post-Fordist regime of accumulation. According to both Aglietta (1979) and Hirsch (1991a), post-Fordism involves a fundamental de-statification of society through which the state becomes decreasingly involved the production of collective consumption goods. Indeed, the automation, commodification and privatization of public services is held to play the same role in the development and social consolidation of post-Fordism as motor car production played in the development and consolidation of Fordism. The development of 'post-Fordist' public services by the state could therefore be seen as a central functional component in the emergence of a new long-wave of post-Fordist accumulation and regulation.

The regulation approach provides a range of very important observations on the development, crisis and restructuring of the state. As I will demonstrate, the restructuring of the water industry has been marked by the development of flexible working practices and computerized control systems which have been developed in response to increasingly rigorous forms of state regulation. Furthermore, the attempt to co-ordinate the water industry through centralized bureaucratic planning foundered on the inability of the state to raise the credit required for large capital projects. For a number of reasons, however, it is difficult to maintain the argument that the crisis and restructuring of the water industry is part of a shift from Fordism to post- or neo-Fordism. The first problem is the teleological way in which the activities of the state are presented. In this approach the state is determined by the inexorable laws of capitalist development and there is no assessment of the role of struggle and agency in determining the form of the state. In this sense capitalist development is reduced to a 'process without a subject'

(Bonefeld, 1991: 45–6). This results from a structural functionalist methodology in which class struggle is subordinated to the structural imperatives of a particular regime of accumulation (Clarke, 1991a: 111–12). The state is seen as being directly functional for capital accumulation. If the Fordist regime of regulation was functional for capital why was it so riven with contradictions and why did it eventually break down? The fundamental problem with this approach is that it remains premised on the notion that the state is relatively autonomous from capital and, therefore, able to regulate away the contradictions of capital accumulation. This does not allow an assessment of the way in which the activities of the state are themselves contradictory and what it is about the particular *form* of the state which prevents the state from effectively regulating the capital accumulation process. This has been the focus of a series of post-Marxist writers, although, as I will show below, this approach also suffers from a failure to adequately theorize the relationship between structure and struggle in the development and crisis of the capitalist state.

The Post-Marxist Approach: The Irrationality of Planning?

The post-Marxist route out of the apparent essentialism of orthodox Marxism is to argue that the crises and contradictions of the welfare state have their own logic which is analytically and institutionally separate from the crises and contradictions of the capitalist economy (see Habermas, 1988, O'Connor, 1973, and Offe, 1984 for a more orthodox formulation of this approach). Offe, for example, argues that the welfare state emerged in order to manage the contradiction between the private ownership and regulation of industry and the increasingly socialized nature of production. In order to maintain the mass loyalty of an increasingly socialized working class the state provided administrative welfare services. In order to provide these services successfully the state has to ensure that resources are generated to resource welfare provision through the successful functioning of the capitalist economy. This required that the state managed the crises and contradictions of the capitalist economy which threaten the commodity form of value. In order to maintain capital accumulation the state has thus to maintain the conditions for capital and labour to engage in profitable commodity exchange. The state attempts to do this through what Offe terms 'administrative re-commodification' in the form of public investment and regulation and through the sponsoring of neo-corporatist arrangements for collective bargaining. The contradiction at the heart of this strategy is that the arrangements set up by the state to encourage recommodification actually result in increasing decommodification and the removal of increasing areas of social life to outside the commodity form and the market.

The above contradiction of the welfare state results in three principal crisis tendencies. First, a *fiscal* crisis develops as the level of resources devoted to recommodification grows uncontrollably. The uncontrollable growth of welfare provision and taxation to pay for it creates what Habermas terms a 'motivation crisis' which simultaneously undermines both capital investment and the capitalist work ethic. Second, an *administrative* crisis or a crisis of *rationality* develops as the state fails to deliver the levels of economic growth and welfare projected by administrative programmes and planning. Third, a *legitimation* crisis develops as the actions of the state appear increasingly particularistic and *ad hoc* and thereby undermine the appearance of the state as an agency of the common good. The response of the state is the increasing 'colonization of the life-world' as increasingly intimate areas of social life are subjected to the scientific/technical rationality of the economic and political subsystems which are mediatized by money and power (Habermas, 1987). This results in new forms of resistance by 'new social movements' which emerge in an attempt to create and defend autonomous spheres of freedom and cultural meaning that straddle civil society and the state (Gorz, 1982; Laclau, 1987; Offe, 1985). The crisis tendencies of late capitalism thus result in the decline of class-based politics within the state and labour process as the 'value form' is politicized and politics is increasingly focused on the imposition of and resistance to scientific/technical rationality.

There are several important themes which emerge from this approach which are directly relevant to the development and crisis of public services. As I will show in Chapter 3, the 'administrative recommodification' that was central to state planning did result in administrative paralysis, and the ineffectiveness and apparent irrationality of the state was a central factor in legitimating the neo-liberal attack on the 'Keynesian' water industry. This approach usefully highlights the way in which the state has responded to the crisis through the increasing domination of state and society by legal and monetary forms of domination. The main problem with the approach, however, is that the reification and analytical separation of the economic, political and socio-cultural subsystems of society suggests that crises result from the structural mismatch between the imperatives of different subsystems of society rather than emerging from social struggle and conflict by social and political actors within the mechanisms of the state. The 'fiscal crisis' of the state which is the principal crisis tendency of the modern capitalist state is presented as an 'objective law' which emerges from the contradictions between reified institutional structures. As I will argue below, it is more useful to analyse the fiscal crisis of the state as emerging from the contradictions inherent in the direct regulation of labour by the state and the direct administration of state services through bureaucratic public service organizations. In other words, the crisis of the state did not develop because of 'political' intervention in the 'economy' but because of the ability of labour to avoid and resist commodification within the state labour process. It is important to see money and the law, therefore, not as symbolic media of communication between reified social subsystems but as material social forms of struggle and domination. I will elaborate on this point further below, but first I wish to consider the contribution that the recent post-structuralist approach can make to the analysis of public service and the development and crisis of the state.

The Post-structuralist Approach

The post-structuralist writings of Michel Foucault, Jacques Derrida and Jean Baudrillard have become increasingly influential in recent years. The most immediate feature of all these approaches is the refusal to acknowledge a central or important role for the state in (post)modern societies (Jessop, 1990: 336). Power is not seen as being centralized within the state but is presented as being diffused across localities, contexts and institutions. Power in these micro-political contexts is intimately related to systems of knowledge codified into 'discourses'. There is no single process of history but a plurality of histories or 'narratives' of history. It is not, therefore, possible to trace the historical development of the state, only the genealogy of particular state discourses. The postmodern approach is, therefore, inherently ahistorical and, as I will argue below, is incapable of providing a conjunctural context for the changes in public services which are explored by writers influenced by this approach.

Michel Foucault has argued that the genesis of state 'discourses' can be traced not to the material contradictions of capital accumulation but to the emergence of the human sciences in the eighteenth and nineteenth centuries. Modern sciences created a distinction between reason and unreason and scientific discourse was embedded in institutional practices which attempted to 'normalize' deviant behaviour (Foucault, 1967). The 'genealogy' of state administration is to be found in the need for new forms of power and discipline in order to respond to the problems raised by rapid social and industrial development. Foucault (1977) argued that during the eighteenth century the principal focus of discipline shifted from the public 'spectacle' to 'surveillance' and forms of 'panoptical' discipline through which individuals internalized discipline and thereby increasingly controlled themselves. The important point is that, for Foucault, these developments are not linked to the systematic development of capitalism. Power is not the product of a structure but constitutes reality through discourses of knowledge (Foucault, 1979). Power is not, therefore, simply a negative phenomenon but is positive through the way in which it produces new capacities and activities through what Foucault terms discursive practices and technologies.

The work of Foucault and other post-structuralist writers has been developed in order to explore the crisis and restructuring of public services. First, there has been a focus on the way in which the development of 'quality management' which has accompanied state restructuring has involved increasing the surveillance of workers and managers through the 'electrical panopticon' of new information technology, and on the way in which this has intensified subjective forms of domination and self-control. Second, there has been a focus on the way in which state restructuring has been legitimated through the imposition of a 'discourse' of enterprise on public services through which an entrepreneurial culture has been developed which subordinates public servants to neo-liberal economic rationality while simultaneously empowering them to become 'entrepreneurs of the self' (Du Gay and Salaman, 1992; Keat and Abercrombie, 1991). Within public services these discourses are presented as powerful 'technologies' which have fundamentally transformed the behaviour of individuals within such services even when these discourses have challenged deeply embedded organizational value systems premised on traditional notions of public service (Hoggett, 1996). Third, these developments have been facilitated by the increasingly symbolic nature of value and the way in which this results in consumption becoming the principal locus of meaning and action (see Baudrillard, 1968, 1970, 1981 for general theoretical discussion and Du Gay, 1996 for application of this approach to the contemporary restructuring of the labour process).

There have also been attempts to develop post-structuralist accounts of organizational restructuring focusing on the 'post-bureaucratic' (Heydebrand, 1989) or 'postmodern' (Clegg, 1990) organization. The shift from modernity to postmodernity is presented as part of a process of 'de-differentiation' through which the boundaries between the public and the private and the organization and its environment begin to break down (Clegg, 1990). Within the public services the development of cost centres and internal markets are presented as important manifestations of this process. The notion of 'postmodern public service' has been developed by Hoggett (1991, 1996), who suggests that the postmodern public service organization is constituted as a 'flawed post-bureaucratic regime' marked by high levels of competition and marketization, a simultaneous centralization and decentralization of control and extended forms of performance management. Hoggett's account is useful as it goes beyond the usual Foucauldian focus on the apparent fragmentation and decentralization of power to highlight the fact that within public services this has occurred at the same time as the development of more remote and less visible forms of centralized power often based on legalistic and monetary control.

On a descriptive level, the post-structuralist account provides a range of extremely valuable insights into the neo-liberal restructuring of public services. As I will show in Chapters 5–8 of this book, restructuring has involved the development of total quality management, which has increased the visibility of workers and managers in the water industry. This has been legitimated through a consumerist discourse which attempts to align the self-maximizing behaviour of individual workers and managers with the valorization imperatives of the organization. This has involved the discursive subordination of water companies to discourses of 'enterprise' which attempt to apply the postulates of neo-classical economics to all aspects of social relations within water companies, between water companies and the state and between water companies and their customers. There is also a useful insight into the new modes of 'governance' which are emerging in public services and which are premised on the remote control of services by legal and monetary regulation, and into how these new modes of control have contributed to the development of new organization cultures and new definitions of public service. The problem is that the post-structuralist account only works at the discursive level of analysis. It cannot say anything about the material factors behind the intensification of surveillance within public service organizations or assess the material interests served by the subordination of public services to a culture of enterprise and consumerism. There is also a failure to assess the role of the state in the development and intensification of new discursive forms of power and domination or to consider whether there are any contradictions underlying this form of domination and control. While this approach is able to contribute useful descriptive insights into the restructuring of public services, it can contribute very little to an effective analysis of the logical and historical development of the state and state-administered public services. I will now consider the contribution that the approaches outlined above have made to the analysis of public service and explore the ways in which these insights can be synthesized into a more developed and holistic analysis of the 'problem of public service'.

Beyond the Fragments

The approaches outlined above provide a range of valuable insights into the development, crisis and restructuring of public services. The pluralist approach demonstrates that the state is institutionally separate from the economy and the representation of the state as an embodiment of the 'common good' has played a central legitimating role in the development of state-administered public services. The approach demonstrates also, however, that the appearance of the state is undermined by the self-seeking and undemocratic behaviour of élite groups and the way in which the increasing complexity of modern social problems may undermine the efficacy of state administration. The industrial relations approach highlights the specificity of state employment and the way in which this has been developed in order to legitimate the public ownership of industries and services, and the way in which the shielding of these workers from the market has contributed to the crisis of public services and the subsequent commercialization and privatization of public services. Neo-liberal writers highlight the essentially *abstract* nature of the 'general interest' in capitalist societies and the way in which the substantive administrative functions of the state undermine this 'general interest'. The neo-liberal approach is important as it has been used to legitimate the 'depoliticization' of public services through the marketization of services and the subordination of public services to legal and monetary forms of regulation. The 'new institutionalists' provide a useful analysis of an increasing convergence between the state and capital and the way in which the political nature of market exchange could pose serious limits to the neo-liberal depoliticization of public services. Marxist accounts illustrate the importance of analysing the development and crises of public services in the context of the contradictions of capital accumulation. The regulationist and post-Marxist approaches provide important examples of the institutional linkages between state and capital and the intimate relationship between economic and political crises. The post-structuralist approach usefully highlights the way in which neo-liberal restructuring of public services has involved increasing the surveillance of managers and workers and the way in which this has been legitimated through an ideological discourse of consumerism.

In this book, I wish to argue that the above accounts provide useful but necessarily partial, incomplete and mystified accounts of the development and crisis of public service. They are partial and mystified because none of these approaches adequately delineates the *material* linkages between the political, economic and ideological aspects of public service. There is also a failure adequately to explore the *historical* context in which public services have developed and the material contradictions underlying the determination of particular forms of service provision and regulation. This is compounded by a failure to relate the development and crisis of public service to the logical contradictions of the social totality of capitalist society. I want to argue that this can be provided by a historically materialist approach which combines the insights explored above into a holistic analysis of the historical process through which public services have developed. Before proceeding in this direction I need to explore a number of important theoretical points concerning the historical materialist method.

There has been a great deal of debate and confusion surrounding the methodological assumptions of historical materialism. The most trenchant criticisms of Marxism usually rest on the 'economic determinism' underlying the base–superstructure metaphor. This approach is, however, quite foreign to Marx's own methodology. Marx elaborated his methodological approach to the study of 'social forms' in the 'Introduction' to the *Grundrisse* (Marx, 1973a: 100–8). There he argued that in order to uncover the social relations underlying a 'social form' the starting point for analysis was a historical elaboration of the simplest and most abstract determination of society. Having isolated this determination the focus of analysis then moves back towards increasingly complex and concrete levels of social reality. This is the method of analysis developed in *Capital*. Historical analysis demonstrated to Marx that the commodity was the simplest determination in capitalist society. Having isolated the commodity he then moved from the commodity to the more concrete and complex determinations of capitalist society. This *dialectical* movement can be traced in the movement between Volumes 1 and 3 of *Capital* (Rosdolsky, 1977: 10–56). We can build on the conceptual edifice of Marx's work to argue that historical analysis demonstrates that the simplest and most abstract determination of the capitalist state is the commodity and that it is possible to move from this simple determination to the more complex and historically determined forms of the state. This is the theoretical focus of this book. The 'capital logic' approach which I outlined earlier went some way towards uncovering the social relations underlying the state as a fetished embodiment of the 'common good'. The limitation of this approach was the failure to consider the historical specificity of the class relations underlying the development of capital and the state. An attempt to overcome these problems is constituted by an approach which attempts to derive the state from the historical materiality of class struggle (Holloway and Picciotto, 1978, 1991; Clarke, 1988: 120–54; Bonefeld, 1992). The form and function of the state are derived from the social relationship between capital and labour in capitalist society – the *capital relation*.

In *Capital*, Marx (1954: 667–724) demonstrated the way in which the 'primitive accumulation' of capital involved the commodification of human needs and capacities. This historical analysis allowed Marx to isolate the commodity as the fundamental and most abstract social form in capitalist society and to highlight the way in which the contradictions of the commodity shaped the historically specific social forms through which the process of capital accumulation took place – capital, money, profit, wages, etc. It is also clear from the historical material presented by Marx that the state played a crucial role in this process through, for example, the passage of 'bloody legislation' which contributed to the creation, disciplining and regulation of the industrial proletariat. While Marx did not elaborate a theory of the state from these observations with the depth and clarity of his analysis of capital, it is possible to utilize Marx's methodology to trace the logical determination of the state and the historical manifestation of public service administration.

As both capital and the state were determined through the generalization of commodity production, an effective analysis of the state needs to begin at the same place as the analysis of capital – with the commodity. In Volume 1 of *Capital* Marx highlighted the contradictions of commodity production and the way in which these contradictions result in the 'fetishism of commodities' whereby it appears that the productive activities of human beings are directed and constrained by the power of things (Marx, 1954: 78–87; Rubin, 1973: 5–60). He thus focused on the importance of *money* as a 'thing' which appeared to direct and co-ordinate the production and distribution of concrete and useful labour. Marx was concerned to uncover the social relations which lay beneath the apparent domination of social production and consumption by money. He achieved this by demonstrating the historical specificity of *capitalist* commodity production, in which money was both a means of exchange (as suggested in the circuit C–M–C) and, through the form of the wage, the way in which capital ensured the production and reproduction of wage labour in the circuit M–C–M' (Marx, 1976: 949–1058; 1954: 193–203). What Marx did not do was to explore in detail the *legal* forms of domination which developed alongside and facilitated the subordination of labour by capital. In order to understand the form and function of the state fully we need to submit the 'juridical' development of capitalism to the same type of logical and historical analysis as Marx applied to the 'economic' forms of capital.

Commodity production and exchange is based on the formal equivalence of all the parties to commodity transactions. The 'rule of law' was necessary in order to create the 'general equivalence' on which commodity production and exchange depends. The development of the legal apparatus of legislature and judiciary was, therefore, the 'legal' manifestation of the fetishism of commodities. They developed into reified things such as laws and statutes which then appeared to determine and to direct the social relations between individual subjects. But this is a mystification, and we need to uncover the historically specific social relations which lay beneath the development of subjective law. As Pashukanis argues:

> In addition to the mystical quality of value, there appears a no less enigmatic phenomenon: law. A homogeneously integrated relation assumes two fundamental abstract aspects at the same time: an economic and a legal aspect ... Subjective law is a social phenomenon attributed to the individual in the same way that value – likewise a social phenomenon – is attributed to the object as a product of labour. *Legal fetishism complements commodity fetishism*. (Pashukanis, 1989: 117; my italics)

The work of Pashukanis is extremely important in highlighting the way in which law is a fetished material category which obscures the social relations on which it is premised. While Pashukanis did not adequately explore the historical specificity of these social relations (Binns, 1980), we can remedy this by a consideration of the role of law in capitalist commodity production and exchange. The law appears as the embodiment of the 'common good' by treating all commodity owners as free and equal in the sphere of exchange. In this sense law supports the circuit C–M–C. As we have seen above, however, the specificity of capitalist commodity production lies in the circuit M–C–M', which is based on the subordination and domination of labour within the labour process. In capitalist society, therefore, law is a contradictory social form; appearing as the fetished embodiment of the 'common good' and obscuring the class relations of bourgeois society.

In any society of generalized commodity production the state would emerge as a 'guarantor of market exchange' or as a separate 'authority' representing the 'impersonal' interests of the system. The institutional autonomy of the state in capitalist society is premised on the 'impersonal' and 'abstract' interests of the capitalist class in the reproduction of capitalist class relations. Money and the law were, therefore, the social forms through which civil society and the state were subordinated to the power of capital through the process of primitive accumulation. Hence:

> Money, the law and the state developed as the complementary *economic*, *legal* and *political* forms of capitalist power: a unity embodied in capitalist property in which money represents the most abstract form of capital, and

> the power of money is institutionalized in the law and enforced by the state. (Clarke, 1988: 15–18)

The capitalist state thus developed as a fetished embodiment of the 'common good' through the way in which it provided a stable legal and monetary framework for the generalization of capitalist commodity production. The capitalist state does not directly represent the interests of capital owing to its separate institutional form, and the resulting institutional autonomy allows for the possibility of state policies which are not directly functional for capital. The capitalist state is, therefore, a highly contradictory social form. The appearance of the state as the 'general will' is premised on the role of the state in maintaining the conditions for the production and exchange of useful commodities as expressed in the circuit C–M . . . M–C. The historically specific form of commodity production in capitalist society, however, results in the state simultaneously maintaining the conditions for the production and reproduction of surplus value as expressed in the circuit M–C–M'. The application of equality by the state results, therefore, in its opposite – inequality. Equality exists only in the sphere of circulation and is constantly undermined by inequality in the sphere of production. The historically specific form of the state is thus a result of class struggle: the struggle of labour to achieve 'political' gains through the state which escape commodification and which precipitates a process of state restructuring which attempts to reimpose commodification on the production and reproduction of capitalist social relations.

In this book, I trace the development of the water industry in Britain in the context of the struggle between capital and labour over the 'form' of the public service state. In the first half of the book I argue that it is possible to trace this development in three phases. First, the development of municipal enterprise in the nineteenth century involved an attempt by the state to resolve the contradictions which emerged from the intensification of absolute surplus value and the physical deterioration of living labour power. As I will show in Chapter 2, the state intervened first to pass legislation to force capital to provide the working class with water services and, when this failed, to administer services directly through municipal enterprises. While there was an initial attempt to regulate services through the abstract forms of law and money, the ability of the working class to organize politically towards the end of the nineteenth century heightened the 'fiscal crisis' of the municipal state as labour was able to force substantive concessions out of an increasingly politicized municipal administration. The crisis of the municipal state was part of a wider crisis of capital accumulation, which forced the recomposition of state and capital on the foundation of accumulation-based centralization, rationalization and the extraction of relative surplus value, which was achieved through the application of Taylorism and Fordism to the labour process. This transformed the crisis tendencies of capital accumulation and redefined the role of the state in the regulation of capitalism. This leads to the second phase in the development of public services as part of the Keynesian Welfare State (KWS).

The main crisis tendency which emerges from the accumulation of capital based on the extraction of relative surplus value is the tendency towards the over-accumulation of capital, as living labour power is constantly expelled from the production process through the introduction of new technology. The KWS emerged as an attempt to mobilize counter-tendencies to the over-accumulation of capital through the administration of aggregate levels of supply and demand and through industrial restructuring which attempted to lower the organic composition of capital and intensify the extraction of relative surplus value. In this period, therefore, the public services became part of the administrative planning apparatus of a centralized bureaucratic state. The separation of public services from the immediate pressures of capital accumulation allowed the development of 'economic', 'political' and 'ideological' practices which deviated markedly from the logic of capital accumulation. This autonomy provided the material grounding for the specificity of public service management and trade unionism and ideologies of public service. As I will show in Chapter 3, the ability of the working class as workers and consumers to force material concessions and benefits out of the administrative apparatus of the state was an important factor in an increasingly serious 'fiscal crisis' which increasingly undermined the effectiveness of state services. The internal contradictions of the KWS and a generalized crisis of capital accumulation on a global scale eventually resulted in a crisis of Keynesianism and resulted in the neo-liberal restructuring of capital and the state in an attempt to resolve the crisis through the resubordination of state and society to legal and monetary forms of state regulation.

The state administration of capitalism is in no way logical for capital as it diverts surplus value away from the poles of capital accumulation and reproduces the anarchy of capitalist competition within the institutions of the state. While the state is necessarily unproductive, the crisis of the state and the resulting restructuring has involved making the unproductive activity of the state more functional for capital. This has involved a restructuring of the relationship between state and society and the restructuring of the state apparatus itself. As I will show in Chapter 3, the managerialization of the water industry was an attempt to resolve the ineffectiveness of the industry. The result of the restructuring was a realignment of the industry and capital which has subsequently facilitated the privatization of the industry. As I will show in Chapter 4, the state has been recomposed on a neo-liberal basis in the form of the Office of Water Services (OFWAT) and this recomposition is premised on ensuring the successful valorization of water capital through legal and monetary forms of regulation. The restructuring of the state in recent years has thus been an attempt to realign state and capital: to establish a unity between those elements which have become independent (Marx, 1969: 513). The three phases of development are not therefore part of an inexorable law of capitalist development, as the regulation approach outlined earlier would suggest, but are forms precipitated by class struggle. Thus, the changing balance between administration and regulation reflects the changing power of labour within the labour process.

In Chapters 5–8 of this book I explore the impact of the realignment of state and capital in the UK water industry on forms of control and resistance within individual water companies. I approach this through an assessment of changing management practices and highlight the way in which the crisis and restructuring of the state has involved a fundamental transformation of the political, economic and ideological social relations within water companies. The important linkages between the spheres of politics and production have been denied both by 'state theorists' and 'industrial sociologists' (Burawoy, 1986: 122). It is important to recognize that the state is not merely 'political' or the production process 'economic', as the 'capital relation' in the sphere of production has political, ideological and economic moments. The economic domination of labour in the labour process is supported by political apparatuses of production and ideological discourses of production which secure the reproduction of labour as labour-power. The restructuring of the state has involved an attempt simultaneously to restructure the political, economic and ideological aspects of the capital relation in both the sphere of production and within the institutional mechanisms of the state (Holloway and Picciotto, 1991: 110). There are therefore important linkages between the 'internal state' of the workplace and regional, national and international modes of regulation and, as I will endeavour to show throughout this book, the exploration of these linkages allows an important insight into the crisis and restructuring of public services.

In developing an analysis of public service that is both historical and logical, and which is able to capture adequately the linkages and contradictions outlined above, I have been faced with a number of methodological issues and problems. In Chapters 2–4 I trace the historical development and crisis of the public service state through a focus on the development of the water industry in England and Wales. In Chapter 2 I trace the municipalization of the water industry and the central role of 'gas and water socialism' in the political and ideological struggle over the form of the public service state. I draw upon the statements made by prominent capitalists in the media, through the political tracts of Fabian socialists and liberals and through the writings and industrial and political action of working-class socialists in order to explore 'gas and water socialism' from a number of *class perspectives* (see Cleaver, 1979, 1992). The sources on which I draw, therefore, represent divergent class perspectives. To take an example from Chapter 2, I explore archival material from *The Times* which highlights the perspective of business, secondary material on socialist and revolutionary trade union theory and practice to highlight the perspective of the working class, and secondary data on Fabian Socialism in order to explore the compromise between capital and labour which emerged through the development of bureaucratic municipal socialism. The sources were not selected on the basis of their reliability and validity as it is understood in its traditional positivistic sense. As Harvey (1990: 202) has noted, in research conducted from a critical, dialectical perspective data is meaningful only in its theoretical context. Cases are selected as 'paradigm cases' in order to represent foci for the analysis of contradiction. The cases which are selected in Chapters 2–4 of the book are therefore meaningful only when placed in the analytical and conceptual totality of a historical and logical exploration of the contradictory development of public services in Britain.

In Chapters 5–8 I explore the way in which the crisis and restructuring of public service has impacted on four water companies in England

and Wales. The main methodological strategy in this section was to present an analysis of ethnographic data that was collected in a series of semi-structured interviews between 1992 and 1993. Clearly my analysis involved deconstructing the managerial and trade union discourses unearthed in the research process. Where my analysis departs from the recent post-structural orthodoxy is in my attempt to develop a 'critical ethnography' (Harvey, 1990: 8–13) which attempts to *reconstruct* these discourses in the context of the historical and logical totality of the capitalist mode of production and the conceptual totality of historical materialism.

The restructuring of public services involves much more than the transformation of 'class' relations within the state and public service organizations. While I have not mentioned inequality based on socio-economic (i.e. sociological) class, gender, race, nationalism, age and sexual orientation, etc., this is not to suggest that these are unimportant. Indeed, the history of public service highlights the deeply gendered nature of public service provision, and research on the recent restructuring of public services has important implications for gender relations (Cousins, 1988; Coyle, 1985; Fevre, 1986). The forms of inequality and domination which do not result from the accumulation of capital, however, operate at a lower level of abstraction than the capital relation. Moving from the abstract to the concrete, the capital relation is overlaid with a myriad of more complex relations based on gender, race, location, nationality, age, sexual orientation and so on. These latter relations are, moreover, constantly decomposed and recomposed through the restructuring of the capital relation. Hence, the neo-Fordist 'feminization' of the workforce (Pearson, 1986) has resulted in a simultaneous recomposition of both class and gender relations in an attempt to increase the rate of surplus value. Thus, the recomposition of gender relations cannot be analysed in abstraction from the recomposition of capital, and the restructuring of gender relations is the historical form in which the recomposition of capital is manifest. It is the logical and historical form of the capitalist state which allows these forms of oppression and struggle to appear as autonomous and unrelated to the process of capital accumulation. In this sense a key objective of this book is to go 'beyond the fragments' of recent sociological relativism in an attempt to develop an assessment of the central and fundamental dynamics of recent changes in the organization of state and society.

2 The Origins of Public Service

Throughout the nineteenth century a central political objective of municipal government was the development of an effective water and sewerage system. The inadequacy of private utility provision forced local authorities to develop municipally owned and managed water and sewerage undertakings. Indeed, the central preoccupation of Fabian socialists with utility provision resulted in their being awarded the rather unflattering title of 'gas and water socialists'. But why were the utilities so important in spearheading the growth of public administration and what were the forces and dynamics behind the growth and development of public service as an ideology and practice? In this chapter I trace the development of the public service water industry in nineteenth-century Britain.

In Chapter 1 I argued that the primary contradiction of capital accumulation during the nineteenth century was the physical destruction of living labour power. This occurred in both production and reproduction, as the intensification of workers' labour in the workplace was compounded by the limited consumption capacity of workers in the sphere of exchange. This resulted in the state becoming increasingly involved in mobilizing the counter-tendencies against this contradiction. Initially, state action was contained within the sphere of exchange through legislation aimed at creating equivalence among utility consumers. In respect of utility provision, legislation was passed enforcing companies to supply on demand, and limiting the prices and profits of utility companies. However, the initial attempt to contain the functions of the state within the legal and monetary form of the liberal state was increasingly undermined by the subordination of labour in the sphere of production. Workers were unable to afford utility services and the state was force to go beyond its liberal form to engage in the direct administration of utility services. Utility capital was initially recomposed into municipal enterprise. Prior to the enfranchisement of the working class this allowed the reconstitution of the liberal state and simply allowed the costs of reproducing the working class to be socialized among the capitalist class. However, the enfranchisement of the working class and the intensification of working-class organization and struggle towards the end of the nineteenth century heightened conflict over how public service provision should be organized. The resulting crisis of the state shifted the locus of class struggle to a struggle over the form of the state. The modern notion of public service emerged out of this struggle and, while the development of Fabian bureaucracy resulted in the partial demobilization of working-class struggle, it also incorporated the demands of the working class within the public service state and set the scene for the further contradictory development of public services through the twentieth century.

The Contradictions of Capitalist Development and the Politics of Improvement

During the first half of the nineteenth century Britain went through a rapid process of urbanization. The development of large-scale industries based on cotton and steel produced new industrial cities to accommodate the new industrial workers. In the decade between 1821 and 1831 Manchester, Leeds and Sheffield grew at a rate of 44.9, 47.3 and 40.5 per cent respectively (Briggs, 1968: 60–86). The rapid industrialization and urbanization of Britain during this period was unplanned and subject only to the anarchy of capitalist competition. The state played a minimal role in planning patterns of social and industrial development and the provision of utilities and other public services was left largely to private enterprise. Where private companies found it unprofitable to provide public services, they were not provided. This rapid and unplanned development resulted in the new industrial cities being plagued by squalor, poverty and disease. The lack of effective sewerage systems turned streets and rivers into open sewers and the lack of clean and wholesome drinking water resulted in repeated epidemics of waterborne diseases such as cholera, typhoid and typhus. The streets of the new industrial cities also became increasingly dangerous, as bands of vagabonds and paupers roamed the unlit streets engaging in acts of crime and violence.

Private water and gas companies failed to provide adequate levels of utility goods to prevent these problems and this resulted in state agencies becoming increasingly engaged in the 'politics of improvement'. The 'politics of improvement' developed in an ideological context dominated by *laissez-faire* individualism. In Britain, *laissez-faire* liberalism was compounded by forms of religious individualism based on religious self-scrutiny and self-responsibility (Lukes, 1973: 94–8). This was particularly evident in respect of public health issues where, for example, *The Economist* mounted a campaign against the 1848 Public Health Act on the grounds that evil and suffering were abominations of nature. Thus, the state should not intervene to prevent the punishment of reckless and indolent individuals who had failed properly to protect and regulate their own health and well-being. The intervention of the state clearly vitiated the Malthusian concern to suppress and marginalize the 'surplus population' which inevitably resulted from the natural development of society (see Engels, 1987: 281–4). As the processes of industrialization and urbanization developed, however, *laissez-faire* individualism became increasingly untenable. It became increasingly apparent that unfettered private enterprise was not providing the utilities required to produce a safe and healthy environment within Britain's growing industrial cities. The development of public service in England occurred, therefore, in the context of a political and religious discourse of *laissez-faire* and self-help alongside increasingly obvious manifestations of the limitations and dangers of these ideologies in practice. The result of these inadequacies was the specifically British phenomenon of 'improvement'.

The municipalization of the water industry

The 1842 report by the Poor Law Commissioners on the 'Sanitary Conditions of the Labouring Population of Great Britain' highlighted both the wasteful effects of competition between water companies and the relationship between poverty and poor health. A further report by the Royal Commission on the Health of Towns in 1845 highlighted the negative effect of the private ownership of water. The report catalogued examples from across Britain in which private monopolies made large profits through the supply of water that was of defective quality and often contaminated by sewage. The poor were unable to secure a supply and obtained water either by begging or by drawing water from grossly polluted rivers. The Commission recommended that the only way to secure an adequate supply of pure water for all citizens was to entrust the service to an independent and disinterested body, and that water companies should be forced to comply with the demands of local authorities. Local authorities were to be given powers to purchase ineffective companies or to establish waterworks where none existed. The process of reform was opposed by the powerful vested interests of private water companies and the 1848 Public Health Act reflected a compromise between the advocates of health reform and the influential private interests of water companies. The Act established local boards of health which were 'enabled' to provide water supplies for their districts; although the Act stipulated that boards could only act with the permission of existing private companies. The imposition of definite obligations on local authorities with respect to water supply was not achieved until the Public Health Act of 1875, which enshrined the recommendations of the 1869 Royal Commission on Sanitation. The 1875 Act gave local authorities the power to supply water to all or part of their districts that were not covered by Statutory Water Companies (SWCs).

The municipalization of water proceeded at a rapid rate in the second part of the nineteenth century, and by 1914 there were 326 municipal water undertakings in Britain constituting 80 per cent of undertakings and accounting for 82 per cent of output (Millward, 1991: 117). The municipalization of water was increasingly accepted as the only effective means of ensuring the proper regulation of water resources. An important landmark was the decision of the House of Lords to allow the passage of the Sheffield Corporation Bill of 1887, which transferred the ownership of the Sheffield Water Company to Sheffield Corporation on the grounds of public policy. Municipalization was responsible for improvements in the quality and quantity of water supply and the development of the public service water industry involved the principles of commercial enterprise being increasingly superseded by the principles of public utility (Robson, 1935: 319). Throughout the nineteenth century the shift was from legal and financial regulation in the sphere of exchange towards more substantive forms of administration in the sphere of production. A similar pattern underlies the development of the modern gas industry.

The municipalization of the gas industry

The early development of the gas industry reflected a total dominance of private enterprise. The growth of the gas industry in Britain reflected cyclical movements of economic activity. The primary periods of growth took place in the cyclical economic booms of 1818–25, 1831–7 and 1842–6 (Falkus, 1967: 495–6). It was, however, inextricably linked to the 'politics of improvement' and the initial business of a company was usually constituted by a contract with the local authority to supply gas for the purposes of street lighting. Indeed, the supply of cheap gas for street lighting was usually a condition of a company being allowed to excavate thoroughfares in order to lay mains. Large companies that required large amounts of capital for their development were usually established by an Act of Parliament that limited liability, and the resulting statute usually imposed strict conditions on the operation of the company.[1]

The early development of the gas industry was marked by increasing public concern over the operational effectiveness and efficiency of gas companies. These concerns included the high monopoly charges resulting from amalgamations, price-fixing and zoning; the health hazards resulting from the duplication and often triplication of gas works through noxious fumes, leakage and the opening of highways; and the poor quality of gas with respect to pressure, neglect of apparatus and the inaccuracy of meters (Robson, 1935: 305–6). In the context of these problems, Parliament was forced to develop increasingly powerful mechanisms of public regulation and control over the gas industry. In 1847 the Surveying Officers Commission reported on the negative impact of competition between gas companies in regard to the interests of consumers. The Report highlighted the short-lived nature of competition and the way in which consumers were forced to pay for contests through rates paid on excess capital when companies merged or went bankrupt. During the 1860s and 1870s state regulation restricted competition through 'districting' and 'zoning', controlled prices and dividends, and placed an obligation on gas companies to supply customers on demand.[2] In the context of these problems there was an increasing trend for gas to be supplied by municipal enterprise, and by 1914 there were over 300 publicly-owned gas companies accounting for 40 per cent of all authorized undertakings (Falkus, 1977: 146–51; Millward, 1991: 116–18). The regulation of public services by the state obviously ran counter to the *laissez-faire* tenets of classical liberalism and the attempt by the state to mediate the material contradictions of capital accumulation simultaneously involved a reformulation of liberal state theory.

Municipal enterprise and the crisis of classical liberalism

The crisis of liberalism developed as the materiality of capitalist development increasingly diverged from the abstract analytical models of classical political economy. The problem of public health became increasingly irresolvable within the liberal paradigm and even economic individualists such as Samuel Smiles and Thomas Macaulay became collectivist on social policy issues (Taylor, 1972: 45–6). The material contradictions of capitalist development and the increasingly important role of the state in mediating these contradictions shifted the concern of liberals away from a defence of unfettered liberal capitalism towards an acceptance of the regulatory role of the state and the need to ensure that the actions of the state were limited, competent and representative (Smellie, 1957: 23–44). The work of Jeremy Bentham and Edwin Chadwick highlighted both the need for reform and the need to constrain the administrative discretion of local improvement commissions by centralized state control.

Local authorities were subject to fiscal constraints in respect of their ability to impose local taxation and this too became an increasing concern of liberal state theory. The increasing functions of the municipal state raised the level of local taxation and resulted in an increasing demand for democratic representation within the local state. The work of John Stuart Mill illustrates the contradictory formulation of the public service state in the mid-nineteenth century.[3] Mill argued that local representative government constituted a central bulwark in the education for and the defence of individual liberty. The democratic representation of 'rate payers' constituted an important rein on the discretionary power of the local state. The status of being a taxpayer was to be not only a precondition for local enfranchisement, but a status which needed to be extended to the poorest members of the community in order to keep down levels of local taxation (see chapter 8 of Mill's *Considerations on Representative Government*: Mill, 1991: 326–45). The work of Mill played a central role in defining the ideological form of 'public service' in Britain and was later to play a defining role in the development of Fabian Socialism (Pease, 1916: 22; Webb, 1962: 78–9;

Webb and Webb, 1963: 397–487). The Webbs argued that the work of Mill played a fundamental role in redefining political liberty on the basis of the 'citizen-consumer' of utilitarian liberalism and Fabian Socialism.

The initial development of public service was, therefore, contained within the liberal moment of the state. Early forms of regulation attempted to resolve the contradictions of capital accumulation through the forms of legal and monetary regulation. The legislation outlined above attempted to enforce equivalence in the sphere of exchange between public service companies and their customers. Companies were forced to supply on demand and the prices and levels of services also became an increasing focus of regulation. The important point is that this form of regulation failed and the state was forced to intervene in increasingly substantive ways in the direct administration of public services. It is in this sense that the contradictions of capital accumulation appeared within the state apparatus as the contradiction between regulation and administration. In the rest of this chapter I want to explore the contradictions and dynamics which resulted in the crisis of the liberal state which, I will argue, was premised on the contradictions and struggle resulting from the enduring inequality between capital and labour in the sphere of production. The crisis and decomposition of the liberal state also resulted in a refocusing of liberal state ideology. The representation of the 'common good' through the 'abstract' individual of classical liberalism was increasingly undermined by the concrete inequalities resulting from the state's inactivity. The focus of liberals shifted, therefore, from a concern with total *laissez-faire* towards a concern with the necessity and limits of state activity. This involved a shift in the representation of the 'common good' away from the abstract individual of classical liberalism towards the 'citizen-consumer' of utilitarian liberalism and Fabian Socialism. I will now demonstrate the way in which the above process operated in the context of the historical and material development of the water industry. I will begin by exploring one of the most significant examples of municipal enterprise – the municipalization of Birmingham in the mid-nineteenth century.

Joseph Chamberlain and the 'municipal ideal' in Birmingham

The city of Birmingham was a pioneer in the development of new forms of municipal enterprise. In the 1860s and 1870s Birmingham was unique with respect to both the prominent role played by capitalists in the public life of the City and the limited organization of labour. These factors facilitated a programme of municipalization developed by Joseph Chamberlain. The programme was based on an explicit concern with the public health of the labouring masses, and was developed in the context of an extension of the franchise to many working people in Birmingham by the 1867 Reform Act. Chamberlain was an advocate of deliberate reformism to protect the interests of wealth (Hobsbawm, 1968: 328) and this resulted in a conscious municipal policy being engineered to address the problem of sewage (Briggs, 1968: 214). Birmingham's sewage was piped into the River Tame at Saltley in a raw state. Following an injunction in the Chancery Court restraining the Council from depositing solid sewage at the Tame outfall, and the rejection of a plan by the 'Gladstonian' Public Works Committee to build a new sewerage works in the Tame Valley, a special 'Sewage Enquiry Committee' was established in 1870. The Committee was dominated by 'new' Chamberlainite Liberals, and produced an important and influential social document that highlighted the appalling state of the city's sanitary system, and demonstrated the way in which this was related to overall and differential mortality rates in the city. Chamberlain used the Report to highlight the disparities of life in the city, the relationship of these disparities to 'pestiferous nuisances', and thus the case for social control. Despite the opposition of private interests, by 1875 the Committee had assumed responsibility for the implementation of a new sewage plan. This was given further impetus by the 1875 Public Health Act, which allowed the creation of 'united districts' for specified sanitary purposes, and which led to the creation of the Birmingham, Tame and New District Drainage Board.

The municipalization of gas played a central role in Birmingham's ambitious plans for the development of a new sanitary system. Chamberlain argued that municipalization strengthened the power and influence of the local council which should be encouraged to become a real local parliament. Monopolies sustained by the state should be in the hands of the representatives of the people, to whom the profits by right should go. A central tenet of Chamberlain's initial programme was that the substantial profits generated by a municipally-owned gas undertaking could be used to improve the health of Birmingham. In 1884 gas was taken into municipal ownership, the purchase of the gasworks raising the borough debt from £0.5 million to £2.5 million.

Chamberlain's argument for the municipalization of water was premised upon the 'great social weakness' of a system that forced the poor to drink water 'which is as bad as sewage before clarification'. Following the 1869 Royal Commission on Sanitary Reform, he argued that 'the power of life and death' should not be left in private hands, and 'whereas there should be a profit made on a gas undertaking, the waterworks should never be a source of profit, as all profit should go in the reduction of the price of water' (quoted in Briggs, 1968: 223–4). The 1872 Public Health Act led to the appointment of a Medical Officer of Health, and his reports, together with a smallpox epidemic in 1874, and the results of the survey of sanitary conditions by the Sanitary Committee which was established following the 1873 local elections, allowed Chamberlain to overcome the opposition of the Birmingham Water Company and the House of Lords, and the waterworks were taken into municipal ownership in 1876.

The reforms undertaken in Birmingham highlighted the way in which the regulatory activities of the state reconstituted the contradictions of capital accumulation within the apparatus of the local state. Chamberlain recognized that the contradictions of capitalist development could not be resolved through legal and monetary regulation and developed the bureaucratic mechanisms that were required to administer water and gas services directly. The local state was now able to produce use-values directly, but its form required that these were produced and delivered through the social forms of law and money – that is, through the social form of the contract. Within the sphere of production this required that gas and water workers were subjected to the wage form, while in the sphere of exchange the costs of water and gas services were socialized but nonetheless delivered on a commercial basis. The appearance of formal equivalence in the sphere of exchange, and the reconstituted basis on which the state appeared to function in terms of the 'common good', both pivoted on the conception of the 'citizen-consumer' of the municipality. The municipal citizenry were all free and equal and entitled to the same levels of service irrespective of wealth and status. The problem was, of course, that the 'citizen-consumers' were far from free and equal, and as workers began to struggle and organize against the exploitation and alienation that they faced in the workplace the tension between abstract regulation and substantive accumulation became increasingly apparent.

The emergence of labour as a class power in the late 1880s threatened to rupture the abstract basis of the municipal state. The working-class response to the contradictions of capitalist development was to develop 'gas and water socialism' as a critique of capitalism and the alienating social relations inherent in capitalist production. 'Gas and water socialism' became an increasingly contested concept and subject to alternative class perspectives. The development of New Unionism was accompanied by the rapid development of revolutionary socialism and this was to play an important ideological role in the development of and the struggle over the public service state.

New Unionism and the Politics of Public Service

The contradictions of the municipal state had initially been resolved through an attempt to mediate the direct production of use-values through the social forms of law and money. As I mentioned above, the implication of this within the sphere of production was the subordination of public service labour to the commodity form of the wage. The direct employment of labour by municipal authorities threatened the abstract basis of the employment relation as it implies the possibility of the partial decommodification of labour. Administration is not directly mediated by the social forms of law and money and is not, therefore, directly functional for capital. The struggle over the social form of the state, therefore, became increasingly concerned with the extent to which social production and reproduction was mediated by the commodity form. In the mid-nineteenth century labour had been demobilized following the collapse of Chartism, and the weakness of organized labour was reflected in the wide-scale subordination of labour to the commodity form. Within the public services the commodification of labour was achieved through the use of contract labour. The remobilization of organized labour in the 1880s, however, threatened to heighten the crisis of the state, as workers challenged the commodification of both their labour and the products of their labour. The proliferation of socialist thought and trade union struggle developed against the material subordination of workers to the commodity form in the production and reproduction of their daily lives.

Within the public services this was manifested in the struggle of workers against the contract system. The disastrous impact of the contract system on utility workers was highlighted by Henry Mayhew in his *London Labour and the London Poor*, where he illustrated the way in which the development of contract labour had reduced the pay and conditions of the London 'sewer flushers':

> It's the old story, I regret to say – a reduction in the wages of the labouring men. But this indeed is the inevitable effect of the contract system ... To contractors the comforts and health of the labouring men must necessarily be a secondary consideration to the realisation of profit. Men can always be found; safe investment cannot. (quoted in Dix and Williams, 1987: 24)

The contract system not only depressed the pay and conditions of public utility workers but was also extremely ineffective, as contractors pursued high profits at the expense of service provision. The result was a rapid increase in the number of municipal workers in the latter half of the nineteenth century as the state took on the function of the direct administration of utility industries. The increase reflected both the concerns of 'ratepayers' groups' with 'local economy' and the increasing organization of public service workers. The initial development of state labour occurred in a context of a weak and fragmented labour movement. Within the utilities the increase in the number of municipal employees was not matched by an increase in trade union activity. Prior to the emergence of New Unionism in the early 1890s municipal employees retained an ambiguous and somewhat hostile attitude to organized labour. However, New Unionism resulted in the rapid unionization of municipal employees and, together with the increasing involvement of organized labour in municipal politics, this raised the contradictions of the municipal state to a new level.

The late 1880s were marked by the emergence of a new wave of industrial unrest led by socialists of the SDF.[4] This resulted in the unionization of large numbers of previously unorganized unskilled and semi-skilled workers, including a large number of municipal public servants. The two moments were linked by SDF members such as John Burns, who was both a key player in the emergent New Unionism and an elected member of the London County Council (LCC). The struggles associated with New Unionism resulted in a vast increase in both union membership in general and the organization of unskilled labourers throughout Britain. The main feature of the New Unionism was a departure from the economism of the labour aristocrats. The new general unions espoused the principles of trade protection, paid few or no benefits and were avowedly political in their aims and objectives

(Hobsbawm, 1968: 179–203; 1984: 152–75). The public, or at least semi-public, structure of the gas industry was one of the most important and enduring foci of activity of New Unionism, and provided an ideal context for the material grounding of political concepts such as 'gas and water socialism'.

Revolutionary socialism and gas and water socialism as revolutionary critique

There has been an established debate within British Marxism on the specificity of the British labour movement. The debate has focused on the perceived failure of the British labour movement to develop into a revolutionary force against capitalism and the intrinsic caution and reformism of British social democracy. The debate reflected the Leninist and Gramscian strands within British Marxism in highlighting either the economic imperialism of a labour aristocracy (Hobsbawm, 1968: 272–315) or the ideological subordination of the labour movement to a deficient and incomplete bourgeois culture (Nairn, 1965, 1972; Saville, 1973, 1988) as primary reasons for the reformist nature of the British labour movement. These accounts share both an essentialism in assuming the existence of a 'pure' form of capitalist development (Wood, 1991) and a tacit acceptance of the Fabian view of history in their acceptance that labour failed to pose a challenge to capital in Britain. Against this latter claim, the following discussion registers the increasing challenge to capital posed by working-class socialists and trade unionists in the struggle over the form of the municipal state. This struggle did not develop in a theoretical vacuum and there is evidence to suggest both that the writings of British socialists became increasingly anti-statist and that this anti-statism was an important influence on the activity and organization of the new unions (Hobsbawm, 1984: 152–75).[5]

Prior to the development of New Unionism oppositional politics was dominated by radical liberalism. The early development of both the Independent Labour Party (ILP) and the Social Democratic Federation (SDF) was dominated by the politics of radical democracy. During the 1880s there was a great flux and diversity in socialist politics and a growing tension between statist and anti-statist currents (Barry, 1965: 133–6). The state-centrist model developed out of radical liberalism, and used the example of the Gotha Programme in Germany to argue for nationalization and the reform of the state in the interests of the working class. This was the initial position of the SDF on its formation in 1884 and the position taken by Marxists such as E. Belfort Bax.[6] There was, however, an important anti-statist current which developed alongside the dominant statist approach. There was, for example, the revolutionary Owenism of organizations such as the 'Land and Labour League'. The League was founded by Joseph Lane and was highly influenced by the continental anarchism of Peter Kropotkin. During the 1890s Lane became increasingly federalist and anarchistic and in 1897 authored the *Anti-State Communist Manifesto.* During the 1890s the position of both the SDF and the ILP shifted towards an anti-statist and federalist position.

The principal focus of socialist theory and practice during the 1890s was the form of the capitalist state. The response of capital to New Unionism included a marked bureaucratization of the state apparatus. In this context, leading socialists of the SDF and the ILP increasingly advocated workers' control and co-operation as a response to the bureaucratic domination of capital and the state. Hyndman, for example, shifted substantially closer to an Owenite position during the 1890s, and increasingly questioned the efficacy of nationalization. In the *Economics of Socialism* (1896), Hyndman developed an analysis of the Post Office which suggested that while the organization was socialistic in form, it was not socialistic in 'nature' (content). The Post Office had the potential to become the 'nucleus of a great co-operative system'. In this system postal workers and their families needed food, clothing and house-room, and all would render useful service in return for these and other necessaries of life.

There is evidence that many socialists conceptualized 'gas and water socialism' as a mechanism that would facilitate an attack upon the alienating relations contained within the capitalist state: that is, that public ownership should raise the status of labour as workers. In 1894 Hyndman and William Morris wrote that workers should be encouraged to take a more direct interest in their enterprises; including the right to elect their own superintendents. This view was taken further by William Morris and E. Belfort Bax, who, in *Socialism: its Growth and Outcome* (1893), developed the argument that socialists should not attempt to capture the national state. In a statement of 'anarchist federalism', they suggested that the growth of municipal government should be seen not as an extension of democracy under the national state, but as a means of destroying the national state. Through the continuous action of federalism and internationalism, the power of the national state would be sapped. The writings of Tom Mann illustrate the extent to which elements of 'anti-statism' were present within the ILP. In *Trade Unionism and Co-operation in the Future* (1897), Mann argued for co-operative production rather than nationalization as the main route to industrial democracy.

The political dynamic of New Unionism was to play an important role in the emergence of independent labour politics. The increasing constitutionalism of the trade unions associated with New Unionism was a result of their defeat in the industrial struggles of the 1890s when the employers counter-attacked (Hinton, 1983: 60–3; and see Hobsbawm, 1984: 152–75 for detailed analysis of the employers' counter-attack). The new unions were successively defeated in the gas and docks industries, and needed to secure formal recognition sanctioned by Parliament. While the counter-attack was to play an important role in the establishment of the Labour Representation Committee in 1900, the partial nature of the attack led to the incorporation of labour through the establishment of collective bargaining frameworks. The labour alliance of 1895–1914 forced socialists on to the periphery of the labour movement and into the structures of local government. The existence of the socialist currents outlined above highlights the way in which the bureaucratic and centralist forms of public service associated with Fabian socialism were determined through struggle, and the existence of a well-developed critique of capitalism, alongside the integration of labour within the bureaucratic state, highlights the way in which public service in its Fabian form emerged as an unstable class compromise.

The persistent anti-statism outlined above found expression in the syndicalist movement and in the industrial unionism that had become increasingly important by 1910. In the context of a fall in real wages and the failure of Labour MPs to win significant economic changes, the working class became increasingly frustrated. With regard to municipal socialism, Ramsey MacDonald was to comment 'After gas and water – what?' The syndicalist movement provided a useful critique of the orthodox strategy of securing nationalization within a capitalist economy. Tom Mann was to claim that the running of industry through Parliament would prove more mischievous than present methods. Syndicalism allowed many gains in both membership and solidarity between 1912 and 1914, and led to elements of workers' control being woven into demands for nationalization. The political programmes and discourses developed by socialists and trade unionists between 1890 and 1914 illustrate the extent to which 'gas and water socialism' was a focus of the political struggle over the form of the capitalist state. Working-class socialists were able to gain control of municipal administration through local elections and thereby to undermine the abstract regulation of labour through a combination of a decommodification of public service labour and a proliferation of capital projects funded by an increase of local taxation.

The contradictory determination of the municipal state form, therefore, allowed real gains for labour and initiated a fiscal crisis of the municipal state form. The political manifestations of the crisis were an emergent anti-statism and anti-centralism with respect to labour, and an attempt by capital to centralize and bureaucratize the state through measures such as the 1906 Liberal Reforms. I will now examine the concrete manifestation of this crisis through an exploration of the relationship between New Unionism in the gas and water industries, the representation of labour within the structures of the municipal state and the fundamental crisis of the state that emerged in the first decade of the twentieth century.

New Unionism in the gas and water industries

The development of New Unionism had a marked impact on both the gas and water industries. In respect of the gas industry, the struggle of the gas workers illustrates the way in which working-class politics was increasingly focused on the form of the municipal state. The organization of the gasworkers in Britain was extremely important, as it demonstrated the distinctive case of the development of nineteenth-century unionism in a sector with the exceptional characteristics of a high degree of public ownership and control; a high public profile and therefore exposure to the pressures of public opinion; and a semi-skilled workforce in a powerful bargaining position (Hobsbawm, 1968: 172–3). The public profile of the gas industry was successfully manipulated by the gasworkers. Following the Reform Acts of 1867 and 1884, and the Local Government Act of 1888, the labour vote had to be considered at a local level. Gas undertakings were both monopolies and, often, municipally-owned. The bargaining power of workers in the gas industry was enhanced through their enjoyment of the dual protection of the law as both consumers and employees. Gas undertakings were legally obliged to maintain supplies and to offer minimum conditions of service to employees.

The London gasworkers were organized by socialists such as John Burns, Tom Mann, Ben Tillet and Will Thorn, who was himself a gasworker. In May 1889, the Gas Workers and General Union (GWGU) was formed. The Union claimed a reduction from a twelve- to an eight-hour day in August 1889, and the gas companies conceded this demand without a struggle. The main impetus to the disruption of 1889 was a combination of the intensification of work in a context of technical stagnation and the successful propaganda of the socialists (Hobsbawm, 1968: 163–5). The companies were forced to concede the demands for wage rises and the eight-hour day as they found themselves at the temporary mercy of the stokers. The gas companies were producing gas without margins of excess capacity and storage, in a technical context of the nascent competition of electricity, and in a political context which, given the municipally-owned and regulated form of the gas industry, forced attention to the emergent labour vote.

The success of the London gasworkers was followed by gas undertakings throughout Britain capitulating to the demand for an eight-hour day. The unwillingness of the gas companies to challenge the demands of the unions was premised upon the successful strike action of workers in Bristol. In Bristol, gasworkers already worked eight-hour shifts. In May 1889, the Bristol United Gaslight Company's Labour Union was formed with 200 members, following a dispute over methods of wage payment. In October, a strike was called after the Company rejected the proposals of the union. In the context of low gas stocks, the Company capitulated in less than 24 hours, on terms costing around £5000 per annum. The victory march organized by the Trades Council, and attended by 10,000 socialists and trade unionists, demonstrated the political significance of the dispute.

Despite the collapse of other general unions, and a sustained counter-attack in the gas industry which included a continuing mechanization programme between 1890 and 1910, the union managed to retain partial control. The gas industry went through a rapid period of expansion during this period and reabsorbed many of those displaced by mechanization. As a consequence, there was no rapid influx of new unorganized labour into the gas industry as a result of restructuring with many of the stokers being retained to operate the new machinery, and this allowed the union to maintain its resistance to the scrapping of existing and expensive capital equipment. In the context of the dual protection of the law alluded to above, the stokers were able partially to retain their bargaining position. The gasworkers had demonstrated the way in which the democratic basis of the state form could be exploited by labour in its struggle against capital.

Turning to the water industry, municipal employees proved to be fertile ground for the growth of trade unionism. In contrast to the unstable and casual employment conditions of other groups of workers affected by New Unionism, such as gasworkers and dockers, local government provided a stable and continual basis for growth. The conditions of municipal employees had improved little since the survey of Mayhew in the 1850s. Combined with the idealism of New Unionism, these factors resulted in a massive growth in the level of trade union membership and activity among public servants (Dix and Williams, 1987: 32–4). Within London, it was the water workers who were to provide the main thrust of this unionization. The LCC main-drainage employees were concentrated at the main sewage outfalls at Beckton and Crossness on the north and south banks of the River Thames. Beckton gas works had been the focus of Will Thorne's activity during the gasworkers' strike, and many of the LCC employees were to join the GWGU – most notably Albin Taylor, who was a leading member of the SDF. During 1889, the men at Beckton threatened strike action unless their demands were met – a 48-hour week, 5 shillings a day, one week's annual leave and the provision of safety equipment. While Taylor and his fellow drainage men were eventually to break with the GWGU to join the rapidly growing Vestry Employees' Union (VEU) – who rejected the class-based unionism of the former in favour of a more traditional concern with pay, conditions, and funeral benefits – the involvement of water workers within the GWGU demonstrates the potency of New Unionism during the earlier 1890s. Moreover, the primary objective of the VEU was to limit the use of contractors and to increase the employment of direct labour; an objective that heightened the crisis of the municipal state because it resulted in the increasing decommodification of labour. While public service labour continued to be regulated through the contract and the wage, these were increasingly established and maintained through bureaucratic and administrative forms of control. Indeed, the recomposition of public service labour in this form became a principle objective of public service unions in their struggle against the liberal form of the state. This can be illustrated through an assessment of the struggles within local government in the 1890s.

Municipal Labour, Class Struggle and the 'Fiscal Crisis' of the Municipal State

The counter-attack by capital against New Unionism in the private sector was replicated within the municipal state through the victimization of union officials by the 'surveyors' who were their *de facto* employers. In London, a prime objective of the VEU became the principle that no employee could be dismissed except through an elected committee of the vestry; the union subsequently winning support for this principle from 'progressive' members sympathetic to labour on the LCC. This had a fundamental impact on the principles and practice of public service trade unionism. Increasingly, municipal workers became aware that they were in a unique position in being able to exert influence on who their employers were. A policy of winning sympathetic influence on local authorities through the ballot box by securing the election of candidates who were sympathetic to trade unionism was, therefore, adopted by municipal employees and soon came to be seen as a priority objective in establishing the union (Dix and Williams, 1987: 41). The increasing incorporation of the working class within the municipal state – as workers, voters and, increasingly, councillors – resulted in a severe and protracted crisis of this form of regulation. The emergence of labour as a powerful class force heightened the contradictions inherent in the municipal form of the state and, as a result, class struggle increasingly took the form of struggle over the form of the municipal state.

The disparaging epithet of 'gas and water socialism' has tended to underplay the importance of municipal politics in the struggle between capital and labour in the period between the 1880s and the First World War. For representatives of the capitalist class the emergence of the organized working class on the municipal stage was far from trivial. The growth of New Unionism was perceived by bourgeois interests as a serious crisis of British industry, but as an article in *The Times* noted on 19 August 1902, equally threatening to the 'national interest' was the 'political' moment of New Unionism as constituted by municipal socialism. The correspondent in *The Times* noted the extent to which, following the Paris meeting of the International Socialist Conference in 1900, which had highlighted the importance of the municipal state to socialist struggle, the major strands of British socialism had all made the successful capture and manipulation of local government an important step on the road to 'unqualified socialism'. The largest threat was constituted by socialists in the SDF and the ILP. *The Times* urged apathetic municipal electors to 'wake up' to this socialist threat, which threatened the entire basis of private enterprise either through direct appropriation, or through the increasing burden on the rates that was posing an increasing threat to levels of profitability. The concrete representation of labour within the institutional mechanisms of the municipal state thus became increasingly manifest through an emergent and increasingly severe fiscal crisis of the local state.

The most explicit manifestation of the fiscal crisis of the state was the growing level of municipal debt. Municipal debt increased between 1874 and 1899 by £183 million to £300 million, against a reduction in the national debt of £137 million; meanwhile taxation for the purposes of local expenditure in England and Wales increased from £17 million to £38 million between 1869 and 1899 (*The Times*, 28 August 1902). The negative impact of the increasing burden of local taxation can be illustrated with respect to the railway industry. Between 1882 and 1901, the local tax burden on the great London railway companies increased by 160 per cent from £76,703 to £199,420. Railways had been forced to contribute to the development of municipal tramway systems with which they were often in direct competition. Railway companies became increasingly unwilling to contribute to the development of 'municipal luxuries' such as water supply and drainage, from which they derived no intrinsic benefit. The direct losses fell on railway shareholders, and municipal enterprise became a subject of lamentation at the half-yearly meetings of all the major railway companies.

Publications such as *The Times* were concerned to develop a 'moral panic' by the suggestion that all municipalization, whether carried out by 'labour' or 'progressive' local authorities, was part of a programme for the socialization of production rather than for the 'improvement' of public service or saving of rates. Articles in *The Times* quoted at length the speeches and journals of the SDF, ILP and Fabian Society which equated municipal improvement with the struggle for socialism. Correspondents were critical of the 'underhand' way in which socialists had been able to secure a hold on local government through the so-called 'Municipal Workers' Committees'. Delegates to these committees were drawn from trade unions, trade councils, socialist bodies and co-operative societies. The committees provided a mechanism both for the formulation of socialist policy and for defraying the expenses of working-class socialists standing in local elections.

The election of working-class socialists on to local government bodies was perceived as a grave political threat. On 8 September 1902, *The Times* fulminated against 'the tendencies towards degeneration' involved in the process through which local authorities were taking on an increasing number of complex functions, while 'businessmen' were increasingly reluctant to stand for municipal office – men willing to govern in the 'general interests of the community' were not always willing to 'keep shop' for their fellow citizens. Businessmen had been dissuaded from standing for municipal office through the increasing demands on their time, the increasing need to bid for municipal contracts, and the 'mischievous' campaigns run by trade unionists against businessmen who failed either to pay union rates or to recognize trade unions.

The crisis of the municipal state resulted from the democratic impact of the organized working class on the administration of public services. The provision of services and the employment of labour according to democratic and bureaucratic procedures and principles heightened the fiscal crisis of the state. The resolution of the crisis required that the administration of labour and service provision was resubordinated to the regulatory social forms of law and money. The regulation of labour in particular could not be premised on the concrete and substantive demands and needs of the working class. The panic of the capitalist class in response to this crisis was reflected in the following letter to *The Times*:

> The expansion on so practical a scale of the fundamental principles of a thorough-going socialism, tends to encourage the entrance into municipal government of men who have axes to grind, who see advantages for their own class in direct employment, who want to promote the expansion of the socialist idea by still further exploiting the municipality. (*The Times*, 8 September 1902)

Articles in *The Times* documented the cases of a gasworker from Blackburn, a street trader from Wolverhampton and a steelworker from a 'northern industrial town' who had all been recently elected as 'labour' representatives. None of the men earned over 30 shillings a week, and they were unlikely to possess 'that practical knowledge of finance and industrial management needed to efficiently run municipal enterprises'. Such men were unlikely to serve the general interest of the community (i.e. ratepayers), were likely to have 'friends' in the trade union movement, and were therefore thoroughly untrustworthy with respect to 'the delicate question of the direct employment of labour'.

The new working-class socialists placed the selfish interests of labour before the general and abstract interests of municipal citizen-consumers. Within the structure of local government the refusal of 'efficient' members to co-operate with councillors whose 'position in life was little better than that of labourers' meant that the latter could not always be kept from the committees where they might do 'harm'. As a result, more and more public work was falling on the shoulders of the 'more qualified' members, and as *The Times* pointed out, in the context of a rapid increase in the amount and complexity of tasks falling on local government, this could have only one consequence – an increase in municipal bureaucracy. Increasingly, the real duties of local government were devolved to permanent officials and experts. In this way, the concrete demands of labour were institutionalized and formalized and thus constrained within the bureaucratic mechanisms of the state. The expansion of the municipal bureaucracy, however, was also a source of political concern to the interests of capital. Permanent officials had a vested interest in the expansion of municipal enterprise. This interest arose both from their sense of 'public service' and from the 'substantial pecuniary benefits' that accrued to them. Municipal officials and experts were increasingly perceived as a 'distinct political force' with a vested interest in the expansion of municipal socialism, and increasingly viewed as a threat to ratepayers, private traders and national industries.

The problems posed by the development of public service bureaucracy were compounded by the direct employment of labour by local authorities. The origin of the direct employment of labour was the establishment of the London County Council Works Department in May 1892. This had followed pressure by socialists on the LCC, such as John Burns, on the issue that LCC contracts should not be awarded to contractors who failed to observe trade union rates of pay and conditions. The inability of contractors to deliver services effectively on these terms led to the establishment of the Works Department. The control of the labour process by elected members of the council engendered an immediate crisis of labour discipline. A Manager of the LCC Works Department highlighted the 'demoralisation' that resulted from a situation in which workers elected their own employers:

> [F]or some time after the Works Department was established there was a tendency on the part of the skilled workmen in our employ not to do the same amount of work for the Council as they would be expected to do for a contractor, and it was only after repeated dismissals that the idea was shaken . . . [T]he visits of individual members of the Council to our works, who enter into conversation with the men employed there, is apt to be misconstrued. Some of the men store up their grievances, real and fancied, until councillors go on to the works, when they are related, and often, I am afraid, in a most exaggerated form. Several of the foremen have complained to me of the bad effect this has on the men, and have stated that their authority over them is very much diminished. (*The Times*, 10 September 1902)

Councillors naturally desired to stay on good terms with men whom they both employed and whose votes they depended on for their re-election. The situation was exacerbated with the emergence of public sector trade unions and the involvement of the unions in municipal workers' committees. In London, trade unions such as the Municipal Employees Association (MEA) had gained in strength owing to the related processes of New Unionism and the expansion of local government employment. These unions pursued demands for minimum wage provision, a 48-hour working week, and uniform wages for all grades in all districts irrespective of competence or efficiency. The unions increasingly used the elective strength of their collective membership to support or veto candidates in local elections on the basis of support for their programmes. The result of these developments was an increasing call for the disenfranchisement of municipal servants and the recommodification of municipal state labour. In other words, it was necessary to re-establish the autonomy of the 'economic' and the 'political' aspects of the capital relation in order to depoliticize public service provision. Sir Thomas Hughes, a municipal notable from Liverpool, is quoted in *The Times* as arguing that there was no great hardship in a man 'ceasing to have a voice in the choice of his master' on becoming a corporation employee. The threat of direct labour was not confined to the question of profit and loss. Direct labour was presented as a central element of the socialist project of transferring all 'remunerative employment' to the state or municipality, and the trade union project of protecting workers from the discipline of the labour market (*The Times*, 10 September 1902).

The democratic representation of the organized working-class within the administrative apparatus of the local state heightened the crisis of the municipal state. The development of municipal bureaucracy was therefore determined both by the struggle of working-class socialists against the state form and attempts to demobilize and institutionalize labour within the state form. As Kay and Mott (1982: 96) argue, 'administration is working class power post festum: working class political victories captured and formalized at their moment of victory'. The contradictory determination of the state, however, means that such formalization can never be complete. The Fabian bureaucratic centralism that emerged from the restructuring of the municipal state in the early twentieth century was a form of class compromise. It emerged on the basis of a partial resubordination of the municipal state to the abstract regulation of the rule of law and the law of money. In the context of local government, this involved an attempt to resubordinate the demands of public service workers to the 'general' and 'abstract' interests of 'citizen-consumers' *qua* ratepayers. Fabian bureaucratization was an attempt to depoliticize the provision of services and this involved restructuring the political, economic and ideological facets of the capital relation as it was manifested within the municipal state. The 'economic' struggle by capital against New Unionism, through an attempt to intensify and recommodify public service labour, was therefore complemented by the 'political' and 'ideological' struggle against municipal socialism. Fabian Socialism provided the legitimation for a political and ideological restructuring of the capital relation – the separation of the 'political' and 'economic' struggles of the labour movement and the reformulation of socialist demands within a statist and reformist ideological discourse.

In the sphere of production, centralized collective bargaining developed in order to ensure that the rewards of public service labour were regulated within the wage form in the context of nationally determined fiscal constraints. The organized activities of municipal public servants were partially demobilized through the development of the centralized and bureaucratic mechanisms of collective bargaining associated with 'Whitleyism'. This established the legitimate 'economic' aspirations of workers as something distinct from their 'political' demands for public services. In the sphere of exchange public service bureaucracy developed as a way of mediating the provision of public services through what appeared to be technocratic and managerialist procedures, but these were ultimately constrained by the necessity of providing services through contract (law) and price (money). The working class were not totally defeated but were demobilized, and their demands were institutionalized through bureaucratic modes of administration. The theory and practice of Fabian Socialism articulated this class compromise and provided the ideological support for socialist strategies premised on the integration of the working class within the state. The crisis of the municipal state was managed on the basis of Fabian Socialism; and Fabian Socialism was to provide the key ideological concepts for the development of the water industry in the twentieth century.

Fabian Socialism and Public Service as Class Compromise

The intellectual domination of Fabianism over the British labour movement has resulted in a widespread acceptance of what may be termed the 'Fabian view of history'.[7] The Fabian view of history equates the development of public enterprise directly with the development of socialism. This view of history presents state socialism as the dominant tradition of the British labour movement, and this provides the political and moral justification for bureaucratic and technocratic forms of public service provision. Fabian Socialism provided the ideological legitimation for the development of public service bureaucracy and its equation with the progressive development of socialism, but it is premised explicitly on marginalist economics and liberal social theory. The emergence of marginalist economics reflected a concern to defend the liberal order against the combined threats of trade unionism, working-class agitation and social reform towards the end of the nineteenth century. Marginalism replaced the classical cost theory of value with a subjectivist theory of value that removed questions of distribution from the domain of economics, and reformulated the rationality of capitalism in terms of its allocative efficiency as a system for the provision of human needs. The 'problem of order' was redefined as 'the problem of reconciling the efficiency of capitalist relations of production and exchange with the equity of capitalist relations of distribution' (Clarke, 1991b: 9). The importance of Fabian Socialism was thus that it did not recognize the inequality which resulted from the subordination of labour within the capitalist labour process.

The Fabians worked within an essentially liberal conceptualization of state and society. The individual was an essentially abstract individual: a citizen-consumer removed from the inequality and contradictions of capitalist social relations in the sphere of production. For the Fabians, the main contradiction of the capitalist order was between the formal rationality of capitalism as a means of producing and distributing goods and the substantive irrationality of capitalism which was caused by members of the capitalist class dominating state and society. In theory, the Fabians held that this contradiction could be resolved through the transformation of private into state property (*ibid.*: 178) – the development of municipal enterprise. In practice the Fabians accepted the political neutrality of money and the law and failed to pose a systematic challenge to the irrationality of the capital relation.

The development of working-class agitation and politics in the early 1890s left Fabian Socialism with the 'problem' of rationalizing the industrial struggle associated with New Unionism. The relationship between Fabian social theory and trade unionism is ambiguous and to some extent contradictory (Melitz, 1959: 554–60). The Fabians accepted the liberal definition of the state as the agency of ultimate sovereignty and the embodiment of legitimate coercion. The state was the most representative agency in society as it represented every individual, and social change and development should only be effected by the state following the agreement of individual citizens expressed through the ballot box. Trade union methods premised on potential coercion, extra parliamentary action and the elevation of the 'narrow interests' of labour over the wider interests of consumers and citizens were problematic. Fabians accepted the theory of wages developed by John Cairnes, which argued that trade unions could not affect general wage levels, and that the actions of organized workers could only be at the expense of their unorganized and less fortunate colleagues.

The explosion of labour activity associated with New Unionism forced a reappraisal of the Fabian attitude towards trade unions, and throughout the 1890s the Fabians adopted an increasingly pro-trade union position. The theoretical differences between Fabian Socialism and trade unionism were tackled by Sidney and Beatrice Webb in *Industrial Democracy* (1920). Collective bargaining was reconciled with neo-classical economic theory on the basis of Alfred Marshall's 'higgling and bargaining' theory of wage determination. Trade unions were reconciled with political liberalism through the focus on the increasingly democratic orientations and practices of trade unions: internally through their representative structures, and externally through their function of sensitizing society to the grievances and claims of the labouring class. The Webbs therefore retained a very narrow view of the role and functions of trade unions, and this was reflected in the Fabian model of 'gas and water socialism'.

The political strategy of the Fabian Society was premised upon the rejection of Marx's theory of value, and the development of a critique of capitalist society within the theoretical confines of the theory of marginal utility developed by Stanley Jevons. Fabian political strategy was premised upon the permeation of existing bourgeois political institutions – particularly local government and the Liberal Party. This position was most clearly set out in the *Fabian Essays in Socialism* published in 1889. In these essays Gas and Water Socialism emerged as a central theme. George Bernard Shaw developed the Jevonian theory of value in order to assert the social origins of wealth, and thus reversed the conclusions of neo-classical economics from its own premises. If wealth emerged from the preferences of individual utility-maximizers, then why should one class of people benefit from this process of mutual utility satisfaction? This allowed municipalism to be directly equated with socialism. Indeed, Sidney Webb argued that the public policy of the Liberal Party in London and Birmingham represented important victories for socialism.

The main concern of the Fabian socialists was the integration of labour within the democratic mechanisms of the state. This integration would resolve the struggle over the state form through the incorporation of individual public service workers as abstract citizen-consumers. Thus the Fabian model of public ownership was essentially a strategy of class compromise. A universal class of citizen-consumers were to be given rights within the representational form of the municipal state. In return organized labour confined its activities to issues around the terms and conditions of wage labour. Citizenship was within the sphere of exchange while the sphere of production was depoliticized, and its management became a technical matter to be undertaken by a hierarchy of experts. This was reflected in the Fabian model of public ownership.

The Fabian conceptualization of public ownership was explored by Annie Besant in the Fabian Essay entitled *Industry Under Socialism.* Besant argued for the development of the co-operative organization of industry under the initiatives of the newly formed county councils and established town councils – the 'municipalisation of industry'. The 'great' industries were already being trustified by capitalists and would eventually be taken over by the state. 'Small' industries, such as the gas and water industries, would be managed locally by committees of the local council. The Fabians did not recommend major changes in the management structures of enterprises taken into state ownership. In *Industrial Democracy* (1897) the Webbs argued that, within state enterprises, policy should be determined by salaried officials of the state or municipality, technical management should remain with experts, and aspects of working conditions should be put in the hands of workers and their union. Workers were to have equal rights in the election of municipal and parliamentary representatives, but were to have no special or privileged rights as employees.

Fabianism provided an ideological justification for the bureaucratization of the workers' movement. The approach of Sidney and Beatrice Webb was to argue that the trade unions had undergone a radical transformation, and as a result the British working class had become thoroughly imbued with Fabian statism, constitutionalism and gradualism. The 'success' of New Unionism facilitated a shift in socialist strategy towards gradualism and constitutionalism. The new approach crushed the 'Revolutionary Owenism' that had emerged during the 1880s, and which, through publications such as *Justice* (1883–9), preached the need for a collective commonwealth of all workers to effect a 'complete international social revolution'. The growth of public service bureaucracy and the resulting administration by 'experts' was an attempt to solve the contradictions of municipal public service.

This contradiction was the contradiction between use-value and exchange-value expressed in a political form: the contradiction between the need for effective water and sewerage services and the necessity that the regulation of these services by the state did not undermine the expanded reproduction of the capital relation. As I have shown in this chapter these contradictions arose because, while the contradictions of capitalist development could not be contained or regulated within the liberal state form, the substantive measures to resolve the contradiction through administration served merely to intensify the crisis tendencies of the local municipal state. Fabian technocracy was the ideological and institutional form taken by the resulting class compromise: a compromise which allowed the partial resubordination of public services to the abstract regulatory forms of law and money to be presented nevertheless as part of an inevitable evolutionary unfolding of socialist progress.

In this chapter I have demonstrated the way in which the contradictions of capitalist development resulted in the emergence of the municipal state, first as a mode of regulation and later as a mode of administration. I have shown how the contradictory form of the municipal state allowed the working class to pursue political demands through the political and administrative mechanisms of the state, and how this resulted in a severe and protracted crisis of the state. This illustrates the way in which public services emerged through a process of crisis and struggle and the way in which the public service state developed in order to contain and institutionalize this struggle. I have illustrated the way in which this containment was legitimated through the ideological discourse of Fabian Socialism and the way in which this laid the basis for the further contradictory development of the public service state in the twentieth century. I will demonstrate in Chapter 3 how the Fabian conceptualization of 'public service', as a management ideology and practice, laid the basis for the contradictory development of the monolithic and centralized 'planner-state' regulation of the water industry throughout the twentieth century.

Notes

1. In Bristol, the charter of the Bristol Gas Light Company, granted in 1819, limited dividends to 10 per cent and stipulated that any surplus would be payable to the Commissioners for Public Lighting in aid of rates. The Company also agreed to supply the Commissioners with gas at a fixed price of £5 per lamp per year, for a period of at least 21 years. See Nabb (1987: 4–5) for a detailed discussion of the conditions under which the Bristol Gas Light Company was constituted.
2. The Gasworks Clauses Act of 1847 limited company dividends to 10 per cent. In 1860 the Metropolis Gas Act attempted to eliminate overlapping and waste through the concept of 'districting'. Successive gas acts from the

1840s controlled the price of gas supplied to private consumers and ensured that gas was supplied on demand. The 'sliding scale' developed from the 1860s directly linked prices and dividends in an inverse relationship, while the Gasworks Clauses Act of 1871 placed an obligation upon gas undertakings to supply consumers on demand. See Williams (1981: 40–4) for an extended discussion of nineteenth-century gas legislation.

3. The attitude of John Stuart Mill to state intervention in the nineteenth-century water industry is explored by Schwartz (1966). In 1842, Mill wrote an article in *The Examiner* that examined a report entitled 'Public Agency v. Trading Companies' that had been prepared by the Metropolitan Sanitary Association in an attempt to agitate for the application of Edwin Chadwick's principles in London. The main convergence between Chadwick and Mill was on the issue of the social costs of bad sanitation: the way in which bad sanitation killed more people than any war, and the way in which infectious diseases were major causes of destitution, widowhood and orphanage. Indeed, the Report led Mill to modify his theory of population: proving that what Malthus called the 'positive checks of population' – misery and vice – did not diminish numbers, but simply kept the population in a younger and more sickly state. Mill highlighted the 'economy of labour' that would result from London being supplied by a single water or gas company under state supervision. A discussion of the role of J. S. Mill in the development of the water industry in London can also be found in Gibbon and Bell (1939: 64–5).
4. See Coates and Topham (1994: 36–123) for an extended discussion of the emergence and development of New Unionism in Britain.
5. This was also illustrated by the ambiguous anti-statism among the working class *vis-à-vis* the Liberal social reforms of 1906. See Pelling (1968).
6. This was the position developed by Bax in *Modern Socialism*, published in 1879. The SDF position was developed in a document published in 1883 entitled *Socialism Made Plain, Being the Social and Political Manifesto of the Democratic Federation.*
7. See Hobsbawm (1968: 250–71) for an exploration of the ways in which the Fabians have successfully disseminated the myths of Fabian history.

3 Public Service and the Contradictions of State Planning

In Britain, public services developed in a decentralized and *ad hoc* way. Following the failure of private enterprise to provide effective services, water, gas and electricity, as well as health and education services, were all initially provided by local authorities or local *ad hoc* commissions and boards. The role of the central state was minimal and was usually limited to the passing of enabling legislation. While this pattern of development provided local authorities with a high level of autonomy from the central state it also limited the ability of local authorities to develop large-scale capital projects. Such projects were obstructed either by conflicts of interests between authorities or by the limited ability of authorities to raise revenue from either local taxation or exchequer loans and grants. As the limitations of municipal provision became apparent there was an increasing concern to *rationalize* public services. At first this took the form of mergers between authorities in order to create joint boards, but following the Second World War, a range of public services were nationalized and thereby transformed into publicly owned commercial companies. The argument behind the creation of publicly owned utilities was that it would allow public services to be *planned* on the basis of public needs. In reality, however, publicly owned utilities turned out to be inefficient and unresponsive bureaucracies, that not only failed to serve public needs, but were also seen to be undermining the national economy through their demands on the Exchequer. The result of these problems has been that over the past twenty years utilities have been restructured according to commercial criteria and returned to the private sector.

In the past 150 years, therefore, there has been a shift from private sector to local authority to nationalized company and finally back to the private sector. The complexity of this historical development highlights the simplicity of many recent attempts to explain the factors behind the crisis of the welfare state and the neo-liberal restructuring of states and societies in the 1980s and 1990s. Neo-liberalism cannot be explained on the basis of an ahistorical conjunctural analysis of the type outlined in Chapter 1, but requires a logical and historical analysis of the contradictions underlying the very notion of public service and the representation of the common interest by the state. In this chapter I explore the development of the water industry in the twentieth century in order to highlight the contradictions of state administration and planning, and the way in which these contradictions resulted in the recent crisis of public service and the neo-liberal restructuring of public services.

Capitalist Crisis and the Contradictions of State Planning

The development of public service has to be analysed in the context of the wider crises and contradictions of capital accumulation and the state form. In Chapter 2 I traced the contradictions underlying the development of municipal public service provision. The municipal state developed in the phase of capital accumulation based on the extraction of absolute surplus value and mobilized the counter-tendencies against the physical destruction of living labour-power. As I argued in Chapter 1, the intensification of labour through Taylorism and Fordism marked the shift to capital accumulation on the basis of relative surplus value and transformed both the way in which the contradictions of capital accumulation became manifest and the form and functions of the state in the mobilization of counter-tendencies against the tendency for the rate of profit to fall (TRPF). Following the shift to capital accumulation based on the extraction of relative surplus value the primary crisis tendency becomes the expulsion of living labour-power from the labour process and the tendency towards the over-accumulation of capital. The counter-tendencies mobilized by the state involved attempts to lower the organic composition of capital (OCC) and to increase the extraction of relative surplus value. The state therefore encouraged the rationalization of production through the introduction of Fordist and Taylorist production methods and pursued a generalized reduction in wage levels, welfare benefits and living standards (Clarke, 1988: 196–203). The state was recomposed as a *planner-state* (Negri, 1988): this involved the development of Keynesian demand management techniques designed to manage levels of 'effective demand' and thereby manage a continual revolution in incomes and investment, in order to eliminate over-investment, increase the marginal efficiency of capital and facilitate sustained economic growth.

The important point is that these developments were not the result of an immanent law of capitalist development but were an emergent result of class struggle. As I highlighted in Chapter 2, a central theme of socialist activity in the period between the 1890s and the 1910s was a working-class struggle for autonomy from both the state and capital. In the 1920s the development of Taylorism and Fordism reflected the 'economic' moment of a more generalized state-led assault on the autonomy of organized labour. The composition of the planner-state recognized the autonomy of labour, but incorporated it within the administrative mechanisms of the state in an attempt to 'plan' the production and co-ordination of relative surplus value. This involved socializing the costs of capital depreciation and ensuring that levels of wages were dependent on increased productivity. The contradictory form of the state, however, implied that the plans of the state could only be realized through the abstract social forms of money and the law. The problem was that the development of the planner-state resulted in the politicization of money through the direct administration of capital accumulation, and this resulted in an increasingly severe 'fiscal crisis'. The socialization and politicization of money by the nation state gave state bureaucrats, public service managers and workers a great deal of autonomy in the way in which the delivery of goods and services was organized. As I will show in this chapter, this autonomy was the principal dynamic in the development and crisis of public service, and state restructuring has been focused on reducing this autonomy through the resubordination of public services to the abstract regulatory forms of law and money. I will begin by exploring the ideological legitimation of planner-state public service by Fabian Socialism, and the way in which this ideology emerged from the material contradictions underlying the direct administration of public services by the state.

Fabian Socialism and the Contradictions of State Planning

As I argued in Chapter 2, the bureaucratic statism of Fabian Socialism represented a class compromise which resulted from the partial demobilization of organized labour. The recomposition of the state in response to the recomposition of capital on the basis of relative surplus value widened the Fabian vision of what it was possible for state planning to achieve. The changing focus of Fabian social theory reflected fundamental changes in the material form of the capitalist state. However, the intellectual traditions of idealism and liberalism which formed the basis of Fabian philosophy resulted in these changes being presented by Fabian writers in a fetished and mystified way. It is, however, possible to deconstruct the fetished categories of Fabian Socialism in order to chart the material contradictions underlying the development of the planner-state in the twentieth century. The intellectual foundations of Fabian Socialism are essentially idealist and moral (George and Wilding, 1985: 69–70) and this allowed the Fabians to reconceptualize the notions of 'common good' and public service on the basis of the material developments resulting from the centralizing and rationalizing tendencies of the planner-state. As the focus of class struggle shifted from the form of the municipal state to the form of the nation state, the Fabians reinterpreted the meaning of public service through an increasingly centralized, bureaucratic and technocratic state ideology and practice. An example of the shift in the focus of Fabian Socialism is to be found in the changing emphasis in the work of G. D. H. Cole.

Immediately following the First World War Cole was interested in the theory and practice of workers' control and the way in which 'Guild Socialism'[1] could transcend the servility of capitalist wage labour (Wright, 1976) to produce co-operative networks of producers and consumers, to determine human needs through direct and functional democracy (Cole, 1920; 1972; 1980). Essentially, Cole turned Rousseau on his head to argue that the 'General Will' finds expression only in the concrete functional needs of individuals, and that it is in the performance of specific functions that the 'General Will' finds its essential expression (Cole, 1973; Vernon, 1980). Direct democracy was thus the only true form of democracy, as voting in a liberal democracy could not alter the distinction between wage-labour and capital. However, the value-form could be mediated politically and Guild socialism provided the institutional mechanism to facilitate this mediation.

Public service for Cole was, therefore, an essentially moral and ethical concept premised on an inherent human desire to serve fellow human beings. However, during the post-war period Cole applied this conception to increasingly centralized and bureaucratic state forms (Cole, 1943: 30–51; 1950). Cole increasingly accepted the inevitability of bureaucratic centralism and the issue became whether the resulting institutions were to be controlled by unrepresentative oligopolists in the public and private sectors or through the democratic institutions of the state – the state acting as the embodiment of public service and the 'common good'. Cole became increasingly interested in the Soviet Union[2] as the desired model for the development of socialism in Britain. He argued that the Soviet Union had transcended the capitalist value form and allowed an expansion in the production of use-values to the productive limits of the economy. Similarly, the development of centralized Keynesian state planning and the nationalization of industry in Britain would also enable the capitalist value form to be transcended and enable managers and technicians to co-operate with workers to ensure the optimum production of use-values as determined by the democratic institutions of parliament. The resulting institutions would unproblematically articulate the morality of public service as the removal of the profit motive would allow managers and workers to fulfil their instinctive desire to serve their fellow (wo)man.

The discourse of Fabian Socialism played a centrally important role in restructuring the ideological form of the state in the process through which the planner-state was formed. The unproblematical acceptance of the neutrality of the state, science, law and money allowed the contradictions of capitalism to be presented as technical problems which could be resolved through the planning and management by relevant experts. This approach was strengthened by the wider ideological currents of Leninism and Stalinism in the USSR and Keynesian liberalism in the West. In this sense Fabianism was the historically specific form taken by Keynesianism in the UK and was given socialist credibility by the weakness of state theory emerging from the USSR – particularly the instrumentalist approach to the state developed by Lenin and transformed into a legitimatory state ideology by Stalin. Hence, the notion that if only socialists could gain control of the levers of state power, then the contradictions of capitalism could be *planned away* became an increasing preoccupation of Fabian writers in Britain. This apparent convergence between Keynesianism and Stalinism strengthened the Fabian utopia of the planner-state.

As I will show in the remainder of the chapter, the planner-state could not overcome the contradictions of capital accumulation as it was ultimately premised on a utopian notion of capital: the illusory communism of capital (Negri, 1988: 32). In bourgeois society capital appears in the form of and exists through *things* (money, factories, houses, machines, utility infrastructure). The democratic production and regulation of these 'things' by the state and the increasing separation of ownership and control through joint stock corporations and trusts makes it appear as if capital has been socialized and thus that capitalist ownership of the means of production has been transcended and with it the exploitation of labour by capital. It is however possible to delve beneath this fetished appearance in order to highlight the illusory nature of this apparent socialization. The state cannot socialize capital because capital is a *social relation* of exploitation and the state is the particular political form of this exploitation. The administrative planning, production and distribution of use-values to serve human needs cannot escape the regulatory forms of law and money which reimpose abstraction on the administrative mechanisms of the state. The ultimate consequence of the planner-state was therefore administrative and bureaucratic paralysis. The state planned improvements in public services through elaborate capital projects. The projects were obstructed by their necessary mediation through the money form. Where administrative projects were funded through exchequer grants and loans the resulting fiscal inflation undermined capital accumulation. The integration of concrete labour within the state and the further development of professional state bureaucrats, therefore, heightened the contradictions on which the planner-state was premised, and the planner-state was increasingly unable to ensure the production of either use-values or values. As I will highlight later in this chapter, this was the context for the neo-liberal restructuring of the 1980s and 1990s. I want to illustrate the above arguments through an analysis of the development and crisis of the planner-state water industry.

Rationalization and the Development of the Planner-State Water Industry

The main dynamic to the development of the water industry in the first half of the twentieth century was the concern of the state with respect to the uncoordinated and piecemeal operations of small *ad hoc* authorities. Undertakers operated either through special Acts of Parliament based on the 1847 Waterworks Clauses Act that laid out sources and limits of supply, the nature and site of works and maximum prices and dividends (in the case of SWCs), or under the general powers of the Public Health Acts. The rapid urbanization of the late nineteenth and early twentieth centuries forced municipal corporations to augment supplies from increasingly remote sources: Manchester, Liverpool and Birmingham procuring supplies from 106, 68, and 74 miles respectively. The result of these *ad hoc* developments was often overlapping and wasteful absurdities such as the competitive pumping of sources and the duplication of trunk mains from remote sources. Undertakers that sought extensions of supply were required to make a fresh application to Parliament in order to extend or modify their powers. The central state lacked both the powers and the knowledge to undertake long-term planning or to devise or enforce alternative and improved methods of supply, and could apply only restrictive and negative mechanisms of control.

The overlapping and waste of *ad hoc* development became an increasing concern of the state. In 1923 an Advisory Committee on Water, constituted by representatives of undertakers, was established within the Ministry of Health in order to make recommendations on changes in water law and practice. This was complemented in 1924 when the Ministry of Health started to encourage the formation of 'Regional Advisory Water Committees', on which the interests of undertakers, county councils and the Ministry of Health were represented. It was, however, the unprecedented drought of 1934 that highlighted the limitations of the *ad hoc* development and fragmented nature of the water industry. The 1934 Water Supplies (Exceptional Shortage Orders) Act gave the Minister (temporary) powers to abolish or modify limitations on abstraction and supply and to force undertakers to supply other undertakers. The 1934 Rural Water Supplies Act facilitated the provision of exchequer grants for the extension of rural supplies that had previously been obstructed by the prohibitive costs of distribution. The 1934 Supply of Water in Bulk Act allowed the transfer of bulk supplies between undertakers with the consent of the Minister of Health. In 1935 the 'Inland Water Survey' was established in order to collect and collate records on underground and surface water resources.

The 1934 drought also resulted in the reconstitution of the Advisory

Water Committee as the Central Advisory Water Committee (CAWC) on which the interests of all aspects of the water industry were represented. Following its inception in 1937, the CAWC published a series of reports that were to be fundamental in shaping the reforms associated with the 1945 Water Act. The reports were concerned with the development of new mechanisms of water planning, the simplification of procedures by which undertakers could obtain additional powers, the supply of water for industry and the development of new river boards to take over the functions of land drainage, the prevention of pollution and the management of fisheries from existing local authorities and *ad hoc* bodies. In mapping out the 'defects in the present system' the 1944 White Paper *A National Water Policy* (HMSO, 1944) was concerned primarily with: the vague and ill-defined responsibilities and powers of both central government and local undertakers; the multiplicity of undertakers; the lack of detailed information on water resources; the lack of a legal obligation on undertakers to supply water for non-domestic (industrial) purposes; and the inadequacy of rural supplies.

The 1944 White Paper laid out the objectives and principles of a 'national water policy': namely, 'to make the best and most economical use of the nation's water resources ... allocation of resources must conform with a *planned* water economy and be based on informed estimates of needs'. This required the development of efficient means of collecting and using information relating to water resources and the development of effective mechanisms to apply this information. What I have termed the planner-state regulation of water was to be premised on three general principles. These principles formed the basis of the 1945 Water Act and highlight the Fabian premises of the modern water industry:

1. *Central control*: the prevention of haphazard and wasteful development.
2. *Democratic control*: the responsibility for the administration of water resources to be placed with the Minister responsible to Parliament at the centre and elected local authorities at the periphery.
3. *Common good*: Sectional interests subordinated to the national interest and the development of mechanisms to permit the political mediation of conflict. (HMSO, 1944: 7)

The 1945 Water Act was designed to rationalize the provision of water in Britain. The Act gave ministers responsibility for promoting the conservation and proper use of water resources and to secure the effective execution by water undertakers, under their control and discretion, of a national policy relating to water. The Act required water undertakers to procure adequate supplies in order to provide a wholesome and continuous supply, and where supplies were sufficient, to make water available for those other purposes, such as industry and trade, on which the life and prosperity of the community depended. The Act facilitated the development of tariff scales that permitted the 'cross-subsidization' of rural water and sewerage services. It also established machinery designed to rationalize the industry with respect to the number of operating units. This included the granting of compulsory powers to the Minister in order to enforce the merging of groups of small undertakers. The Act finally reconstituted the CAWC on a statutory basis with enhanced powers that enabled it to make representations to ministers on any questions within its terms of reference.

The reforms of 1945 attempted to impose centralized co-ordination and control on the (democratic) municipal provision of water services. As I will show later in this chapter, the result of the reforms was institutional paralysis. The administrative and technocratic planning of water resources constantly came up against the problem of securing financial resources in order to put the plans into effect. Neither central nor municipal authorities were able to raise the finance that would allow the effective co-ordination and operation of the industry. The management of the post-war water industry was indeed marked by an increasingly technocratic and systematic approach to the augmentation and conservation of water resources. However, as we will see below, the divergence of interests at different stages of the 'water cycle' and the increasing need to control the public sector borrowing requirement undermined the operational effectiveness of the industry. This institutional paralysis provided the context for the managerialization of the water industry, together with a reformulation of Fabian conceptualizations of public service and the common good in an attempt to resolve an increasingly serious fiscal crisis of the state.

Fiscal crisis and the crisis of Fabian Socialism

The substantive operation of the planner-state was not to live up to the Fabian utopia. The utopia had therefore to be rewritten, and it was rewritten in the form of managerialism. The Fabians were not of course alone in arguing that the separation of ownership and control implied by the development of the joint-stock corporation and the nationalized industries had fundamentally transformed the locus of power and politics in modern state and society (Bell, 1961; Burnham, 1945; Galbraith, 1969). What was unique about Fabianism was the way in which it applied the theory of managerialism to the crisis and contradictions of the British state. The problem was that the planner-state was increasingly unable to deliver the goods, services and benefits that were required to alleviate the inequalities in power and resources that marked post-war Britain. The planner-state was unable to implement administrative programmes fully without simultaneously threatening its own tax-base: the crisis and contradictions of the planner-state thus appeared as an increasingly serious *fiscal crisis* by which the ability of the state to satisfy social needs was increasingly constrained by prohibitive costs. Fabian socialists presented the crisis of the planner-state as a technical problem that would be resolved through the application of science and technology by managerial experts.

The debate within Fabianism focused on the way in which science and technology were to be applied and controlled by the planner-state. The crisis of the planner-state was thus conceptualized as a technical problem that would be resolved through the application of expertise to the administrative mechanisms of the state. Fabianism reflected the material contradictions that were emerging from the substantive failures of planning. The debate between Richard Crossman and Anthony Crosland during the 1950s focused on the Fabian response to the crisis of the planner-state and illustrated the tension between the liberal and technocratic moments of Fabianism (see for example Crossman, 1956; Crosland, 1952). Crossman attempted to maintain the autonomy of the state from the 'economic' and 'political' power of the capitalist class while Crosland realized that the crisis of the planner-state would be resolved only if the products of state planning were mediated by the abstract social forms of money and the law. Crossman and Crosland were therefore engaging with the increasingly apparent contradiction between administration and regulation as the political form in which the contradictions of capital accumulation appear.

The liberal Fabianism of Crossman theorized the crisis of the planner-state in terms of the democratic unaccountability of oligopolistic managers in both the public and private sectors. Through the extension of public ownership and democratic planning Crossman envisaged that managers would become the servants rather than the masters of the nation. The planner-state controlled by the Labour Party unproblematically represented the 'common good' and it was equally important for Crossman that the sectional interests of organized labour were subordinated to the democratic control of Parliament. The planner-state, therefore, would resolve the problems of inequality and poverty through the democratic control and planning of technological and scientific development on the basis of a politically-defined notion of the 'common good'. Individual freedom and liberty would be expanded through the process of 'planning for freedom'.

The technocratic Fabianism of Crosland was different. It highlighted the limits of administrative discretion and the extent to which the crisis of the planner-state would be resolved through the regulation of production and reproduction through the abstract forms of money and the law. Crosland argued that the combination of Keynesian planning and the separation of the ownership and control of industry had produced a distinctively new form of society which he termed 'statism'. The defining feature of statism was the emergence of the state as an independent and intermediate power dominating the economic life of the nation. The emerging 'managerial class' was increasingly motivated by its contribution to the 'public good' rather than the pursuit of higher profits and dividends. The worst excesses of liberal capitalism had been transcended by progressive fiscal policies and the maintenance of full employment. From this perspective the main obstacle to the further elimination of inequality was the irrationality and irresponsibility of organized labour.

For Crosland, the further development of the welfare state needed to be financed by increases in economic efficiency. The main obstacles to an increase in productivity were the trade unions, and Crosland ultimately resolved the crisis of the planner-state with regard to the problem of labour: his solution being the recommodification of labour within the public sector labour process and a reapplication of the rule of law to address the deteriorating state of UK collective bargaining. This was to become an increasing preoccupation of the Wilson and Callaghan administrations, manifested in developments such as the concerns around the report of the Donovan Commission and the 'Social Contract' (Hyman, 1989a: 26–54).

Crosland grasped in an incomplete and mystified way the internal decomposition of the planner-state. The planning of and for labour by the state was having increasingly serious consequences which became manifest politically as administrative paralysis and economically as inflation. As a result the 'problem of labour' became an increasing concern of the state during the 1960s and 1970s: specifically, the need to reduce unofficial stoppages and to link wage increases to increases in productivity (Hyman, 1989a: 203–12). Attempts to solve the 'problem of labour' also found concrete expression in the managerialization of the state sector during the early 1970s. The Fabians had assimilated and developed the utopian conceptualization of capital articulated by Keynesianism, and rationalized the oppressive and repressive edifice of the planner-state as a part of the progressive and harmonious movement towards socialism. However, the socialistic and democratic legitimation of the planner-state was increasingly undermined by the technocratic and bureaucratic reforms developed in response to the contradictions of this planner-state. The case of the water industry highlights the material processes underlying the crisis and internal decomposition of the Fabian conception of public service.

The Managerialization of the Water Industry

The crisis in the planner-state administration of water was largely perceived as a technical problem which resulted from the fragmentary nature of the industry. The problem with respect to the design and development of major water and sewerage schemes was that they were constrained by natural watersheds that seldom coincided with local authority boundaries. The 1945 Water Act failed to provide an effective mechanism for the planning of water resources. The need for such a system was highlighted by the Report of the Proudman Committee that was established by the CAWC in 1955 in order to consider anticipated increases in the demand for water and the problems associated with meeting these expected increases. The Committee reported in 1962, and projected that on the basis of an increase in demand of 2.4 per cent per year between 1955 and 1960, the demand for water would double by 2000. Moreover, rainfall was heaviest in the north and west of England and in Wales, and demand was projected to grow most rapidly in south and east England. The projected increase in demand therefore required the development and conservation of existing resources and major capital works to facilitate the movement of water over long distances. The recommendations of the Committee, for 'comprehensive new authorities' to manage the overall resources of a river basin and the need for a national water policy, were incorporated within the 1963 Water Resources Act with respect to the creation of 29 hydrologically-based river authorities and the Water Resources Board (WRB).

The WRB was established in order to provide a national agency for the collection of data, research and planning, and was intended to act as an advisory body to river authorities and the Government. The members of the board were appointed on the basis of their scientific expertise in the field of sanitary engineering or chemistry, and were expected to provide technical assistance in the development of major hydrometric schemes. The WRB undertook a series of influential hydrological surveys which highlighted the need to plan water resources over increasingly large areas (Water Resources Board, 1973a). With data supplied by river authorities and water undertakers, the WRB undertook a survey of the projected resource requirements of England and Wales: this highlighted the increasing need to undertake major hydrological projects such as the transfer of water between river basins, the regulation of river flows and a series of complex and expensive capital projects in south-east England and Lincolnshire – most notably a plan to build a huge tidal barrage across the Wash.

The 1963 Water Resources Act was an explicit attempt to develop a more systematic and technically efficient framework for planning water resources. The new river authorities were based on natural watersheds, and were given responsibility for land drainage, fisheries, the control of pollution and water conservation. However, the majority of the members of the new river authorities were representatives of local government – who were also concerned with the cheap disposal of sewage effluent. The function of controlling pollution had been taken from the 'inefficient' local authorities by the 1948 River Board Act, and successive legislation had given river boards the power to impose increasingly rigorous 'consents'. The 1960 Clean Rivers (Estuaries and Tidal) Act gave river authorities the power to control all significant new discharges into estuaries, and the Secretary of State had the power to make orders under the Rivers (Prevention of Pollution) Acts concerning existing discharges. Given the make-up of the river authorities, however, the increasingly rigorous consents were not exercised in any meaningful way, and no orders or consents were issued for any of the major estuaries in the post-war period.

The perceived failure of the 1963 reforms resulted in the CAWC being reconvened in September 1969 in order to consider

> [h]ow in the light of . . . technological and other developments the functions relating to water conservation, management of water resources, water supply, sewerage, sewage disposal and the prevention of pollution . . . can best be organized. (DoE, 1971: 1)

The Committee reflected the conflict between competing users of water resources at different stages of the water cycle, and in particular the conflict between organizations with an interest in augmenting public water supplies in order to meet anticipated increased demand for drinking water and organizations with an interest in using water resources as an industrial raw material or as a conduit for the disposal of sewage and industrial waste. The 1971 Report by the CAWC highlighted the way in which Government 'loan sanctions' had effectively blocked the 'consents' that required the construction of new sewerage works. The report resulted in the 1973 Water Act which attempted to subject the administrative functions of the water industry to the abstract regulatory power of monetary regulation. The 1973 Water Act removed water services from the control of elected municipal authorities and facilitated the development of more technical and bureaucratic mechanisms of interest mediation and planning based on integrated river basin management by large multi-function regional water authorities (RWAs).

The 1971 CAWC Report highlighted the extent to which the projected increase in the demand for water was likely to increase the importance of water quality. Projected increases in demand, it argued, would be most efficiently met through the extensive and systematic reuse of water resources. In order to meet anticipated increases in demand upon resources for water supply, water would increasingly have to be drawn from the lower reaches of rivers, which involved the reuse of diluted sewage effluent as drinking water. The problem of augmenting raw water supplies of suitable quality, quantity and cost was presented as an administrative problem which resulted from the conflict of interest associated with the procurement of new resources for water supply. The 1945 Water Act obliged water undertakers to procure adequate supplies in order to provide a wholesome and continuous supply for domestic purposes. However, the 1963 Water Resources Act also obliged undertakers to obtain a licence to abstract water from the relevant river authorities who were given a duty to take actions for 'conserving, redistributing ... or augmenting water resources in their area'. While river authorities needed to have regard to the duty of undertakers to provide water for domestic purposes, there was a strain between the conservation interests of the river authority and the financial and quality concerns of the undertakers.

The fragmented nature of the water industry inhibited the effective application of the joint and national hydrometric schemes that had been developed by the WRB. Schemes involved more than one authority, and given the way in which costs and benefits would necessarily apply to the river basin as a whole, and the way in which the balance of costs and benefits might change at some future date, the apportionment of costs between authorities and agencies was highly complex and increasingly problematic. The conflict of interest was particularly acute between sewerage authorities discharging effluent into a river, and water supply undertakers wanting to abstract water for drinking water farther downstream. Higher expenditure on sewerage treatment would only benefit authorities and agencies further downstream.

The conclusion of the 1971 CAWC Report was that these conflicts, and others involving land-use and the siting of industry in catchment areas, could only be mediated effectively through the development of effective and comprehensive mechanisms of planning. Water management was a problem for, and a benefit to, the whole river basin, and what was needed was a framework that would allow the equation of costs and benefits in naturally determined hydrological areas. The CAWC Report argued that a comprehensive 'water management plan' should be developed for every river basin, and that this required fundamental organizational and financial reforms to the existing regulatory framework. The Report recommended that the water industry should be restructured in order to facilitate effective co-ordination and planning.

Regional water authorities (RWAs) were to be responsible for the development of 'Action Plans' that would establish the short and medium term priorities *vis-à-vis* the implementation of a 'National Plan'. The 'Action Plan' would specify the amount of finance (aggregate value) that Central Government had decided to commit to projects in the regions. This amount was to be calculated on the basis of the projected future demand for water and the current state of the economy. In addition to the development of Action Plans, the RWAs were to develop long-term 'Regional Plans' that would project and interpolate the National Plan with future Action Plans on the basis of the projected growth in population and industrial activity. The CAWC, however, stressed the enduring 'public service' conception of water services and argued that provision should adapt in accordance with other factors and authorities (DoE, 1971: 45).

The 1973 Water Act restructured the water industry on the basis of 'Integrated River Basin Management', by which ten new RWAs were made responsible for all aspects of the water cycle within their naturally determined hydrological areas. The RWAs took over the assets of local authorities, joint boards and river authorities, and were to act as public utilities operating within commercial criteria and financial objectives laid down by the Secretary of State. The objectives of the RWAs were to develop systems which would allow the efficient management and co-ordination of planned capital investment programmes. The 1973 Act laid the basis for the development of charging systems and investment appraisal mechanisms which were to enable the full value of water resources to be realized and which were to prevent 'over investment'. The economic and financial objectives of the new RWAs were:

1. The development of charging systems which ensure that the demand for services (and hence investment) is not exaggerated by the supply of services at prices which are too low in relation to the value of the resources used. Charges should not be seen as a way of getting the necessary revenue and allocating the cost fairly among different users of the service, but to ensure the optimum use of available resources by making users aware of the cost of supplying the water which they use. The best way of ensuring this is to relate the charge for the water used directly to the cost of that water.
2. The development of techniques of investment appraisal which ensure that demand is met in the most efficient way with due regard to the timing of investment.
3. To ensure that revenue is sufficient to balance recurrent expenditure over a period of years. Like the nationalised industries, the RWAs will require target rates of return on capital. (DoE, 1973: 31)

The 1973 Water Act determined the form of the 'managerial' water industry. The organizational structure preferred by ministers and civil servants comprised a chairman appointed on the basis of his or her proven ability in guiding complex organizations and a board of 10–15 persons appointed on the basis of technical expertise or membership of major local authorities. Owing to the enduring influence of local government representatives on the CAWC, however, the final Act produced boards which were made up of a majority of local government nominees, and large, cumbersome boards of up to 50 members were established. Furthermore, the maintenance of sewage distribution systems remained with local authorities, who were to act as the agents of the RWAs (Jordon *et al.*, 1977: 330–1). The Government, however, refused to follow the recommendations of the CAWC and develop a 'national water authority'. Planning functions were retained within government departments and the National Water Council (NWC) was established in order to provide a consultative and advisory body at national level.

The reforms of the 1970s resulted in the managerialization of the water industry. The industry was removed from local democratically elected bodies in an attempt to resolve the fiscal crisis of the planner-state through the application of rational planning and administration. The crisis was resolved through the development of 'integrated river basin management' that would focus on the reuse of existing resources rather than developing more costly new resources: an attempt to solve the fiscal crisis of the state through technical and scientific planning. The focus shifted from a concern with water quantity to a concern with water quality. The reforms illustrate the strain between the administrative and regulatory moments of the state: authorities could plan (administrate for) the production of water services but the realization of these services outside the money form heightened the crisis of the planner-state and forced a tightening of the regulatory mechanisms to which the administration of water services was subject. Managerialism was an attempt to solve the crisis and contradictions of planning through further planning. It was for this reason that, rather than solving the crisis of the planner-state, managerialism intensified the crisis and laid the basis for the more thoroughgoing commercial restructuring of public services in the late 1970s and early 1980s.

Managerialization was legitimated on the basis of 'public service'. However, the increasingly strict financial targets imposed on the water industry further inhibited the effective production of water services (i.e. use-values) and further undermined the rationality of the planner-state. Managerialization removed the water industry from democratic control and subjected the industry to bureaucratic rationality. Earlier, the contradictory form of the capitalist state had allowed the administrative activities of the planner-state to be legitimated on the basis of a democratic Fabian centralism. Planning reflected the democratically expressed wishes of the electorate and the demands of the electorate were to be delivered via Parliament and local authorities by technocratic and managerial administrators. The managerialization of the water industry removed the democratic basis for determining levels of service and investment, while the fiscal crisis of the state forced water authorities to cut costs, reduce capital spending and intensify the labour of waterworkers.

Managerialism precipitated heightened levels of fiscal inflation and evoked increasingly stringent bureaucratic controls on finance in order to ameliorate the fiscal crisis of the state. The contradictions of managerialism resulted in serious cuts in public spending and the managerialist water industry was forced simultaneously to reduce service and increase prices. Managerialization reflected the recomposition of the state. It involved resubjecting the administrative activities of the state to the abstract regulatory forms of law and money. Increasingly, contractual and monetary relationships replaced administrative relationships. In this sense the managerialist state was a 'transitional' form of state between the Fabian planner-state and the neo-liberal state which has emerged from the ruins of the planner-state.[3] The political and economic decomposition of the planner-state therefore made the ideological representation of the planner-state as an embodiment of the 'common good' increasingly untenable. The Fabian ideology of the planner-state as progressive was increasingly undermined by the state imposing legal and monetary restrictions on the ability of the water industry to meet public needs. The planner-state was an attempt to manage the crises and contradictions of capital accumulation. The state, however, is a contradictory social form of the capital relation and, in the context of a wider global crisis of over-accumulation, the contradictions of the state became increasingly manifest. The result was an increasingly serious crisis of crisis management.

The Crisis of Crisis Management: Public Service and the Law of Money

The crisis of the planner-state water industry has to be seen in the context of the wider crisis of Keynesianism as a global form of capital accumulation. In this sense the crisis of the KWS is a reflection of the way in which the crisis of the international monetary system interacted with the specificity of the British state (Clarke, 1988: 287–341). The managerialization of the state took place in the context of a severe and protracted crisis of over-accumulation. Keynesianism was dependent on US expansionism and the hegemony of the US dollar in maintaining international liquidity. While this form of accumulation resulted in periodic crises of over-accumulation, nation states were able to mobilize counter-tendencies effectively through the stop–go policies that were a characteristic of the 1950s and 1960s. The 'oil crisis' of the early 1970s ruptured global Keynesianism, and the restrictive US monetary policies which followed forced other national governments to pursue similarly restrictive policies.

In the UK the state attempted to counter the inflationary impact of increased public spending and incomes by incorporating organized labour within the state and attempting to manage the relationship between wages and productivity through a series of incomes policies. The UK, however, lacked effective dirigiste mechanisms of corporate concertation to link the administrative and regulatory moments of the state. As a result, increases in public spending and public sector pay resulted in inflation, unemployment, a reduction in international competitiveness and the opening up of divisions between workers in the public and private sectors. The contradictions of the KWS allowed the Callaghan government to engage in a populist assault against public spending and organized labour. The contradiction between the social democratic form and the monetarist content of the Callaghan Government allowed the monetarist challenge to be intensified by the post-1979 Conservative administrations, who were able to exploit the alienation and dissatisfaction of workers in regard to the KWS to pursue neo-liberal policies which attempted to resubordinate state and society to the rule of money and the rule of law.

The development of the water industry in the 1970s has to be seen in the above context. As I mentioned above, the managerialization of the water industry involved the recomposition of the state in an attempt to restructure the industry in order that administrative activities were mediated by the abstract regulatory forms of money and the law. In particular, during the period following 1973 the reforms were marked by the introduction of increasingly rigorous financial controls over the RWAs. Between 1974 and 1983 the RWAs were subject to a system of controls through capital allocations, and in 1983 these controls were tightened through the introduction of External Finance Limits (EFLs)[4] which limited the amount of external finance that RWAs were permitted to procure per annum. EFLs contained an inbuilt tendency for entitlements to be underspent, as the RWAs needed to pay due regard to the way in which changes in the financial climate could increase borrowing requirements and result in the EFL being overshot. In 1982/83 these controls resulted in the capital allocation for the water industry in England and Wales being under-utilized by £193 million, only £219 million of a total EFL of £412 million being used (National Water Council, 1983: 19). The overall impact of this measure was to reduce both the borrowing and capital investment of water authorities during the early to mid-1980s. The RWAs were subjected to further financial controls through the development of 'financial targets'. In 1981 the Government announced that RWAs should be earning a rate of return on the net value of their assets of at least 1.25 per cent by 1983/84 (Water Authorities [Return on Assets] Order 1981). By 1986 this figure had been increased to 1.95 per cent – requiring a near doubling of water industry profitability in five years. The main mechanism by which this was achieved was through the introduction of 'performance aims': a Government-imposed target for 'efficiency' improvement in order to ensure that financial targets were not met simply through the introduction of higher charges or reductions in service.

The reimposition of the law of money required fundamental changes to the institutional structure of the water industry. Most fundamentally, it required the marginalization or exclusion of labour at the micro and macro levels of the industry. The appointment of sympathetic people to the boards of nationalized industries has been central to the neo-liberal project of 'Thatcherism' (Gamble, 1988: 103–4): this facilitated the 'depoliticization' of the state sector, and the breaking of the micro-corporatist structures associated with the KWS. In the water industry the boards of the RWAs were increasingly constituted by businessmen, accountants and supporters of 'Thatcherism'. Within the management structures of the RWAs, entrepreneurial skills became increasingly important and engineers were increasingly replaced by accountants and professional managers. The 1983 Water Act resulted in the abolition of local authority and trade union representation on the boards of water authorities and the abolition of the macro-corporatist arrangements associated with the NWC.

In capitalist society the production of commodities is simultaneously a labour process and a valorization process. The reimposition of the law of money and the rule of law required the recommodification of labour, and an undermining of the power of organized labour has thus been a central feature of the neo-liberal project (Gamble, 1979: 15–17). The 1983 Water Act coincided with a serious confrontation between the state and organized labour in the water industry. The dispute demonstrated the extent to which labour in the state sector presented an important obstacle to neo-liberal restructuring. The 1983 waterworkers' strike involved a claim by manual workers for a pay settlement that would restore their earnings to the 'upper quartile' of manual worker earnings. The claim was rejected on the grounds that such an increase could not be conceded without commensurate increases in productivity, and that comparisons with the gas and electricity industry were unfair given the higher proportions of skilled workers in these industries. The NWC played a key role in the dispute. It provided a 'national focus for information'; set out the employers' case in the national press; arranged media briefings; co-ordinated a national campaign to conserve supplies; and commissioned an opinion poll of the attitudes of the 'general public' in order to augment the argument of the employers that their offer should be accepted (National Water Council, 1983: 25).[5] Nevertheless, the abolition of the NWC by the 1983 Water Act weakened the structures of national collective bargaining and devolved most meaningful issues to individual RWAs. National negotiating mechanisms were subsequently abolished with the privatization of the water industry in 1989.[6]

The restructuring of the water industry, and the recomposition of the state which this implied, required a fundamental restructuring of the capital–labour relation. It is in this sense that the restructuring process was a process of class struggle. Managerialism involved the recommodification of labour and the products of labour within the water industry. The marginalization and exclusion of labour from within the administrative mechanisms of the water industry was, therefore, the central focus of the restructuring process. The culmination of this process was the 1989 Water Act, which transferred the RWAs into the private sector and established OFWAT as the neo-liberal state regulator.[7] The privatization of the industry represents a reconvergence between state and capital. The contradictory determination of the state initially allowed the planner-state to administrate the production and consumption of water services in a way which escaped the immediate mediation of legal and monetary regulation. The costs of these forms of administration were socialized, and thus regulated by legal and monetary relations in and through the corporate institutions of the nation state. This decommodification reflected the relative strength of labour within the labour process. The dynamic of managerialism involved an assault on the power of organized labour in order to reimpose the logic of capital, and the neo-liberal restructuring of the water industry has resulted in the reconstitution of water-capital on a national and international scale. Managerialism thus constituted an attempt to resolve the fiscal crisis of the state through the application of capitalist rationality to the institutional mechanisms of the state. Managerialism facilitated therefore the reconvergence of the state and capital.

The neo-liberal restructuring and privatization of the water industry has facilitated the development of a major programme of capital spending. In 1990 the projected investment programme for the water industry to the year 2000 was £28 billion, including capital spending in excess of £2.5 billion in each of the years 1991 to 1994. These levels of capital spending involved at least a doubling of capital spending for all the companies following privatization (OFWAT, 1991: 15). In the context of a global crisis of over-accumulation, managerialism created large efficient entities capable of operating as capital in the context of surplus capital looking for investment. Managerialism allowed a realignment of labour and valorization processes within the water industry, and this has allowed the recrudescence of water capital within a recomposed neo-liberal global system. The restructuring and privatization of industries such as water has had a significant impact on UK and international capital markets, and utilities are becoming an increasingly important sector of the UK stock market. In 1987/88, it would have represented 8.5 per cent of turnover, 13.7 per cent of pre-tax profit and 18.5 per cent of quoted UK PLC, ranking second only to the oil industry with regard to turnover and pre-tax profit (£42 billion and £6.3 billion) and having the largest operating capital of any sector (£47.5 billion). The UK water industry employed operating capital of £8.4 billion in the year to March 1988, ranking the industry alongside medium-sized sectors such as electronics.

There are important international ramifications to the neo-liberal restructuring of the water industry in Britain. The Morgan Stanley index ranks utilities as the largest non-financial sector, with 6.3 per cent of global capitalization (Buchanan and Clapham, 1988: 1, 12–14). Two large French multinationals, Générale des Eaux and Lyonnaise des Eaux, have increasingly constituted a growing international water sector. These companies have interests in over 150 companies worldwide, including 50 per cent of General Waterworks Corporation, the USA's second largest operator, and Saudi Arabia's water and waste system, and have launched joint ventures with large UK multinationals such as John Laing and Trafalgar House. In turn these UK-based multinationals have accrued large stakes in the UK's statutory water companies (SWCs), and by 1989 French multinationals owned 12 out of the 29 SWCs and had substantial interests in a further six (*Financial Weekly*, 30 November 1988; *Financial Times*, 4 November 1989).

Neo-liberalism and the Crisis of Public Service

The analysis of the development and crisis of the planner-state has important implications for the debate concerning the origins and nature of the neo-liberal project associated with 'monetarism' or 'Thatcherism'. The most influential analyses have presented neo-liberal state projects in terms of external responses to economic crisis constructed and legitimated at the political (Bullpitt, 1986; Gamble, 1988; Jessop *et al.*, 1988, 1990) and ideological (Hall, 1983, 1988) levels. The crisis of the planner-state regulation of water illustrates the weakness and inadequacy of these approaches. In this chapter I have attempted to demonstrate that the planner-state decomposed from within because of its contradictory and crisis-ridden form. The state embodies and reproduces the contradictions of capital accumulation in a political form. This is manifest in the contradiction between the formal equality of individual citizens in respect of the administrative and democratic activities of the state and the necessary mediation of administrative and democratic activities through the abstract regulatory forms of money and the law, which ultimately ensure the production and reproduction of the capital relation. The planner-state allowed the institutional decommodification of labour and public services: the separation of labour and valorization processes. This is what allowed the state to appear as an embodiment of the 'common good' but also what threatened constantly to rupture the appearance of the state as the embodiment of the 'common good'.

It is in this sense that the state decomposed from within and has been recomposed in order to mobilize counter-tendencies in the form of re-uniting labour and valorization processes through an attempt simultaneously to restructure the political, ideological and economic aspects of the capital relation. The economic restructuring of the capital relation has involved imposing the law of value on the production and reproduction of public services. In production this has involved the intensification of labour and the increasing use of contract labour. In the sphere of exchange this has involved replacing administratively defined tariffs and modes of delivery, which as I argued earlier defined the form of the planner-state, with contractual modes of payment and delivery. The political restructuring of the capital relation has involved the destruction of class-based collective modes of interest mediation and their replacement by individualized and non-class-based modes of interest mediation. An example is the exclusion of organized labour from the administrative apparatus of the state and the development of individualized forms of representation through developments such as the Citizen's Charter. The ideological restructuring of the capital relation has involved an attempt to destroy the collective social democratic ideologies of public service on which the planner-state was premised, and to replace them with individualistic ideologies based on the fulfilment of individual needs and the centrality of individual self-interest. In the next chapter I explore in more detail the specific form of the neo-liberal state which has emerged as a response to the crisis of the planner-state and the resulting realignment of state and capital within the water industry.

Notes

1. Guild Socialism was centred around the National Guilds League and a monthly journal *The Guildsman.* In addition to G. D. H. Cole the main exponents of Guild Socialism were Bertrand Russell, R. H. Tawney, S. G. Hobson, A. J. Plenty and A. R. Orage. The most important examples of Guild Socialist literature are listed in Cole (1980: 217–18). The intellectual origins of Guild Socialism lie in the English Romanticism of William Morris, John Ruskin, Hilaire Belloc and G. K. Chesterton.
2. The attitude of Sidney and Beatrice Webb to the Soviet Union also illustrates this point. Soviet planning was Gas and Water Socialism taken to its logical conclusion. In a letter to Charles Sarolea in June 1924 Beatrice Webb

wrote 'My Husband and I have always been against the Soviet System, and have regarded it as a repetition of Russian autocracy based on a creed – a very Eastern conception' (Mackenzie, 1978: 207; see also Webb and Webb, 1923: 161–2, for a discussion of the early attitude of the Webbs to Bolshevism). However, following a trip to the Soviet Union in 1932, the failure of the 1924 and 1929 Labour Governments and the economic crisis of 1931, Sidney and Beatrice Webb became increasingly preoccupied with the Soviet Union as the 'New Civilisation' (Webb and Webb, 1937; see also the letters written by Beatrice Webb to Harold Laski, H. G. Wells and R. H. Tawney between November 1941 and July 1942, in Mackenzie, 1978: 452–60).

3. A similar point is made by Saunders and Harris (1994: 38), who argue from a neo-liberal perspective that '[t]he privatization of the water industry was, in a sense, the logical end-point to the reorganization process begun in 1974'.
4. The imposition of EFLs was common to all the nationalized industries. See Fine and O'Donnell (1981) for an assessment of the impact of EFLs on the nationalized industries and Ferner (1985, 1987) for an examination of the impact of EFLs on British Railways.
5. A more stark illustration of the role of the state in smashing the macro and micro corporatism associated with Keynesianism is provided by Beynon and McMyler (1985), who explore the role of the National Coal Board in the 1984 miners' dispute.
6. The impact of decentralized bargaining and negotiation on individual water companies is explored in Chapter 8 below. See also Sheldrake (1991) and Ogden (1992) for a discussion of recent changes in the structure of water industry collective bargaining. More recent changes in the bargaining arrangements within the privatized water companies are explored in the Industrial Relations Review and Report (*IRS Employment Trends*: 469, August, 516, July 1992) and O'Connell Davidson (1993: 58–66).
7. The 1989 Water Act was part of a wider consolidation of legislation pertaining to water in England and Wales. In 1991 five new acts (the Water Act (1991), the Water Resources Act (1991), the Statutory Water Companies Act (1991), the Land Drainage Act (1991) and the Water Consolidation (Consequential Provisions) Act (1991)) replaced the morass of overlapping and confusing statutes relating to water.

4 The Monetarization of the Water Industry

In the last chapter I highlighted the way in which the implosion and decomposition of the planner-state resulted in the discrediting of social democratic conceptions of the 'common good' on which public service has traditionally been premised. In this chapter I explore the way in which the resolution of the crisis of the planner-state through the reapplication of the law of money and the rule of law has involved a fundamental transformation of public service as a state ideology and practice. The neo-liberal restructuring of public services has attempted to resolve the contradictions of the planner-state through a fundamental restructuring of the political and economic rights of workers and consumers and a radical reworking of the ideological representation of what constitutes the 'common good'. The neo-liberal restructuring of the water industry has redefined the concept of the 'common good' on the basis of the abstract postulates of neo-liberal social theory. This has facilitated a marked depoliticization of the institutional mechanisms of the water industry and, more widely, has resulted in the citizenship rights of individuals becoming more abstract and formal. In this chapter I explore the ideological, political and economic forms of the neo-liberal state as it impacts as a regulatory form on the water industry. This involves an analysis of the functions and responsibilities of the Office of Water Services (OFWAT)[1] and a discussion of the way in which this state form is underpinned by an essentially abstract definition of 'citizenship' taken from neo-liberal social theory. I will begin by exploring the way in which neo-liberal social theory conceptualizes the rights and duties of individuals in contemporary capitalist societies.

Neo-liberal Theory and the Abstract Individual

Neo-liberal social theory is premised on the individualist postulates of micro-economic theory. Neo-liberal economics is premised upon a conception of the individual as a rational utility-maximizing consumer. The action of calculating utility-maximizers spontaneously and impersonally interacting in the market results in both individual liberty and economic efficiency. The market allows individuals to incorporate all their consumption behaviour into a personal consumption plan that spontaneously produces the optimum allocation of social resources (Barry, 1987a: 52–3; 1987b). The 'market' is central to this project as a result of its individualistic premises. The market has no ends or purposes and consequently resources are allocated on the basis of subjectively determined values through the competitive dynamic of supply and demand. The existence of imperfect competition in no way vitiates the efficacy of the market. Competition is not an 'end state' but a 'process' through which the dynamic and rivalrous competition between transactors continually corrects market imperfections and pushes the system towards a hypothetical equilibrium.

The public benefit is maximized unintentionally through the actions of individual marginal-maximizers pursuing their own self-interest. The imperfections of real markets heighten the importance of 'property rights' which provide incentives for entrepreneurs to create profits through the identification of price differences in real markets. The state lacks the knowledge that is available to decentralized entrepreneurs, and planned systems of provision therefore fail to deliver the optimum allocation of resources. Liberal social theory is thus premised on the utilitarian notion of 'unanimity' and is critical of tendencies towards the politicization of economic life. The 'public interest' is derived from the interests of autonomous and anonymous (abstract) individuals and (abstract) economic freedom constitutes the fundamental basis of social power. What unites liberal social theory is a rejection of any substantive administrative role for the state. The recent liberal renaissance has been concerned to demonstrate the necessary relationship between spontaneous (i.e. unplanned) social development and individual freedom and sovereignty. Neo-liberal theory is constituted by a diverse body of literature, but a brief review of the Chicago, Austrian and Virginia schools of neo-liberalism highlights the important relationship between neo-liberal ideology and the reformulation of the 'common good' within the institutional apparatus of the neo-liberal state. As I will demonstrate below, neo-liberal theory has guided the material restructuring of the state apparatus and provided the intellectual justification for an assault on the collective notions of the 'common good' which were embodied within the planner-state.

The most notable example of the Chicago School of neo-liberalism is to be found in the work of Milton Friedman (Friedman, 1982; Friedman and Friedman, 1980). Friedman argues that the public interest is constituted by state policies and institutions that promote the interests of each individual as an anonymous (abstract) member of the public. The economic freedom of individuals in the sphere of consumption constitutes the direct and most immediate form of freedom. The political co-ordination of economic affairs is necessarily coercive. Political channels of decision-making tend to force conformity as politicians are faced with a limited number of yes/no decisions. The market constitutes a form of economic proportional representation through which the unrestrained decisions of individuals lead to 'unanimity' without 'conformity'. The market allows voluntary co-operation between private individuals and prevents interference in the affairs of individuals through the separation of economic and political power.

The state has important 'economic' functions with respect to countering the effects of 'technical monopoly' and 'neighbourhood effects'. Technical monopoly relates to industries and services such as water where 'voluntary exchange' would be either exceedingly costly or practically impossible. In such cases, technical and economic efficiency are best achieved by one producer or enterprise delivering the good. In the context of technical monopoly there are three alternative production/regulation configurations: public monopoly, public regulation and private monopoly. For the neo-liberals, private monopoly is the least distasteful of these unpalatable alternatives. In the context of rapid technological change, the factors leading to technical monopoly are likely to be transient and a private monopoly is the most likely to be eliminated by technological development. Similarly, when it remains public monopoly or regulation should be organized in a way which permits competition. The work of the Chicago School highlights the importance of maintaining the separation between the economic and political spheres of society and the way in which this implies an essentially abstract conceptualization of individual rights and freedom. A further theme alluded to by Friedman is that the rights of producers are necessarily subordinate to the rights and power of consumers. The pay and conditions of individual workers are, like any other commodity, determined through the impersonal mechanism of the market. From this perspective, therefore, the collective organization of workers through trade unions or the employment of workers in state bureaucracies amounts to a form of monopoly which undermines the freedom of individual consumers by forcing them to pay higher than necessary prices for goods and services.

The most notable representative of the Austrian School has been Friederich A. Hayek (Hayek, 1944, 1960). Hayek has been concerned to demonstrate the 'epistemological absurdity' of a single institution such as the state having sufficient economic and social knowledge to enable it to 'fine-tune' the economy. State control of the money supply results in 'cheap money' and 'mal-investments' that move the allocation of resources away from the pattern of allocation that would most benefit an 'anonymous [abstract] society'. The Austrian School highlights the way in which concrete administrative decisions undermine the abstract power of money and reduce the marginal efficiency of capital. The Virginia School of 'public choice' liberals highlights the way liberal democratic processes allow utility-maximizing politicians to pursue their own rather than the 'public' interest. They apply the microeconomic calculus to public life in order to question the extent to which political actors behave in a 'public spirited' and benevolent way (Buchanan and Tullock, 1962). For them, the operation of a plurality of interest groups in a corporatist framework destroys the interests of 'anonymous individuals' and is against the public interest (Olson, 1965, 1982).

The various strands of neo-liberal thought outlined above all share an overriding emphasis on the essentially abstract nature of the 'common good'. Neo-liberal theory focuses on the importance of mediating social production and consumption through the rule of law and the law of money. There is a concern to demonstrate the way in which the administrative and substantive policies of the state undermine the 'common good'. The 'common good' is premised on abstract individuals pursuing their own interests in civil society. The role of the state is to ensure the maintenance of the 'common good' by ensuring that social interaction is properly mediated by monetary and legal transactions. As I mentioned above, neo-liberal theory has guided the material restructuring of state apparatus and provided the intellectual justification for an assault on the collective notions of the 'common good' which were embodied within the planner-state. This can be illustrated through an exploration of the way in which neo-liberal concepts and categories have informed the development and operation of OFWAT as the neo-liberal regulator of the water industry in England and Wales.

Neo-liberalism and the 'Citizen-consumer'

The National Consumer Council played an important role in determining the institutional form of regulation imposed on the water industry following privatization in 1989. The NCC produced a Report (NCC, 1989) which was concerned with the form of state regulation most likely to stimulate competition and thereby protect the interests of consumers. The Report argued that the political imperatives of the planner-state had resulted in forms of state regulation that undermined the interests of individual (i.e. abstract) consumers. The essential nature of utility goods had resulted in 'equity' being a major element in utility regulation. The utility commodities were presented as 'merit goods' that had a 'strategic' role at the macro-economic level and utilities were used as instruments of social and economic policy. Statutory regulations obliged utilities to supply on demand through uniform tariff structures that divorced price from production costs (values) via the principle of 'cross-subsidization'. The interests of consumers were undermined through the use of the pricing and investment structures as instruments of macro-economic policy, and the views of 'consumer councils' on prices and costs were marginalized by the broader social and economic objectives of the state. The planner-state form of the utility industries thus resulted in the exploitation of 'inefficiency opportunities' and the resultant over-staffing and managerial slack legitimated the 'privatization' project of the New Right. According to the Report, private ownership would have important advantages for consumers as private sector managers would have the positive incentive to increase profits and the negative incentives of the threat of bankruptcy and takeover that were not present in the public sector.

The principal concern of the Report was the development of a regulatory mechanism that would allow the operation of property rights in the water and electricity markets. The monopoly status of utilities did not allow consumers to 'signal' their wishes through their buying power and the power of utilities over their markets gave them *de facto* powers of taxation. These powers provide the *raison d'être* for the establishment and operation of utility regulation, and the role of regulation was to establish a market 'proxy' which would protect consumers from excessive prices and poor standards of service. Regulation needed to shift the focus from the workers and owners of an industry to those that use its products: a shift in the locus of social power from producers to consumers.

The primary consideration of the NCC was the development of an essentially liberal form of regulation. Regulation needed to be based on individual contractual relations between water companies and customers and the profit motive needed to be institutionalized within the industry. In other words, the absence of competition required the creation of a 'market proxy' to ensure that the production and consumption of public services was subordinated to the law of money and the rule of law. Regulation needed to be concerned with both price and quality because companies operating in a competitive market would lose market share if they attempted to raise profit levels by either raising prices or reducing quality *vis-à-vis* their competitors. In competitive markets consumers made judgements about, and traded off between, price, quality and service. In a monopoly situation consumers could be exploited along all three dimensions, and regulation needed to be concerned with all three dimensions. The NCC highlighted the deficiencies in the regulatory frameworks that had been developed for the gas and telecommunications industries. The prices charged by the privatized gas and telecommunications industries were regulated through price-capping. The regulator predicted an outcome premised on the achievement of a 'normal' rate of profit and the difference between prediction and reality provided incentives for increased efficiency but also an incentive to reduce quality. Regulation needed to result in the establishment of specific quality standards in order to ensure that incentives for increased profits through greater efficiency were not offset by a reduction in quality.

The NCC was concerned that OFWAT would operate as a perfect market proxy. Quality standards would be set in advance, with penalties more onerous than cost savings if these were not met. An effective link would be established between the quality of service an individual received and the individual price they had to pay – with compensation being payable if standards were not met. The ability of regulatory agencies to make reasonable and informed decisions was dependent upon the ability of the regulator to collect and process information. The ability of regulators to collate information would be improved through the restructuring of utility industries in a way that would facilitate comparative competition; providing examples of 'best practice' and helping to prevent regulators being 'captured' by the utility company. The NCC highlighted the danger that companies could be motivated by factors other than profit-maximization; in particular, employees and managers exploiting monopoly on their own behalf in terms of over-staffing or higher wages and thereby increasing prices or reducing quality. The human resource aspects of utility operations also needed to be a legitimate concern of regulation. As I will show in later chapters, the regulatory framework established by OFWAT has had a marked indirect impact on conditions of employment through the development of new information auditing systems – although OFWAT has not become involved in the operational human resource management of water companies. Clearly, therefore, the neo-liberal regulatory regime does not go as far as the framework envisaged by the NCC in subordinating the interests of managers and workers to the 'abstract' consumer-citizen of neo-liberal theory, and this has important political implications which will be explored in later chapters.

Despite the above caveat the institutional form of OFWAT following the 1989 Water Act does indeed closely resemble the 'ideal' consumers' state presented in the Report of the NCC. This highlights the way in which the neo-liberal water industry has been recomposed on a neo-liberal basis and the way in which this has resulted in the emergence of new state ideologies based on the interests of the abstract marginal-maximizer of neo-liberal social and economic theory. I will now consider the regulatory role of OFWAT as quasi-market. This shows the way in which simultaneous regulation of price, quality and service involves an attempt to impose an abstract form on the institutional mechanisms of the neo-liberal water industry. This will provide the context for the following four chapters, which explore the impact of neo-liberal state regulation on management and labour processes within individual water companies.

OFWAT and the Regulation of Abstraction

The 1989 Water Act created OFWAT as the agency responsible for the economic regulation of the water industry and the National Rivers

Authority (NRA)[2] as the agency responsible for the environmental regulation of the water industry, while the Drinking Water Inspectorate (DWI) was created to regulate the quality of drinking water. The Act privatized the RWAs and enforced a separation between the 'core' monopoly functions of supplying water and disposing of sewage and other 'enterprise' functions. The 'core' business operations of the former RWAs and the existing SWCs were taken over by 'Water Supply Plcs' (WSPLCs), and these were licensed to supply water and dispose of sewage by OFWAT. The licence established charging limits and performance standards and managers were left free within this framework to make profits while meeting quality standards. The function of the regulator was to establish a framework that safeguarded the 'public interest' while providing incentives to efficient management (HMSO, 1986: 16–7). OFWAT provides a proxy for the competitive market. The market proxy was constituted by the development of measurements of comparative competition and the threat of mergers and takeovers. OFWAT has the function of establishing the licence conditions of the WSPLCs, and 'regulating' compliance with the licence conditions through the collection and application of data on operating and capital costs, levels of service and customer care. This range of data was stipulated in the conditions laid out in licence agreements and forms the basis of the comparative competition through which 'the market' assesses the efficiency of water undertakers. In the following three sections I outline the way in which OFWAT regulates prices, quality and service. The central point to note is that in respect of all these functions the operation of OFWAT has been to depoliticize, individualize and monetarize the provision of water services in a way which corresponds with the neo-liberal form of the OFWAT regulatory regime.

OFWAT and the Regulation of Prices

In the water industry price increases are regulated by the formula (RPI + K). The value of 'K' is a function of what a company needs to finance the provision of services to customers while taking into account the amount needed for capital expenditure and operating costs, offset by improvements in productivity and proceeds from the sale of land. In order to finance a proposed £25 billion investment programme in improved drinking water quality and reduced pollution in the ten years following privatization, all water companies were initially awarded positive K values (an average of 5.5 per cent for the first five years and 4 per cent for the second five years). The levels of K were reassessed in 1994 and the reductions in K have resulted in a situation in which the resources for improved standards will have to be found from increases in operating efficiency (*Guardian*, 29 July 1994).

The regulation of prices is the responsibility of the 'Charges Control Division' of OFWAT. The Division is responsible for advising on adjustments to 'K' either on an interim basis or via a periodic review. The Division undertakes the collection and analysis of financial information, encourages comparative competition, and undertakes periodic efficiency studies. It monitors the performance of companies and the costs and benefits of changes in service standards; limiting charges 'to those that would be charged by companies competing directly with each other' (OFWAT, 1990a: 13). The 1989 Act gave each WSPLC the power to fix charges for its services within (RPI + K) within the limitations of 'Licence Condition E', by which they are required to ensure that no undue preference is shown to, and that there is no undue discrimination against, any class of customers or potential customers (OFWAT, 1990b, Annexe 1: 1). The Charges Control Division is also responsible for developing policy on tariff structures and charging methods. OFWAT has been concerned to promote the informationally advantageous, though economically prohibitive, method of metering in order to provide customers with 'a sensible price message to enable them to affect their consumption pattern' (OFWAT, 1990b: 16). The context of the exercise was a situation in which, owing to the need to finance improved quality standards, water charges are set to rise by between 22 per cent and 122 per cent by 2000, while the 1989 Water Act prohibited charging by rateable value on new properties immediately and on all properties after 2000. The determination of individual charges needed to be considered within the (RPI + K) formula. While compulsory metering has been resisted by water companies on the grounds of cost and impracticality, the general policy of OFWAT on this matter illustrates the neo-liberal ideology underlying the institutional form of this state agency.

The 1989 Water Act attempted to depoliticize the tariff structures of the water industry. The Act prohibited the calculation of water charges on the basis of 'ability to pay'. This objective has subsequently been taken up by OFWAT. The agency has argued that in respect to the balance between 'standing' and 'variable' elements of water bills the latter was the more important as it was more closely related to individual consumption. Standing charges weighed heavily upon small properties with low consumption, and households that 'chose' to use large amounts of water needed to have this reflected in their water charges. The customer needed to be able 'to control his [*sic*] consumption and expenditure in the light of his needs and resources' (OFWAT, 1990b: 9–10). The 'objective' of providing 'simple incentives' to customers and companies was 'to help ensure that the right level of service is provided at the right price . . . to achieve improved economy and efficiency and to ensure that resources are well allocated'. Tariff structures needed to 'provide clear price messages which encourage companies to meet customers' demands, subject to achieving statutory environmental and health objectives, at the lowest price' (OFWAT, 1990b: 9–11). In order to provide incentives the tariff structure needed to be organized on the basis that, if a customer changes the volume of water or sewage services demanded, the change in his/her bill would broadly reflect changes in both capital and environmental costs.

The vast capital expenditure programmes required to meet increasingly rigorous environmental standards highlighted the relationship between the economic and environmental aspects of regulation (OFWAT, 1990b, Annexe 2: 1–5). Environmental considerations were central to decisions on future investment programmes, the structuring and monitoring of investment programmes and the nature and implementation of charging systems. 'Economic efficiency' required that both the costs and the benefits of environmental decisions should be a concern of the regulator. Customers both benefited from, and shared the costs of, environmental programmes and it was important that the costs of initiatives were presented in a way which indicated their implications for individual water bills. It was important to allow customers of water services to make judgements about the value they place on environmental benefits. Regulation needed to be premised upon the relationship between the economic and environmental operations of the water industry. Decisions on new (environmental) obligations needed to be translated into investment programmes and prices, and implementation needed to be structured within a medium-term framework that gave customers certainty regarding their charges but also gave the industry space to manage.

The establishment of distinct roles for the NRA, OFWAT and WSPLCs made it important that prices reflected the environmental costs attributable to distinct stages in the use cycle (abstraction, treatment, discharge). Increasingly tight environmental standards necessarily implied higher charges for customers. The 'Municipal Waste Water Directive' (MWWD) required an end to the dumping of sludge at sea by 1998, and the expansion of treatment to the sewage outflows that flow into estuaries or the sea. Between 1991 and 1994 around £2.5 billion per year was projected for water industry capital investment, and of this, between £0.8 billion and £1.25 billion was required to meet existing and future environmental improvements. The costs were spread unevenly across the ten WSPLCs.[3] Improvements were to be financed through the bills paid by customers as determined by (RPI + K), and this needed to be reflected in the process of environmental planning and decision-making. OFWAT has argued that customers would not welcome further price rises unless they were confident 'that [price increases] are justified and provided good value for money' (OFWAT, 1990b: 15). New obligations needed to be reduced to prices before decisions on environmental improvements were taken. The action of quality regulators on new environmental initiatives, the costs of these initiatives and the differential impact upon the investment programmes of individual companies needed to be analysed in the context of the likely impact upon the bills of individual customers. The final decisions on proposals would fall on ministers, who would need to balance the cost of making the improvements and the consequences for customers' bills against the environmental benefits. The main concern was the development of tariff structures that adequately reflected the subjectively defined values placed on utility services by individual consumers: a development which addressed and attempted to resolve the fiscal crisis of the Fabian water industry.

Technocratic Fabianism attempted to meet the politically-defined needs of consumers through the planning of large-scale capital investment projects. The neo-liberal regulation of the water industry is an attempt to resolve the fiscal crisis which resulted from this form of Keynesian planning and to depoliticize the provision of water services. This means that the development of improvement programmes with respect to drinking water and sewage disposal has to be equated with the prices paid by individual consumers. Hence, the operation of OFWAT in respect of pricing policy has attempted to depoliticize the provision of services and decisions on capital investment programmes and subordinate service provision to individuated monetary and legal relations. The regulation of prices by OFWAT highlights the way in which the substantive political and democratic content has been emptied out of public service as a form of state practice, and utility provision has become increasingly premised on the abstract individual of neoliberal social theory.

OFWAT and the regulation of quality

The 1989 Water Act placed a duty on OFWAT to promote competition and encourage efficiency and effectiveness through the mechanisms of 'inset' appointments,[4] comparative competition and mergers. The licences of water companies lay down the detailed accounting information that is to be made available to OFWAT in its function of encouraging comparative competition. Comparative competition is designed to allow OFWAT to make conclusions on the benefits to consumers and allows the financial markets to make judgements about the different quoted companies. The technical, engineering and scientific aspects of water company performance are monitored by the 'Engineering Intelligence Division' of OFWAT. The Division reports on and certifies information submitted by WSPLCs. The Division is intended to establish a mechanism that ensures

> [t]he development of the necessary reporting arrangements to enable OFWAT to monitor and compare a company operating performance, levels of service, and investment expenditure . . . [and] to support planning for periodic reviews and the efficient and economic integration of new obligations. (OFWAT, 1990a: 21)

The 1989 Act required WSPLCs to develop detailed, long-term 'Asset Management Plans', which together with investment and levels of service projections formed the basis of the K setting. The projections were designed to improve the service provided to water customers, and it is the function of OFWAT to ensure that projected developments are achieved on time and at the lowest acceptable cost to customers. In order to balance arm's-length regulation with an assurance that water customers' monies are being effectively and economically managed, OFWAT requires companies to submit an annual report. The Report provides

> a framework for the submission of the majority of information required to enable OFWAT to monitor progress and compare performance . . . [enabling]

> the generation of time-series information and facilitating non-financial comparisons. (*ibid*: 22)

Companies report on their medium-term progress *vis-à-vis* the 'Asset Management Plan'. Through this plan companies must outline their investment procurement strategy, provide quantitative data relating to service 'outputs', highlight their progress in meeting drinking water and sewage compliance programmes, and provide an outline of the methodology and procedures adopted to enable the accurate representation of levels of service indicators. Outputs are measured and monitored by a series of quantitatively defined quality standards that are laid down by the operating licences.

The regulatory auditing developed by OFWAT has had a fundamental impact on the managerial structure of water companies through the way in which the collection and auditing of performance data has resulted in a massive investment in new IT management information systems and provided a major dynamic in the development of 'total quality management' and 'constant improvement programmes' within the water industry. The output measures have been central in the recent organizational and management restructuring of water companies. They have been incorporated into management control strategies by forming the basis of the appraisal and performance-related pay of senior managers and through their centrality to the development of new 'quality systems', monitored and audited by an increasingly important 'customer service' function. In these ways the regulatory activities of OFWAT have played a central role in the intensification of labour within the water industry and have facilitated a range of regulatory indicators which have embedded the dynamic of 'constant improvement' within the organizational structure of water companies.

The regulation of quality by OFWAT provides an important illustration of a neo-liberal alignment between state and capital in relation to the privatized water industry. The OFWAT regime not only provides the major dynamic in the adoption of constant improvement programmes but determines the indicators around which constant improvement is structured. The OFWAT quality audits attempt to institutionalize the dynamic of constant efficiency improvements within the organizational form of the water industry and ensure that the organization of both the labour process and the systems of service provision are subordinated to the abstract and indifferent power of money and the law. As I will show in the following chapter, however, such subordination is necessarily partial owing to the contradictory form of the capitalist state and the way in which the policies and procedures developed by OFWAT are mediated by bureaucratic and democratic pressures and constraints. There is, therefore, an enduring struggle over the definition of 'quality' which cannot be totally resolved by neo-liberal restructuring.

OFWAT and the regulation of service

The 1989 Water Act gave OFWAT particular duties with regard to existing and potential customers of the water industry. The Consumer Affairs Division is responsible for the development of policy *vis-à-vis* the consumer aspects of regulation. The 1989 Act requires OFWAT to establish and nationally co-ordinate Customer Service Committees (CSCs) which correspond to the areas formally covered by the former RWAs. The CSCs have the functions of protecting the interests of rural, elderly and disabled customers, investigating complaints, and approving and modifying codes of practice. The members of the CSCs are appointed on the basis of nominations invited from business, agriculture, local government, the voluntary sector and consumer organizations. The CSCs are independent of the water companies and have a statutory duty to 'keep under review matters of interest to customers and to consult and make representations to companies; to investigate customer complaints; and to advise and report to the Director General' (OFWAT, 1990a: 28).

The 1989 Water Act gave OFWAT and the CSCs a duty to investigate unresolved customer complaints. The licences under which WSPLCs operate stipulate that companies must have both a procedure for handling complaints and staff trained to deal effectively with complaints. WSPLCs are given an opportunity to respond to complaints prior to OFWAT becoming involved. Complaints are initially dealt with by the CSCs; though matters such as drinking water may be considered by the Director General, who may forward them to the DWI. OFWAT pursues complaints on a 'case by case' basis to secure compensation or rebates where 'the product or service supplied is below the standard for which the customer has paid' (*ibid.*: 29). Licence Conditions G, H, and I obliged the WSPLCs to submit to OFWAT three codes of practice: these covered relations with customers and CSCs, guidance to customers who have difficulty paying their bills (procedure prior to disconnection), and leakage from metered supplies. These codes of practice were formulated jointly by the industry and OFWAT with important input from the NCC. OFWAT is also responsible for administering the 'Guaranteed Standards Scheme' by which the failure of a company to meet certain prescribed standards entitles customers to a payment of £5 (or £5 per day for certain sustained failures).

The regulation of services by OFWAT highlights the way in which citizenship rights have been recomposed through the neo-liberal restructuring of the state. Following the neo-liberal restructuring of the water industry, the users of water services have no democratic input into the way services are managed and provided as they did within the planner-state, but rather, users are treated on a contractual basis as individual customers, with monetary penalties being payable as compensation if pre-agreed standards of service are not met. The consumer is the abstract consumer of neo-liberal social theory. The ideology and practice of public service has thus been redefined on the basis of the micro-economic postulates of neo-liberal economics and the function of regulation in relation to service provision is to ensure that individual customers receive value for money. The regulation of prices, quality and service therefore illustrates the way in which OFWAT developed as part of the neo-liberal recomposition of the state. The intellectual discourse of the New Right and a wider discourse of 'consumerism' has guided the material restructuring of the state and provided the intellectual justification for the assault on collective notions of public service. I have demonstrated the way in which OFWAT was designed in an attempt to subordinate the substantive activities of water companies to the abstract regulatory forms of law and money.

The primary function of OFWAT is to ensure that the production and consumption of water services is subordinated to the law of value: that concrete use-values are mediated by exchange-value and that the labour process is simultaneously a process of valorization. The problem is that the neo-liberal recomposition of the state has not resolved the fundamental contradiction of the capitalist state form. Neo-liberal state regulation involves the substantive administration of public utilities. Interest groups and public utility professionals are involved in the development and execution of policies which have emerged from bureaucratic and/or democratic pressures on the state. The neo-liberal state continues to embody and reproduce the contradictions of capital accumulation. OFWAT cannot completely formalize the contradictions and this highlights the fragile and contingent nature of capital's success in recomposing the state in a neo-liberal form. In the following chapters I illustrate the above proposition through a consideration of the impact of the crisis of the planner-state and the neo-liberal restructuring of public service on the managers and workers involved in the production and distribution of water services.

Notes

1. See Taylor (1996) for an extended discussion on the role of OFWAT in the restructuring of the post-privatized water industry.
2. See Bowman (1992) for a detailed analysis of the role and function of the National Rivers Authority.
3. Costs have fallen heaviest on WSPLCs with long tracts of coastline. The percentage increase in investment required to meet MWWD is: South West over 35 per cent; Southern, Welsh, North West, Northumbrian 15–20 per cent; Yorkshire, Anglian 10–15 per cent; and Severn Trent, Thames, Wessex less than 10 per cent (OFWAT, 1991: 16). The overall impact on water prices has been far more marked. The average increase in domestic water charges in the area covered by South West Water between 1989 and 1994 was 74 per cent. This has led to heightening protests from consumers in counties such as Devon and Cornwall where pressure from the EU and tourists for cleaner beaches have meant onerous increases in water charges (*Guardian*, 28 July 1995).
4. Inset appointments allow industrial customers using large amounts of water or customers on 'greenfield' sites to be served by an undertaker other than the WSPLC or SWC covering the area in which they are situated.

5 State Restructuring and the Restructuring of Management

In the previous two chapters I highlighted the way in which the regulatory regime that was created by the 1989 Water Act developed through the crisis of planning and managerialism. The 1989 Water Act was a key moment in the process through which the substantive administrative activities of the water industry have been subjected to the abstract mediation of law and money in an attempt to 'depoliticize' the public service state. The Act privatized the RWAs and made provision for the SWCs to convert to PLC status. The resulting WSPLCs were restructured in order to separate 'core' monopoly functions that were to be the subject of regulation and other 'enterprise' functions. The WSPLCs were constituted as public 'group' holding companies with water supply and sewerage functions being undertaken by subsidiary 'service' companies and other functions such as engineering and training by subsidiary 'enterprise' companies. The 1989 Act also substantially recomposed the regulatory form and functions of the state. In particular, the Act created OFWAT as a 'market proxy' in order to ensure that the water industry is subjected to the rigours of competition. The Act created the NRA and DWI to regulate river quality and drinking water respectively – although these have subsequently been incorporated into the Environment Agency.

As I have already argued in previous chapters, the restructuring and privatization of the water industry is part of a reconvergence of state and capital corresponding to an emerging neo-liberal global order of capital accumulation. The managerialist water industry, and the forms of state regulation associated with it, resulted in the development of large efficient entities capable of operating as capital in the context of a global crisis of over-accumulation. The privatization of the RWAs and the transfer of the SWCs to PLC status has therefore coincided with a

£25 billion programme of capital investment. The successful valorization of this capital, however, is dependent on the production and exchange of water services being subordinated to the abstract mediation of monetary and contractual relations. The valorization of water capital is ultimately dependent on the subordination of waterworkers within the labour process through the intensification and commodification of labour. In the second part of this book I explore the way in which the restructuring and privatization of the water industry has impacted on the management of the industry.

In earlier chapters I argued that the neo-liberal restructuring of the state has involved an attempt to re-establish the appearance of equality in the sphere of exchange. This has been attempted through the ideology of the 'customer' and the 'empowered citizen' of John Major's Citizen's Charter or the Labour Party's 'stakeholder society'. The realignment of state and capital has seen a similar concern to propagate an ideology of empowerment and consumerism within the management structures of public service enterprises. The most obvious manifestation of this is the increasing preoccupation of utility managers with various forms of human resource management (HRM) and total quality management (TQM). Indeed, I will demonstrate the key role that has been played by the state in facilitating the development of HRM/TQM in the water industry. In the following chapters I present a series of case studies which highlight the emerging gap between the rhetoric and reality of HRM/TQM in the water industry. I develop the argument that the gap between rhetoric and reality highlights the enduring contradictions not only of capitalist forms of management but wider ideological representations of the 'common good' on which the rhetoric of public service is ultimately premised. Before moving on to this analysis I want to mention briefly the methodological assumptions underlying the fieldwork on which these chapters are based.

Talking to Managers: The Research Design

In order to explore new forms of state regulation and management in the water industry I undertook a series of semi-structured 'key informant' interviews between summer 1991 and spring 1992. The interviews took place at a time when the water industry had been in the private sector for between two and three years. The interviews were focused on managers working within the water industry who were either directly involved with managing the relationship between their company and state regulators or managers concerned with the 'human resource' implications of the new regulatory regime. The managers interviewed ranged from senior management executives to junior managers and supervisors and the focus of the interviews was to explore the way in which new forms of state regulation had impacted on the social and technical organization of their companies. I interviewed managers at four water companies. The companies share the characteristics of having pursued 'quality management' strategies, and have developed new computerized management information systems following the pressures of regulation. Two of the companies were former RWAs involved in water supply and sewage disposal and two were former SWCs involved in water supply only.

Despite these similarities, the companies do have some distinctive features. In outlining the main features of these companies I have given each company a pseudonym for reasons of commercial confidentiality. WESTWAT is a former RWA privatized by the 1989 Water Act. The company has focused on the development of 'quality management' and has established a special department to facilitate the development of 'quality management' throughout all the company's activities. The company has pursued an aggressive 'industrial relations' strategy and has replaced the bargaining and negotiating arrangements with trade unions with a 'company council' arrangement. EASTWAT is also a former RWA and has focused on the application of information technology to the development of 'quality management' and the development of a polyvalent and flexible workforce. CITYWAT is one of the larger SWCs and supplies a large urban area with water. The company transferred to PLC status following the 1989 Water Act and in the context of pressure from the City has undertaken a major restructuring exercise involving the commercialization of relations between different departments and functions within the company. SHIREWAT is one of the smaller SWCs supplying water to a predominantly rural area. The company is a subsidiary of a large multinational corporation and the parent company has provided the dynamic for a major restructuring of the company's operations. The company has drastically reduced staffing levels and has attempted to replace technical/bureaucratic forms of management with commercial management.

My exclusive focus on managers in the water industry obviously raises important methodological questions concerning the reliability of data drawn from such a narrow cross-section of water authority employees. A series of useful empirical studies have, for example, demonstrated that privatization in the water industry has impacted differently on different groups of workers and has enjoyed different levels of support among manual, white-collar and managerial staff (O'Connell Davidson *et al.*, 1991; Saunders and Harris, 1994: 77–98). The main finding to emerge from these studies was that while privatization was deeply unpopular among all water industry employees, it was less unpopular among managerial and supervisory staff than among manual workers. Indeed, Saunders and Harris (1994: 82–3) claim not only that support among managers has increased since privatization, but also that a majority of managers considered that both their pay and job satisfaction had increased following privatization.

Clearly, therefore, the management restructuring which has followed privatization has not had a uniform impact across management hierarchies. Indeed, as Legge (1995: 50–4) has argued, both line managers and personnel managers are important 'stakeholders' in the development of HRM and TQM. Returning to my methodological comments in Chapter 1, therefore, the managers that I interviewed were selected in order to provide 'paradigm cases'. These are cases which have subsequently allowed me to deconstruct management 'rhetoric' on HRM/TQM and to 'reconstruct' the data provided by the interviews in the context of the 'totality' of the neo-liberal restructuring of the capital relation. Interviewing managers provided a rich source of data from which the contradictions inherent in the neo-liberal project could be deduced and elaborated in the context of the enduring contradictions of capital accumulation.

State Restructuring and the Restructuring of Management

The neo-liberal restructuring of the water industry has resulted in the widespread introduction and development of HRM and TQM by privatized water companies. Managers working within the industry suggest that the competitive pressures generated by OFWAT and international financial markets are the principal dynamics underlying the introduction of these new management forms. According to this view the competitive pressure to which water companies have been subjected following privatization has forced managers to be more responsive to the needs of their customers. As a result there have been attempts to transform the organizational culture of water companies according to the principles of 'total customer satisfaction'. However, as I have already demonstrated earlier, the neo-liberal restructuring of the water industry has involved subordinating the substantive and concrete demands of waterworkers and water consumers to the abstract mediation of monetary and legal regulation. There is, therefore, a fundamental contradiction at the heart of the neo-liberal regulation and management of the water industry. There is an attempt to limit the representation of the customer in both state and management ideologies to the role of a purely formal and abstract customer, while the administrative provision and control of water services by utility companies and the state remains substantive and concrete and involves real customers with substantive demands and concerns. In other words, the neo-liberal restructuring of state and society cannot magic away this fundamental underlying contradiction of capital accumulation.

In this chapter I want to begin by outlining the main features of the HRM approach and its implications for the restructuring of the labour process. I will argue that many accounts of HRM/TQM are over-generalized and that an effective analysis of the introduction of HRM/TQM in the water industry must consider the specificity of the industry in respect of state restructuring, valorization imperatives and established patterns of labour relations. I will then explore the way in which the neo-liberal recomposition of the public service state, in the form of OFWAT, has played a central role in facilitating the development, and to some extent in determining the form, of HRM in the water industry. Finally, I will explore the limitations and contradictions inherent in neo-liberal conceptualizations of 'customer care' and 'quality'. This will mean exploring the way in which the development of HRM/TQM in the water industry is a key moment in attempts to recompose the meaning of 'public service' on a more 'abstract' basis, and the way in which this involves the subordination of both waterworkers and water consumers to the valorization of capital.

Human resource management

The discourse of human resource management (HRM) has dominated the recent restructuring of management in both the public and private sectors. While there are clear continuities between HRM and early forms of personnel management there are, at a rhetorical level at least, a series of distinctive features of the HRM approach (Legge, 1989). First, HRM is a strategy directed at managers and core workers rather than the workforce as a collectivity. Second, HRM is a strategy involving line-managers as 'business' rather than 'people' managers, who therefore direct their primary attention to reducing the 'bottom-line'. Third, HRM as a strategy is principally directed at the management and manipulation of organizational culture – in particular the development of an 'enterprise culture' or a 'culture of excellence' within organizations. The main impetus behind the development of HRM has been 'the search for competitive advantage' in what is presented as an increasingly competitive global capitalist system. The defining features of HRM are therefore the elevation of the personnel function to a strategic corporate goal and an attempt to develop a culture within organizations based on competitive individualism and entrepreneurship, in an attempt to raise efficiency and profitability. The main material developments of HRM include total quality management (TQM)/just in time (JIT) programmes and customer care. The water companies examined below have seen the development of both quality management and customer care programmes and so it is important to explore the main principles of these forms of management.

The key focus of TQM is the transformation of organizational culture according to the principles of 'total customer satisfaction' and continuous improvement. The central human resource implication of this form of management is the commercialization and individuation of social relations within organizations. The theoretical basis of TQM can be summarized in the form of a number of core assumptions and principles (Hill, 1991a: 400–1, 1991b: 554–6, 1995; IDS, 1990; Sewell, 1990). TQM involves top–down restructuring through which top management develop quality objectives and systems. The focus is on the totality of the organization, with quality systems being presented in the form of a 'quality triangle' or 'quality chain' the points of which represent 'management commitment', 'statistical process control' and 'team-working'. The interdependence of these elements to customer satisfaction is represented through the analogy that the chain may break at any point (Oakland, 1989: 2–3). In contrast to earlier forms of participatory management such as 'quality circles' which broke down as a result of middle management mistrust and opposition (Bradley and

Hill, 1983, 1987; Brennan, 1991; Hill, 1991b), therefore, TQM is fundamentally top–down and senior management commitment is a central feature, with senior managers acting as 'role models' in disseminating TQM culture throughout the organization. This dissemination of TQM is usually dependent on management 'steering teams', and line-managers and supervisors play a crucial role in the introduction and development of TQM.

TQM involves the incorporation of 'continuous improvement' into organizational design through the development of 'high trust' participatory forms of management alongside the systematic control of work, setting of performance standards and statistical assessment (Wilkinson *et al.*, 1993: 1–4). The focus on the quality of design and conformance to quality specification facilitates the elimination of waste, and the 'cost of quality' is presented as being between 20 and 35 per cent of the operating costs of large companies. TQM involves the development of cross-functional management in order to co-ordinate the development of quality improvement both vertically and horizontally through an organization: a core component of this is the 'commercialization' of relations between horizontal units through the concept of 'internal customers'. Managers occupy the central position in the process of quality innovation, with middle managers being particularly important as they occupy a nodal position between vertical and horizontal management processes. In this sense a central aim of TQM is to release the 'entrepreneurial propensity' of managers through the debureaucratization and decentralization of organizations. TQM involves the development of rigorous and systematic techniques of issue identification and problem solving and a corresponding focus on the availability of accurate information in order for problems and solutions to be measured and quantified effectively.

TQM is premised on fundamental cultural change within organizations: in particular, the development of 'high trust' social relations including greater involvement in decision-making, open communications and an absolute commitment to and internalization of the ethic of 'customer satisfaction'. The stress on the 'customer ethic' is part of a more generalized commercial culture within organizations, as the responsibilities of managers and workers are presented as an empowering relationship premised on 'ownership'. In many public service organizations the latter has involved the development of a 'customer care' approach, including the introduction of customer care departments to co-ordinate and appraise the performance of staff in respect of customer care issues (IDS, 1995; Walsh, 1995). These developments are premised on extensive quality 'training' for all levels of the workforce. In essence, TQM is defined by management textbooks as the institutionalization of planned business improvement assessed against the satisfaction of customers: where quality improvement is addressed to the totality of organizational operations and therefore involves the development of both quality systems and a quality culture.

An important impetus towards many companies attempting to develop quality management has been the pursuit of the British Standards Institute's Quality Systems standard BS 5750, which regulates quality assurance, quality control and quality management. Since 1987, BS 5750 has also conformed to the international standard ISO 9000 and this standard is becoming an increasingly important quality guarantee for companies competing in the global market-place. By 1990, 6500 UK companies had achieved BS 5750 (IDS, 1990: 8) and all the water companies explored below had been awarded or were currently pursuing BS 5750. There are, however, important differences between BS 5750 and TQM and in some areas the two may be mutually incompatible. The main difference is that BS 5750 is concerned with the written systematization of process and quality control while TQM is primarily concerned with individual responsibility and the breakdown of rigid guidelines and functional demarcations.

HRM and the restructuring of the labour process

There is a developed academic debate concerning the impact of HRM/TQM on the organization of the capitalist labour process. There are three main strands of argument which have emerged from the debate. First, a 'managerialist' approach highlights the positive and empowering implications of TQM for labour. Second, a Foucaldian approach presents TQM as part of a shift from the structural to the discursive domination of labour within the labour process. Third, a critical approach highlights important continuities between HRM/TQM and earlier forms of management, and the way in which HRM/TQM involves the intensification and subordination of labour within the labour process. The first two approaches are both premised on the notion that HRM/TQM is the result of a qualitative break from earlier modern forms of Taylorist and Fordist labour organization. The latter approach is concerned to demonstrate the essential continuity of modern forms of subordination and exploitation in the capitalist labour process. As I will seek to demonstrate in the chapters below, however, while the former approaches are clearly deficient there *have* been important changes in respect of the *form* of subordination associated with TQM.

The advocates of TQM have tended to develop the regulationist approach outlined in Chapter 1 in order to argue that TQM is part of the flexible empowerment of labour associated with the shift from Fordism to post-Fordism. Hill (1991b) points to TQM as an effective post-Fordist alignment between capital and labour and an effective form of management for flexible organizations. For him TQM is qualitatively different from earlier forms of participative management, such as the 'quality circle' movement in the 1980s, in the way in which it addresses the cultural and institutional totality of organizations and delivers cost reductions while simultaneously aligning with the self-interest of managers and the demands of workers for more participative and egalitarian forms of management. The main problem with Hill's account, however, is his tendency to play down the way in which the devolution of responsibility has been accompanied by the centralization and intensification of managerial control.

The centralization and intensification of management control has been achieved by TQM through the way it increases management 'surveillance' of the labour process. The concept of surveillance was a central focus in the work of Michel Foucault and as a consequence Foucauldian concepts have dominated the analysis of TQM. The category of surveillance can provide valuable insights into the impact of TQM on the labour process. Sewell and Wilkinson (1992), for example, combine the work of Foucault and Braverman to argue that in making the labour process more visible TQM is a 'regime' which reinforces the asymmetry of power between capital and labour in the labour process and facilitates the more effective transformation of labour into labour-power. Sewell and Wilkinson usefully develop the work of Edwards (1979) on the limits and contradictions of 'bureaucratic control'. They argue that bureaucratic control, based on a pyramidal organizational structure, results in the distortion of information flows, and allows workers the 'time' and 'space' to escape management control and engage in various forms of 'making out' or 'idle time'. TQM is the reordering of time and space according to the principles of the 'panopticon': the result being a more direct and detailed form of 'low trust' control involving devolved responsibility and intensified central control. TQM has undoubtedly increased the surveillance of the labour process, but as I will now seek to show there are problems with importing other Foucauldian concepts into the analysis of the labour process.

According to Foucauldian writers the development of TQM is part of a reconstitution of power, marking the shift from modernity to post-modernity. Intensified control is facilitated through the ways in which panoptical control facilitates the reconstitution of power on the basis of the identity-sustaining practices of subjective individuals. The Foucauldian approach highlights the discursive nature of power and the way in which the 'sequestration' of knowledge through surveillance facilitates the subjugation of individuals to the totalizing impact of organizational discourses. The resulting 'self-management' and 'self-control' is a central component in the focus of TQM on the 'responsibility' which workers have to customers, and their active engagement in the process of 'continuous improvement'. TQM thus involves devolving responsibility to work groups in order to exploit the collective ingenuity of labour while intensifying centralized strategic control through the development of an 'electronic panopticon'. The development and maintenance of the means of surveillance emerge from the contradictions of TQM as the principal means through which management authority is maintained.

The Foucauldian approach presents TQM as consequence of the increasingly subjective locus of 'governmentability'. TQM involves the manipulation of organizational culture in order to make it congruent with the personal 'projects' of self-governing individuals: the refocusing of organizational culture around discourses of 'enterprise', the 'customer' and 'continuous improvement' aligns with the personal projects of self-reflexive individuals constituted as 'entrepreneurs of the self' (Du Gay and Salaman, 1992; Grey, 1994; Rose, 1989). Du Gay and Salaman present TQM as emerging from the rigidities of 'Fordist' bureaucratic control and argue that empowered 'post-Fordist' customers are forcing organizations to be more customer-oriented. According to this argument, organizational restructuring through TQM is primarily a process of cultural transformation. The discourse of enterprise has sought to align the autonomy and creativity of individuals with the valorization imperatives of organizations through the encouragement and 'normalization' of entrepreneurial values among individuals, manifested in a project of 'total customer responsiveness'.

A major weakness of both the managerialist approach and the Foucauldian approach is the implication that TQM represents a fundamental break with the past. The Foucauldian approach presents TQM as a postmodern economic form with the further implication that the materialist analysis of the labour process developed within the Marxist tradition is incapable of providing an adequate 'deconstruction' of the essentially discursive domination implied by TQM. The managerialist approach aligns the interests of capital and labour in a post-Fordist settlement which resolves the contradictions and exploitation inherent in the capital relation. There have, however, been a number of studies which have sought to demonstrate the gap between the rhetoric and reality of TQM and which together undermine many of the claims made above.

There are problems with the core claims that TQM empowers and increases the autonomy of workers (see Delbridge *et al.*, 1992 and Walsh, 1995 for a discussion in the public service context). TQM increases the visibility of the labour process and thereby reduces the choices available to workers in respect of task and time execution. In this sense TQM is a shift in the frontier of control which reduces the ability of labour to develop a degree of counter-control within the labour process. The shift in the frontier of control has been allowed by the development of new information systems which have increased the means of surveillance available to management through the visualization of the labour process. The responsibility and accountability of supervisors and line-workers implied by TQM has resulted in the reversal of the separation of manual and mental labour. However, numerous studies have demonstrated that polyvalence has involved 'multi-tasking' rather than 'multi-skilling' and any 'empowerment' has to be placed in the context of the enhanced surveillance capacity of a managerial élite. Thus, TQM primarily involves a shift in the frontier of control, in a strategy designed to reduce the porosity of the working day and thereby to intensify labour. The difference between TQM and earlier forms of management is the way in which the intensification and exploitation of labour is obscured through the ideology of the 'customer'. Internal customers exert peer control over workers, while the production process *in toto* appears to be driven by the market rather than by management. Indeed, through the process of 'continuous improvement' workers are expected to contribute to the intensification of their own labour. In this sense capital appropriates both the mental and manual skills of the workforce and deepens the subordination of labour.

There is a real sense in which HRM and TQM do constitute 'old wine in new bottles'. There are many similarities between HRM and both 'unitarist' (Fox, 1985) and 'soft humanist' models of personnel management (Nichols, 1980; Nichols and Beynon, 1977). TQM also embodies a series of logical and empirical contradictions: between commitment and flexibility, between flexibility and quality, between individualism and teamwork and between quality and commitment (Legge, 1995: 39). Furthermore, there is little evidence of HRM being pursued as a coherent strategy. Rather, it would appear that elements of HRM are being pursued by managers in an opportunistic and *ad hoc* way in order to exploit a socio-political climate marked by high unemployment and a weak and demobilized labour movement. There is also the problem that much of the literature exploring HRM has focused on non-unionized 'greenfield' manufacturing sites. As Scott (1994) notes, the introduction of HRM methods has been mediated by existing patterns of collective bargaining arrangements. In the case studies explored by Scott the most successful implementation of HRM was in a context in which it was introduced through established 'pluralist' patterns of collective bargaining, and attempts to impose HRM through unitary approaches met with suspicion and hostility from workers.

Clearly, the public services are a distinctive sector with their own tradition of collective bargaining and personnel policies. In analysing the introduction of HRM in the water industry the specificity of the sector must therefore be a central concern (Walsh, 1995). As I mentioned above, a key feature of the restructuring of public services has been a shift from the regulation of labour through bureaucratic planning to the organization of state and labour process according to the impersonal and abstract power of money and the law. There are several contributions that established approaches to the study of TQM can provide in respect of contextualizing the analysis of public services. The importance of money in the restructuring of public services is picked up by post-structuralist writers such as Du Guy and Salaman (1992: 620), who highlight the importance of enterprise culture and entrepreneurialism. Du Gay and Salaman also highlight how the contradictions of bureaucratic compulsion played a key role in the crisis of the state, though they fail to develop the implications of this in respect of the origins and significance of TQM. Sewell and Wilkinson usefully highlight the dysfunctions of bureaucracy as an important dynamic in the development of TQM. This is a useful insight but needs to be accompanied by a more detailed analysis of the crisis of the bureaucratic state form and other bureaucratic forms of labour regulation more generally. There is also the problem that TQM and JIT are ideal types and there are important empirical variations in the scope and intensity of quality systems between and within organizations (Jenkins, 1994). The monolithic conception of power in Foucauldian approaches fails to allow for either empirical variation or nodes of resistance to the development of TQM. What needs to be addressed is the historical specificity of TQM as a management ideology and practice (Nichols, 1980: 298) and the material determinants underlying its adoption in particular industries at particular times.

In respect of the water industry I will develop the argument that HRM/TQM developed in response to the limits and contradictions of the bureaucratic planner-state and reflects the increasing convergence of state and capital. The quality systems that have developed as part of a quality management approach in the water industry have developed in response to, and mirror the form of, the liberal moment of the state. The quality systems create quantitative data that allows competitive pressure to be imposed on the water industry both by the state in the form of OFWAT and capital in the form of international capital markets. The quality systems also confirm the status of consumers as essentially abstract and formally equal customers, recognized only through the abstract mediations of law and money. However, water services have to be provided by real workers and managers for real consumers and the substantive inequalities and contradictions which emerge from this process highlight the enduring contradictions of public service in its neo-liberal form.

The origin of TQM in the water industry can be found in the crisis of the planner-state and the resolution of this crisis through the subjugation of the industry to the abstract power of money and the law. This involved the depoliticization of the water industry and the re-establishment of management autonomy in respect to the political and economic relations within the industry. The shift to more abstract forms of regulation was a principal dynamic in the development of quality management in the water industry. The development of quality management in the water industry in response to the regulatory pressures of OFWAT and the City has indeed had a marked impact on management control and information systems. New systems have been developed which are premised on the need to obtain 'total customer satisfaction' in an increasingly competitive environment. However, the exploration of how these systems have developed within the case study companies outlined below highlights both the problematical notion of 'competition' in respect of a sector like the water industry and the highly ambiguous and contradictory notion of the 'customer' on which customer care programmes are premised. These problems reflect the impossibility of totally depoliticizing public service provision and the serious and enduring contradictions underlying the form of the neo-liberal state.

The Origins of TQM in the Water Industry

I will now explore the way in which managers working within the water industry perceive the origins, development and consequences of state and managerial restructuring and the contradictions underlying new forms of management ideology and practice. Managers grasp the way in which the origins of quality management are intimately related to the fiscal crisis of the planner-state and the way in which neo-liberal restructuring constitutes an attempt to resubordinate the water industry to the abstract imperatives of the law of money. The Senior Personnel Manager at EASTWAT, for example, argues that the primary dynamic to the development of TQM was the changes to the financial structure of the company. The old culture reflected a situation in which the organization was obliged to go to the Government for the funds it needed to finance important capital projects; money that was increasingly unavailable as the cuts in public expenditure began to bite from the late 1970s onwards. This contrasts with a situation in which the company is now *free*, within the constraints of its 'K' formula, to determine its own financial profile. Managers are now free to manage, in a company that is a PLC; that is, 'just like Marks & Spencer or IBM'. Importantly, this 'opening out' of the company's financial profile has had the effect of 'opening out' the lives of all the individuals within the organization. People have been able to escape from a hierarchical and safe approach, to one of dealing with constant change and constant improvement. This manager described with great precision the contradictions and limitations of the managerialist form of the water industry, the contradiction between rising consumer expectations and the fiscal crisis of the state, and the way in which the contradiction is resolved through the imposition of the law of money on the water industry:

> How would we have been able to respond, if you take a recession and the Government says 'No more money!'? You can't respond, so somewhere or another there would have been some sort of clash – something would have to give. You would say to the customer 'Forget it! We're not going to replace those old sewers . . . '. And it would even rock the Government: 'You're rotten, give them more money!' In the 1990s it would come out as an absolute shriek! The Greenpeaces of this world would really be going on. They'd be going to the Government, and we'd be a pawn – as a water authority in all that – whereas now we're the focus of it. The Government have deflected that because we're now a standalone company – it's up to you to perform. And we have got an out. We've got an out that says 'We put our charges up'. We can go to the market and get more money. We can also say to the customer 'No, we're not going to do that!' – provided that we can get people on our side.

'Quality management' has developed in the water industry in response to the contradictions of managerialism and state planning, and a key dynamic in the introduction and development of 'quality management' has been the development of new forms of neo-liberal state regulation. The OFWAT regulatory regime established by the 1989 Water Act has put increasing pressure on water undertakers to develop systems for the measurement and monitoring of levels of service and standards, and this has been legitimated through the notion of 'total customer satisfaction'. The efficiency of water companies is measured by a series of operational targets that are defined and set by OFWAT, and these form the basis of the (RPI + K) formula (the indicators are set out in the Appendix). The formula determines the amount water companies are allowed to charge for their services in order to cover projected capital investment and, therefore, the values imposed by the formula impact directly on marginal rates of profit. The (RPI + K) formula has an inbuilt element of efficiency improvement. The information is required by OFWAT in order to measure the performance of companies against a series of predetermined targets in key areas, and the data provides the basis for the comparative competition by which capital markets are able to assess the efficiency of water companies. The systems developed in order to collect, monitor and report this information have had a marked effect on the operational and managerial structures of control within water companies and have provided the major dynamic in the development of TQM.

The collection and monitoring of regulatory information has resulted in the development of new management information systems and the establishment of new departments and posts which relate directly to the processes of regulation. In order to satisfy the new regulatory regime, water companies are required to collect and process vast amounts of information relating to the performance indicators. Thus the main effect of the new regulatory regime has been to compel the introduction and development of increasingly sophisticated management information systems. Within the new regulatory framework, companies have to present a detailed account of their performance to OFWAT each year through the 'July Return'. The preparation of this document has imposed a significant new workload on water companies, and has had a significant effect on staff and resources. The main consideration in the development of new information systems has been the need to produce data that are quantitatively commensurable and auditable. Across the water sector companies have adopted new management information systems and these systems have played a central role in the development of TQM.

The importance of traceability and repeatability is illustrated with respect to the new information systems developed at WESTWAT. The systems highlight how the concepts and methodologies of TQM have addressed the regulatory activities of the state. The most important consideration in the development of the new systems was the need to have a vigorous 'audit trail'. It is important that all information, whether for internal purposes or for OFWAT, be traceable to where it originated. For an area such as 'interruption of supplies' (Condition J Level of Service Indicator DG3), a document exists which specifies the staff who have responsibility in this area and what those responsibilities are. The systems were developed in response to the pressures of regulation and have fundamentally increased the level and type of information continually available to senior managers. Managers have the ability constantly to monitor information relating to the level and costs of service, relate this to corporate policy and appraise and reward managers and staff accordingly.

The Condition J and other OFWAT performance indicators have been incorporated into the corporate and managerial strategies of water companies. This is reflected at WESTWAT, where the level of service indicators features in the 'key results' of the business, and the ability of managers to monitor performance against the indicators is considered vitally important. The new systems have increased the information available to senior managers and enabled them to monitor the performance of subordinate managers and staff more effectively. The new systems have thus provided the basis for the restructuring of strategic asset and labour power allocation and planning. The Business Systems Controller at WESTWAT is responsible for collating information from the various areas of the company, and compiling a 'consolidated report' for the 'Senior Executive Team'. He suggested that the new systems will both increase the availability of operational information to senior managers and embed the procedures by which this information is collated within the technical and bureaucratic structure of the company. The new systems have allowed a reduction in the number of managerial levels in order to make the managerial function more 'hands-on work' and 'encourage managers to manage'. Given the surveillance capacity of the new IT systems, the primary consideration of the newly empowered managers is increasingly a focus on 'costs' and the performance of their department or section in the context of wider business objectives.

The new IT systems have given managers speedy access to the information that is required in order to monitor the line-managers and foreman to whom responsibility for operational effectiveness has increasingly been delegated. However, in this regard there are two contradictory trends at work within WESTWAT. Functional managers have been given greater autonomy and responsibility in an attempt to introduce 'hands-on management' within the company. On the other hand, the development of management information systems has increased the ability of senior management executives to monitor and control middle and line-managers. The substantive administrative activities of managers are, therefore, increasingly measured and appraised by systems designed to impose abstract logic on the operational activities of water companies. This contradiction is experienced by managers as the increasingly important objective of subordinating the concrete and substantive activities of water companies to the abstract power of money. Within the organizational structure of water companies it has resulted in the increasing dominance of management accountants.

At WESTWAT the OFWAT-inspired systems have thus played a central role in flattening out the managerial hierarchy within the company and devolving responsibility to first-line managers and supervisors. In essence, the new management ethos has involved pushing the locus of managerial responsibility further 'down the line'. The development of TQM has transformed the technically-oriented supervisor who dominated the Fabian form of public service into a 'business manager' engaged in the direction of support functions towards business goals (see Legge, 1995; Storey, 1992: 198 for wider discussion). This new approach utilizes the skill and expertise of the staff directly involved in the operation of water distribution and sewerage systems, rather than relying on a 'hierarchy of experts'. The OFWAT-inspired systems have also shifted the central focus of management information systems towards the control of costs and allowed management accountants to replace engineers as the hegemonic management group within the water industry (see Storey and Sisson, 1990 for a discussion on the wider implications of this trend). The important point is that within the water industry these developments mark a shift in the focus of management away from operational concerns with delivering water services to more 'abstract' concerns with ensuring that water services are delivered at minimum cost through contractual relations with customers rather than through a technical relationship with a consumer. In this way quality management is a state-sponsored attempt to impose the law of money and the rule of law on the water industry in response to the crisis and contradictions of the forms of public service associated with the planner-state.

Quality management as the law of money

The imposition of the law of money on the operational structure of the water industry is perceived by managers working within the water industry in terms of an increasing focus on finance. The Business and Customer Services Director at CITYWAT suggested that an inevitable result of recession is that 'the accountant comes to the top'. In the former SWC sector this has been compounded by the transfer of many companies to PLC status and the resulting change in the relationship between water companies and the City. When companies such as

CITYWAT were SWCs, investors could add CITYWAT shares to their portfolios in the expectation of a low but fixed return. As a result, the City had little interest in the performance of the company. The transition to PLC status has totally transformed this relationship. The City now scrutinizes the performance of the company in great detail, and this has increased the focus on finance at every level. The impact has been particularly sharp with respect to line-managers and supervisors and, as a senior operational manager at CWL suggested, between engineers and accountants:

> It's helped focus on costs and things like that. There are the endless clashes between 'I'm an engineer and what I say is right!' and 'I don't care who you are, you're not having the money to spend!'. So there have been the fairly classic arguments . . . But there is an increasing concentration on cost, and that makes life increasingly difficult for the line managers, and that in itself brings some tensions – some which are quite creative and good for the company and some of which can be distractive. [*sic*]

The new regulatory framework has also had a marked impact at SHIREWAT through a shift in the organizational structure and culture of the company. The 'Customer Services Manager' at the company suggested that the main impact of regulation has been a marked shift in the cultural orientation of the company from an emphasis on the 'product' to an emphasis on the 'customer'. SHIREWAT was formerly a company dominated by engineers concerned only with the production and distribution of water. The new regulatory framework required an increasing emphasis on the 'customer':

> This company was product-orientated. We were concerned about the water. And if we got the water out of the ground, and we got it pushed out to people's taps, that was our job done. We didn't really believe that the end user, the person that paid the bill, had got any right to ask any questions and anything else. We were run by engineers, the engineers filled all the top slots, and, therefore, they were totally product-orientated. When it came to customer service, 'Well, what service do they want?' It was that kind of operation. The regulation that came with privatization made a dramatic difference – because all of a sudden we had to start counting things and collecting information. And it was a major shock to the company's culture.

The pressure to 'count things' and 'collect information' was a direct result of state-imposed pressure to improve efficiency. This was facilitated through the efficiency improvements that OFWAT and the DoE have built into the company's 'K' profile. The pressure has resulted in a fundamental restructuring and rationalization of the company's operations. Immediately following the introduction of the new framework, the company employed a team of management consultants to look at the scope for reducing staffing levels either through rationalization or through increasing the use of subcontractors. The result of this was a 30 per cent reduction in the workforce through a voluntary redundancy programme that drastically reduced the age-profile of the company. The restructuring programme had a 'marked benefit' for SHIREWAT with respect to the removal of staff with entrenched 'concretist' attitudes. In the water industry these staff were labelled 'concretist' because they were (mostly) civil engineers interested in the development of (real) concrete structures such as reservoirs, sewerage works and water towers in response to technically-defined needs of consumers and used these criteria in order to determine the commercial and operational imperatives of the organization. However, the constitution of the (Fabian) managerialist labour process rendered the removal of these staff extremely problematic from the point of view of the operational effectiveness of the company. A major feature of the managerialist form of the company was that 'nobody wrote anything down', and the result of the voluntary redundancy scheme was the disposal of a vast amount of experience 'tied up in employees' heads'. The immediate impact of the scheme was, therefore, operational ineffectiveness and heightened levels of unrest and disquiet among the remaining staff. The primary management strategy for dealing with this situation has been the development of new 'quality management' systems that codify operations within formal procedural systems and which resystematize some of the information that has been lost through the voluntary redundancy scheme.

The development of TQM in the water industry thus reflects several important pressures that have been imposed on the industry. The industry has been exposed to the pressure of scrutiny by the state and the city, and the resulting competitive pressures have required a form of management which allows for the quantification of performance and the institutionalization of constant improvement. The pressure of competition has also forced companies to reduce staffing levels, and to the extent that this has focused on the more experienced workers there has been a need for a form of management which codifies the knowledge of workers within management information and control systems. These developments have been legitimated through claims that a movement towards ever greater levels of 'quality' benefits the customer, and 'customer care' units of various kinds have become increasingly important loci of power within the industry.

OFWAT and the 'Marks-and-Spencerization' of the Water Industry

An important component of TQM where it has been developed in the service sector has been 'customer care' programmes (Walsh, 1995; Wilkinson *et al.*, 1993: 7). This is the specific manifestation of the way in which all TQM programmes embody an ethic of 'total customer satisfaction'. The development of TQM in the water industry has indeed been accompanied by the increasing importance of the 'customer care' function. The resultant 'customer care' departments have come to occupy an increasingly nodal position in the control structures of water companies; occupying the interface between customer complaints, OFWAT and the monitoring and auditing of operational performance. This increasing tendency towards 'customer management' (Fuller and Smith, 1991) is manifested in the water industry in the increasingly detailed control of the labour process by a management function ostensibly premised on the interests of the 'customer'. In turn the development of new forms of state regulation and management have been legitimated through the way in which they benefit the customer.

The principal dynamic for change is perceived by managers working in the industry as 'competition'; an abstract dynamic that demands an ever-increasing emphasis on 'customer service'. The competitors are increasingly seen as the exemplars of the UK private sector. Water companies compete with Marks & Spencer and Boots rather than each other. How is this competitive pressure perceived by managers working within the industry, and what has been its impact on the operational and managerial structure of the industry? A senior operational manager at WESTWAT, who is in front-line contact with OFWAT, suggested that the role of OFWAT in facilitating comparative competition is simply one element in the increasingly competitive social context in which the water industry operates. OFWAT has had a marked impact with respect to the pressure to develop increasingly complex management information systems and audit trails. The notion of competition, however, extends far beyond the pressures exerted by OFWAT:

> I think [the pressure of comparative competition] is in there, amongst several other aspects, whether it's competition against Marks & Spencer, or whatever. I think there are aspects of customer service which aren't necessarily unique to the water industry. Therefore, if it's a question of how quickly you respond to a telephone call, or whether it's the appearance of the inspector when he arrives on your doorstep, a matter of keeping an appointment, then I think the comparisons are legitimate outside of the water industry. I was aware last week when my wife rung up and the dishwasher had broken down. The lass on the other end of the phone said 'We'll be around tomorrow morning'. That was something that was beyond my expectation. But that is your competition.

The competition faced by water companies is essentially abstract competition – a competition to maximize the valorization of capital rather than a competition to maximize the utility provided to real customers. A senior operational manager at CITYWAT highlighted the point through the argument that the idea that water companies compete against each other is completely ludicrous. Customers only deal with one company, and the diverse specificity of the geographical and hydrological situations of individual companies makes comparisons between companies, as developed by OFWAT, 'irrelevant' as far as the individual customer is concerned. Customers look to the 'big market-place' and compare companies with Marks & Spencer and with the other utilities:

> That is what they compare you with because that is what they know. They don't get served by two water companies so they can say 'It's much better on Tuesday!' They know you, so they compare you with your market-place, which is the big market-place . . . It would be wrong to suggest that all companies should provide the same service, quite wrong – completely. You're dealing with different areas, you're dealing with different waters, different things, different expenses. Similarly you get a different service from Tesco, Marks & Spencer's, Sainsbury's. But you have a choice between the service of Sainsbury and Marks & Spencer's. So we must live with that sort of comparability.

It is through these perceived changes in the 'outside world' that managers think about both the increasing importance of abstract management and competition, and the contradictions inherent in the very notion of competition when applied to the water industry. Managers are able to grasp, albeit in a highly mystificatory way, the contradictory notion of competition articulated by the neo-liberal state form, and this highlights the importance of the state in the restructuring process. There is a convergence between the abstract regulation of OFWAT and the abstract management of TQM in that both attempt to minimize costs and maximize efficiency in order to achieve customer satisfaction and maximize competitive advantage. However, both the conception of the customer and competition are essentially abstract, and we will see that these constantly break down when set against the substantive and concrete reality of water industry operations. I will now explore the way in which the neo-liberal restructuring of the state and water industry has been legitimated on the basis of the 'customer' and the implications of this in respect of social relations within water companies.

OFWAT and the Problem of Total Customer Satisfaction

The new mechanisms of control have been legitimated through the discourse of consumerism. The notion of 'customer care' has legitimated the 'commercialization' of social relations within water companies and between water companies and their consumers (O'Connell Davidson, 1993: 142–59). The OFWAT performance measures have been embedded in the bureaucratic structures of water companies through their incorporation into the managerial ethos and the rewards system of such companies. The existence of an outside regulator has acted as an important stimulus to increasing levels of monitoring within water companies and the generalized ethos of monitoring has subsequently been extended into areas not covered by the DG measures. The increasing importance of monitoring has been legitimated through the discourse of 'customer care', as is illustrated through the impact of the DG measures on managerial control systems and labour processes at SHIREWAT.

OFWAT and the customer care unit at SHIREWAT

The DG performance indicators have had an important impact on the organizational structure and culture at SHIREWAT. The indicators in respect of dealing with complaints and billing queries have become an important element in the company's culture. Staff who work in these areas are fully aware of the time-frames and constraints attendant on them with respect to OFWAT, and these constraints and time-frames have been built into the new management control systems. The company has developed a system that automatically sends out warnings to customers in respect of interruptions to supply (Condition J Level of Service Indicator DG3) and has established a special unit with the exclusive function of maintaining and monitoring adequate pressure (Condition J Level of Service Indicator DG2). The most important impact, however, has been with respect to the establishment of the 'Customer Service Unit'; a unit that has provided an important catalyst in increasing the importance of 'customer care' throughout the organization.

The unit is staffed by two women selected on the basis of their experience of many aspects of the company's business, and has the function of dealing with any 'customer problems' that are referred to it. It has the objective of ensuring the satisfaction of the customer; of pursuing customer problems through relevant departments until they are resolved and then reporting back to the customer. The unit is part of an initiative within the company to focus awareness on 'customer care' issues: to inject 'customer care' into all aspects of the company's structure and culture. The Customer Services Manager at SHIREWAT suggested that 'customer care isn't just about those people that speak to the customer – it's about all the things that we do in the organization'. Thus, every member of staff at SHIREWAT has undergone between four and six days' 'customer care training'. The programme highlighted the importance of keeping customers 'informed' and emphasized the extent to which most complaints arise from a lack of information rather than poor performance.

The 'customer care' function at SHIREWAT is made up of three elements: developing the CSU, heightening the awareness of 'customer care' and improving the way customers are kept informed. The CSU has played a central role in the latter two developments by making managers from across the organization focus on the issue of 'customer care'. The main function of the unit is dealing with written complaints; although it also deals with overspill from the telephonist and other departments and with any 'nasty' calls received by the company. The CSU also deals with OFWAT on a day-to-day basis. Incoming complaints are logged on to a computer system and passed to the appropriate head of department. The system is a continuous auditing system, and there has to be a file in existence for every complaint number that is logged. This allows the system to be audited each year for OFWAT. Thus the system develops an audit trail for every complaint, and highlights unresolved complaints and complaints where the customer has not been reported back to within the specified time-frame. The CSU continuously monitors the system, and has the function of chasing up outstanding complaints with managers and heads of department.

This has had an important impact with respect to managerial control within the company. On a day-to-day basis, the complaints received by the company (for example, poor water quality or pressure) were previously assigned to the inspectors and mostly 'left to drift', with nobody following the complaint up unless the consumer recontacted the company. With the introduction of the new systems, the complaint is logged on and assigned a number, following which it is assigned to an individual inspector who receives a print-out of the complaint and has the responsibility of reporting back on the complaint. If the complaint is not 'signed off' by the inspector it is followed up by the CSU. A member of the CSU team at SWL suggested that the unit has provided an important discipline with respect to instilling 'customer care' into managers and staff within the company. The unit has 'improved' the realization among staff that there is a 'consumer at the end of the line' – particularly among departments which have little or no customer contact. The new IT systems have played a central role in this process and have allowed the CSU access to the performance of managers across the organization.

According to my informants, the CSU initially met with a great deal of hostility and suspicion. People in the organization were not used to being 'answerable' to anyone, and this allowed complaints to fester away unanswered. It was felt that these unresolved complaints constituted the raw material which was developed by the press in order to give the company a bad name. Staff initially failed to recognize that the increased monitoring and control of their activities was in fact a process designed to make the company more efficient on behalf of the company and the customer. A member of the CSU commented:

> When we first started to tighten up on it, people kind of felt that we were looking over their shoulders to see what they were doing – instead of looking

out for the company and the customer interest. And it's all for your PR at the end of the day – if you give good service then you get good reports.

There is, therefore, an important gap between managerial rhetoric and the material implications of the 'customer care' function. The 'customer care' function has played an important role in respect of both the intensification of the labour process and the tightening up of management control structures. Through the introduction of dedicated new systems of information technology the CSU has acted as a catalyst for the restructuring of all aspects of management, employee and customer relations within the company. The increasing focus on 'customer care' is also illustrated by developments at WESTWAT, where the ethos of 'total customer satisfaction' has also been applied to the relationship between departments and individuals within the company.

The Internal Market and the Development of 'Customer Service Teams' at WESTWAT Ltd

The process of collecting and monitoring levels of service information has had a marked impact on the organizational structure of WESTWAT, primarily through the development of 'Customer Service Teams'. Within each operating area of the company a 'Business Services' Department' has been established in order to co-ordinate all the functions that are not directly concerned with the treatment, supply and distribution of water, the treatment of sewage, or plant and buildings maintenance. The departments thus co-ordinate the administration, finance and planning functions. The 'Customer Service Teams' have direct first-line contact with customers, and operate the 'Customer Services System' through which every contact with a customer is logged and can, therefore, be traced and audited. The 'Management Information Group' is concerned with both the dissemination of information from the centre and the collection of performance data from within areas of the company. The Group is responsible for gathering information on levels of service and comparing performance against performance targets. The information is transmitted to the centre and forms the basis of the 'Monthly Report' to the Managing Director. The Report contains basic financial data, reports from all the executive directors to the Managing Director and, in summary detail, all the levels of performance which are both presented in aggregate form and broken down by (operational and geographical) area.

The structure of management accountability and control associated with the 'Business Services Department' represents an important, if not fundamental, change in the organizational structure of the company. The team leaders within the 'Business Services Department' report directly to the Business Services Manager, who is responsible directly to an area manager, who in turn reports directly to the Operations Director. According to my interviewees, the main dynamic for the establishment of the new structure was to acquire consistency and co-ordination in the way in which the company dealt with information relating to customers. The functions that are now contained within the 'Business Services Department' have always existed in some form, but the new system brings them all together under one manager. Prior to restructuring, the management information and finance functions would have reported to the Divisional Accountant, the customer services function to the Distribution Manager (who dealt mainly with water), and the administrative function to the Personnel Manager.

Thus it is claimed that the customer service function is an important element in developing the company into a 'quality organization' that delivers a 'quality product'. A senior operational manager argued that the Customer Service Teams are able to act as a catalyst for infusing the culture of 'customer care' throughout the organization:

> I think the fundamental issue associated with how well we treat the customer is, how well do we treat each other internally? What I think is that the Customer Service Team have the need to speak to everybody, because they don't know what the next customer call is going to be about . . . and therefore, they have the need to speak to everyone in an area. It's from the comments of our Customer Service Teams that you learn what's going wrong with these internal communications . . . and things like the continuous improvement programmes that are currently under way, there is a lot that the Customer Service Team are able to put into that.

The production of a customer-conscious, quality organization has resulted in the breaking down of functional rigidities within the company. This has been particularly marked with respect to the area of the company–customer interface where the Customer Service Teams have provided an important catalyst for change. The comments and concerns of staff working in the Customer Service Teams have been used to develop and define company policy on customer service and standards, and these have been incorporated into quality management procedures. The development of quality management, and the concomitant development of the 'Customer Service Department', represent important changes to the organizational structure and culture of WESTWAT. However, senior managers confuse the demands for improved services from real customers with the competitive pressures emanating from the regulator and the City and the way this involves subordinating public services to the abstract power of money. One senior manager commented as follows on the origins of the customer culture:

> The main dynamic, I think, is the culture of this country – I would broaden it out to that extent. I think that these days, because of things like the Citizen's Charter, because of increased competition and the desire to achieve greater market share through improving customer service, through the pressure from the Customer Services Committee (i.e. OFWAT), through all sorts of different reasons, I think there is a culture and an expectation there on the part of customers, that they expect certain standards of service . . . I think that any company would be foolish to necessarily 'jump off the cliff', and say 'yes, I'll spend whatever it takes!'. Everyone's got their budget as to what they can afford, and you've got to achieve a balance. But that balance is achieved only by being aware of the world around, and what that world demands.

The customer service teams have thus developed the important role of balancing the ever-growing expectations of customers with the ultimate constraint of the law of money. In managing this balance the units have provided a particular catalyst for the intensification of labour within the labour process. The same senior manager observed:

> If you look at the basic operations on the part of the workforce, and the basic methods and systems that they employ, there's been no change at all. I think that like any other industry, if you get the person at the sharp end actually doing the work, digging the hole, or whatever, that privatization, or regulation, hasn't actually made any difference to them, I wouldn't say in the way they do it, but certainly in what they do, it hasn't changed. What I would suggest, however, is that the way in which they do it, and the attitude and manner in which they do it, is changing.

The customer care units have, moreover, contributed to a fundamental intensification of management control systems. The development of TQM is part of a process through which the law of money has been reimposed on the bureaucratic structures of control developed through managerialism. The ideology of consumerism materially represented in the form of the 'customer care' function has simultaneously legitimated and obscured the contradictions inherent in the neo-liberal form of 'public service' which has emerged from this process. These contradictions emerge from the way in which the 'common good' represented by neo-liberal public service involves an attempt to subordinate the producers and consumers of water services to the abstract power of money capital. The extent to which this process can only ever be partial highlights the enduring contradictions underlying neo-liberal public service management and regulation.

The Contradictions of 'Customer Care'

The function of management within the neo-liberal water industry has increasingly become the mediation of operational service activities through financial constraints. In the neo-liberal production/consumption configuration the form of the state will be determined through the (re)subordination of public service labour processes to the expanded reproduction of capital (valorization process). This is part of the neo-liberal alignment of state and capital which has developed in response to the contradictions of Keynesian state planning. The alignment, of course, can never be total owing to the contradictory determination of the capitalist state. One manifestation of this enduring non-alignment is the struggle between state and industry over the irrationality of OFWAT's substantive policy formulations. This highlights the enduring contradictions underlying the concrete administrative activities of the state. It is in practice impossible to depoliticize the regulation of the water industry. The (RPI + K) formula limits the prices that water companies are allowed to charge for their services and provides a framework in which companies are free to pursue profits and set dividends to shareholders in line with improvements in efficiency. It has, however, proved politically impossible for OFWAT to allow companies to make huge profits and pay high dividends, irrespective of whether these are the result of efficiency increases. Hence,

> [i]n the water industry, where real prices are rising rather than falling, where

> there is no effective competition from alternative suppliers, and where privatization was and remains very unpopular with most of the electorate, big profits swiftly provoke a hostile reaction in the media and among opposition politicians and pressure builds on OFWAT to 'show its teeth'. (Saunders and Harris 1994: 66–7)

The result has been that OFWAT has constantly intervened in the industry between the 'periodic reviews' in an attempt to reduce prices and limit the dividends paid to shareholders.[1] When this is combined with the 'legitimate' function of OFWAT to ensure that quality standards are maintained, the result has been a high level of regulatory intervention in a visibly politicized context. The contradictory premises of OFWAT are perceived by managers working within the water industry in terms of the 'unrealism' of the regulator. Senior managers are critical of the regulator in respect of the unrealistic way in which OFWAT interprets performance indicators and the negative image that OFWAT develops of the industry in public statements. Senior managers are concerned that the industry must learn to 'manage' the regulator better. OFWAT is felt to have a great potential in helping customers to 'understand' the arguments concerning the costs and benefits of capital spending projects. The criticism of OFWAT is that it highlights deficiencies in service without accompanying this with an assessment of remedial costs. The depoliticization of the industry implies that capital spending is met from either revenue or borrowing, and both options result in higher water charges. It is here that OFWAT is failing to fulfil its potential as a truly neo-liberal state form. A senior operational manager at CITYWAT argued:

> [OFWAT] doesn't seem to be doing much in terms of public understanding of the industry. It tends to help the *Sun* with its next banner headline. The banner headline has a case, but only one side of the case. I don't think it's helping in the construction of the debate about some of those other things. Now, I appreciate that it's immensely difficult, [but] you should never underestimate the stupidity of the customer. To get general debates over the question of water is very difficult. Similarly, I think that most people are intelligent enough to understand the basic arguments, and I think that's where OFWAT has a big role to play.

The same manager outlined two examples of where the water industry and the regulator could work together in order to temper the voracious appetites of consumers for greater quantities and increasingly effective use-values:

> There are areas where the regulator should be working more closely with the industry to help the customer. For example, a lot of the stuff about leakage, a lot of the stuff about water quality. Yes, you could improve the water quality! Yes, you could reduce the leakage levels! The awareness argument is 'Oh my God, 30 per cent of this is wasting away and it's costing £500 million'. It would be helpful for us to debate – well if it's costing £500 million for it to leak away – but it may cost you £15 billion to put it right. So that is where I think OFWAT can help the industry. I think it can help because it will make it possible for the public to understand and make some choices, because it is truly independent. Similarly, the things about water quality, you know: 'It's terrible! Lead in the water! Must reduce it!' But one person has their life shortened by ten minutes because of a lead pipe. Is it better to spend another £5 billion getting lead out of the system or would you be better putting an extra crash barrier on the M1 or whatever? It's that sort of thing we're thinking.

The contradictions of customer care are also highlighted in the institutional arrangements that have developed for the representation of 'customer' interests and opinions within the neo-liberal water industry. There are ten Customers Service Committees (CSCs) in England and Wales corresponding to the areas covered by the former RWAs. In contrast with the Consumer Consultative Councils (CCCs) they replaced, the CSCs are not embedded within the institutional structure of the water industry, but form part of the regulatory apparatus and are constituted as independent bodies within OFWAT. The CSCs are constituted by a full-time secretariat made up of employees of OFWAT and part-time members of the committee who are drawn from a variety of interest groups. These developments have had a marked impact on the institutional structures of water companies. Water companies have developed managerial posts and systems in order to 'manage' customer representation. While organized labour has skilfully been excluded from any involvement in the CSCs, the bodies nonetheless represent the development of a form of neo-liberal corporatism which involves various user-groups in the formulation of water company policy.

The scope and limit of CSC involvement within the water industry are tightly controlled. The CSCs are not involved in the day-to-day regulation of the company's operational performance. The involvement of

CSCs tends to assume two basic forms: consultation prior to major new developments and initiatives, and direct contacts between full-time CSC members and 'Regulation Group' employees in respect of customer complaints which have not been dealt with adequately by water companies and have been reported to OFWAT. The day-to-day contact between the company and the CSC is at the level of the full-time secretariat. The most important function of the ordinary CSC members is consultation and facilitating the dissemination of information on service issues.

This is reflected at CITYWAT, where the most important point of contact between the company and the CSC has been in response to guidance notes issued by OFWAT: such notes have included guidance on 'Debt and Disconnection' (23 May 1991) and 'Services for Disabled and Elderly Customers' (9 October 1991). The company has been required to give presentations to the CSC outlining its response to guidelines of this type. Contact with the CSC has been necessary when complaints have been made against the company and referred to the CSC for adjudication, and the company has used the CSC as a 'sounding board' prior to new developments and initiatives. The CSC was, for example, consulted over changes to the design of the water bill prior to these being sent out to customers.

The main problem CITYWAT has faced with regard to contact with the CSC has been with regard to the CSC function of resolving customer complaints. The CSC has tended to undermine the neo-liberal premises of OFWAT by generalizing complaints, and hence repoliticizing the regulatory relationship. A senior operational manager at CITYWAT outlined the way he perceived the problem as follows:

> One of the problems that we've had with the CSC is that they will often be trying to get us to do things for the population as a whole, based on the 1 per cent sample that they are dealing with. Now sometimes it makes sense, but other times it just doesn't, and you can end up with a bit of a conflict. Because they are trying to resolve particular complaints, they will resolve that complaint and then say to us 'Well look, you could avoid all of these in the future if only you'd do all that'. Well, probably 99 per cent of our customers aren't interested. So it might help OFWAT with their work, but it doesn't actually help the bulk of the customers.

What seems to be emerging is a conflict between the textbook customer who is derived from the abstract postulates of neo-liberal theory and the real customers to whom water companies supply water services. This is reflected, at SHIREWAT, in the way the Customer Service Manager is concerned by what she considers to be a serious conflict between the quasi-customer constituted by OFWAT and the real customers to whom SHIREWAT supplies water. This conflict has been recognized and addressed by OFWAT, which has ruled that all water companies will have to undertake 'market research' as part of future periodic reviews. Indeed, SHIREWAT has already addressed this issue through the appointment of MORI to conduct a series of comprehensive surveys in order to measure the opinions of SHIREWAT's real customers. The customer service manager at SHIREWAT outlined the concerns that led to this development:

> OFWAT is supposed to be the quasi-customer [and] I've got concerns about that because they take what I call a rational and logical view of things. And with the best will in the world, the general public are not always rational and logical. So many of the things I see coming from OFWAT where it says 'We believe this is the customer's view', it doesn't tie up at all with our perception of customer's views that are relayed to us by people getting on the phone or writing to us. In many cases they are not logical. But they just feel very strongly about something and logic just goes straight out of the window. So I don't really think that either OFWAT or the CSCs truly represent the customers' views.

The reason for the CSC not truly representing customer views emanates from the narrow base of interest groups on which it is constituted. The SHIREWAT representative on the CSC suggested that the Committee's constitution – it is made up of local councillors, and representatives from agriculture, small business, and disabled and charity groups – prevents the Committee developing what she termed a 'balanced view'. In considering the Committee's lack of rationality, she highlights the extent to which conflict is increasingly premised on the commodification of water:

> On the one hand – I've actually heard it within the CSC – you'll get one member saying 'Well, I believe that it's wrong for other water-company payers to pay the bills of those people who won't pay, therefore water companies ought to disconnect supplies'. And then in the same committee you've got another member saying 'That's terrible, to disconnect people that can't pay their bills'. So we do tend to get mixed messages coming from them.

The extent to which the water industry is now premised firmly on the rational abstract individual of liberal social theory is reflected in the way the same manager conceptualized the logical and ultimate development of 'customer sovereignty' – the freedom to receive *poor service*:

> I was speaking to Ian Byatt [the Director General of OFWAT] about a month ago, and he was saying the selfsame thing, because I posed the question, the hypothetical question, 'What if our customers would actually prefer a lower level of service at lower cost?'. Because OFWAT is always talking about improving levels of service, but obviously, all these have a cost attached to them. And I'm actually turning the tables and saying, what about if they actually say 'Well, we don't want this level of service, but will you knock 10 per cent off our bill?'. What would OFWAT's reaction be to that? And he sort of mulled it over for a while, and he said: 'Well, if that's what your customers really want, it would not be right for OFWAT to say no, they can't have it!'

The weakness and problems associated with consumer representation in the neo-liberal water industry are perceived by managers as emanating from the illogicality, irrationality and stupidity of real consumers. The contradictions of 'customer care' are manifested in the struggle between OFWAT and water companies over the level of abstraction at which the interests of consumers are to be considered. The development of quality management has been part of a process which has attempted to contain the needs of consumers within an administratively-generated and -mediated law of money within water companies. So far, I have explored some of the ways in which this has involved the mystification of – and problematic responses of the industry to – real consumer needs. However, as I highlighted in Chapter 1, capitalist production is a unity of valorization process and labour process. I now want to analyse how the realization of surplus value within the water industry also, and necessarily, results in the intensification and subordination of labour within the labour process. This highlights the alienating and oppressive content underlying the ideological form of TQM. In the next chapter I elaborate on this issue through a detailed analysis of the forms of TQM developed within the water industry and the impact of TQM on social relations within individual water companies.

Note

1. This is explored in more detail by Saunders and Harris (1994: 55–76), who also highlight similar tendencies working in the state regulation of telecommunications, gas and electricity. They argue that these developments amount to a *de facto* shift from the 'price-cap' method of regulation to the US method which regulates utilities by limiting rates of return on investment.

6 TQM in the Water Industry

The particular form taken by TQM has developed through the contradictions of managerialism as part of an increasing alignment between state and capital. In this chapter I explore the specific forms of TQM which have developed in the water industry. The quality initiatives have been introduced through the pressures of the regulatory/financial regime that was created by the 1989 Water Act. In the following chapter I will show that the quality systems have had a marked impact on management and labour processes within water companies through the deskilling of technical and professional workers, the development of new bureaucratic management control systems and a resulting intensification of labour. I will demonstrate the contradictions underlying both TQM and neo-liberal forms of public service. In doing this I will show that the restructuring of the water industry illustrates the need to explore the development of TQM in the water industry within the context of the valorization imperatives of senior management executives and the regulatory form of the state.

The central feature of TQM is the dynamic of 'constant improvement'. The regulatory activities of the state have played a fundamental role in institutionalizing 'constant improvement' within the institutional form of the water industry. The financial targets imposed by the state prior to privatization and the (RPI + K) regime imposed by OFWAT following privatization have institutionalized the need for constant improvements in efficiency within the management control systems of the water industry. This provides the material basis for the articulation of ideological forms of management premised on TQM. As I have already begun to demonstrate in the previous chapter, TQM is the ideological form taken by the abstract imperatives of the valorization of capital in the neo-liberal water industry. TQM has a particular poignancy in the public services owing to how it can be presented as a way of liberating managers and workers from the stultifying and oppressive constraints and contradictions of managerialism. The need for increased flexibility and efficiency has thus been legitimated through the way in which TQM facilitates the simultaneous development and improvement of both the individual and the company.

As I mentioned in the previous chapter, post-structuralist writers have pointed to TQM as an example of the increasingly discursive nature of power and domination in the (post)modern workplace. Clearly, TQM does involve an attempt to align the subjectivity of managers and workers with the valorization imperatives of capital. Post-structuralist accounts of restructuring are useful in pinpointing the forms of 'ideological' manipulation that have accompanied the development of TQM. However, these accounts are flawed as they fail to explore either the material connections between TQM and the dynamic of capital accumulation or the relationship between the recomposition of the workplace 'regime' and the restructuring of the state. As Burawoy (1986: 151) has argued, the development of quality management is part of a shift in the form of factory 'regime' from 'hegemonic' to 'hegemonic despotism', as signified by an attempt by management to invade spaces created by workers under the former regime. TQM can thus be seen as an attempt to depoliticize the 'internal state' through the regulatory forms of law and money. This has involved the recomposition of 'industrial citizenship' on the basis of TQM in order to recompose management and labour processes on the basis of individual 'stakeholders' with rights, duties and obligations whose tenure and remuneration are related to the valorization of capital in increasingly direct ways.

TQM has thus evolved into a form of 'organizational game' (Burawoy, 1979: 77–94) which attempts to secure the consent of workers to the despotism of neo-liberal capitalism. The usefulness of the 'game' metaphor is that it diverts attention to the way in which the production of surplus value is both secured and obscured by the game-like institutional practices which emerge from struggle and bargaining within the workplace. The effectiveness of the game in securing the active consent of workers to their subordination lies in the notion that is impossible to 'play the game' while simultaneously 'questioning the rules'. The practice of games has the effect of both individualizing social relations within the workplace and deflecting conflict in a lateral direction – thus obscuring the class oppression of labour in the labour process and dissipating collective resistance against management. In this sense TQM is a very effective game. The notion of 'internal customers' directs conflict laterally through peer pressure and control. Furthermore, TQM is legitimated through the way in which it involves reducing uncertainty and risk and, as Burawoy (*ibid.*: 87) notes, the most effective games are ones in which uncertainty is neither too great or too small, so as to make workers indifferent to their possible outcome. The development of TQM in the water industry is thus part of a realignment of state and capital facilitated by the depoliticization of the global and factory regime, which attempts to secure the active consent of workers to the despotism of neo-liberal capital accumulation. I will begin by exploring the way in which the crisis of managerialism and the development of TQM involves a fundamental change in the 'rules of the game'.

Expunging the Town Hall

A key feature of HRM/TQM is the need to align the self-maximizing behaviour of individuals within the organization with the maximization of corporate performance. As I mentioned above, it is useful to conceptualize the creation of consent within the capitalist employment relation as a game. If workers are unable to 'play' or refuse to accept the rules then they have to be expelled from the game. The introduction of TQM has involved changing the rules of the game for the remaining staff. This has been a primary objective of senior managers in the water industry. With the development of HRM/TQM, an individual's 'fit' within the organization becomes increasingly important and having the 'right' people in the 'right' jobs becomes an increasingly important management objective (Legge, 1995: 36). Consequently, the processes of selection, appraisal and 'exit' become increasingly important within companies pursuing a 'quality' strategy. These processes have all become increasingly important in the post-privatized water industry. But what qualities are water companies looking for when they select, appraise and 'exit' managers and other staff? The immediate answer given to this question by managers is to get rid of the 'town hall culture': managers and staff wedded to an outdated bureaucratic and technocratic conception of public service.

Within the water industry this type of attitude is given the epithet of 'concretism': a pun reflecting the notion that the engineers that have typically dominated the management of the industry were only interested in the concrete out of which the industry's reservoirs and sewerage works are constructed and had little interest in abstract bodies of management science and the control and accounting systems which they spawn. Senior managers have led a veritable crusade against these type of staff owing to the way in which they threaten the restructuring of the industry on a more abstract basis. TQM has been the top-down strategy through which senior managers have attempted to expunge concretism from the water industry. If managers and workers have resisted organizational change they have been replaced. For these managers of change, the introduction of a culture of 'constant improvement' has been obstructed by a pre-existing 'town hall culture' marked by concretism and bureaucratic inertia. A senior manager from EASTWAT observed:

> It reflects itself occasionally when a group of people say 'No! We're not going to do that!', when they're given something different or something new. A 'What's in it for us?' scenario. And to be fair, it is a bit much to expect the local government tradition to change in three years to something that is, not a Japanese mentality, but a new realism.

The process of expunging the remnants of town hall culture at EASTWAT has involved senior managers within the company taking on the role of 'cultural ambassadors'. The role of cultural ambassador has been particularly important with respect to the senior managers in the 'Senior Management Personal Contract Team', whose close proximity to the 'leader', and whose employment in terms of performance-related pay and individual contracts, make their cultural importance particularly significant. The development of the new organizational culture at EASTWAT has involved an increasing focus on the 'quality of management'. Senior managers have developed a critical awareness that a manager who does not 'buy into' the new culture constitutes a serious 'log-jam' within the organization. A central feature in the process of becoming a 'quality organization' has therefore been the existence of an effective but supportive 'exit policy'; a vital element of the process which facilitates the disposal of the old 'entrenched' managers who did not feel 'comfortable' with the new organizational culture.

The obverse of the 'exit' process is development, coaching, career counselling and upskilling. The impact of the 'exit policy' has been significantly to reduce the age-profile of management within the company; a process that has prioritized the process of management development through the pinpointing of what could be called 'abstract' or 'generic' management skills among younger employees. This process has been developed alongside a new managerial employment relation premised upon a formal appraisal system, fixed-term contracts and performance-related pay. The development of quality management has thus involved pinpointing the potential of existing and potential managers to become 'generic' managers while reconstituting the management employment relation on an abstract basis so that tenure and remuneration reflect the contribution that a manager makes to stated business objectives. I will explore this through a series of case studies and conclude the chapter by assessing the impact of TQM on the reinterpretation of public service as a management ideology and practice.

Quality Management: Dynamics, Ideologies and Resistance

In this section I trace the factors behind the strategic decision of senior managers to introduce quality management at the WESTWAT Group, the ideologies developed by senior managers in order to legitimate the development of TQM and the problems which have resulted from the quality strategy. It is clear from the case study that the fundamental dynamic powering the introduction of quality management has been the drive to reduce *costs* in the context of increasing pressure from the City and OFWAT. The process has, however, been legitimated through the way it benefited water industry staff and their customers – internal and external customers. It is important to note that the unitary perspective embodied in the TQM philosophy, and which was articulated by senior managers in terms of maintaining management control of the quality process, sat uneasily alongside the stress on team-building and co-operation. The result was the distrust and opposition of many workers to the introduction of TQM.

The focus on 'quality' at WESTWAT was a clearly articulated top-down strategic policy adopted alongside the changes in corporate structure which followed privatization. This involved the creation of a corporate holding group (WESTWAT Group Plc (WWG)) which is made up of WESTWAT Ltd, a wholly owned subsidiary concerned with the 'core business' of water supply and sewerage services (90 per cent of Group business) and 29 'enterprise companies'. The decision to develop quality systems at WWG was taken by the board of directors, and a 'Group Quality Manager' was appointed with a brief from the Chief Executive to 'facilitate, encourage and cajole' people through the process of developing quality systems. The strategy has been to apply 'corporate encouragement' to the process of subsidiary companies developing quality systems appropriate to their market/regulatory position. The main consideration facing the Group in the development of quality systems was the perception of the City. The 'golden share' of the Group was issued in 1994, and senior managers felt that it was strategically important to have quality systems covering all the Group's 48 subsidiary companies prior to the issue.

The development of 'quality management' within WWG has been an important, if not fundamental, aspect of management strategy in the post-privatized environment. Indeed, WWG has made the achievement or development of quality systems the major consideration with regard to the purchase of subsidiary companies. Enterprise companies which were previously departmental functions of WWG prior to privatization (environmental engineering, training, technology department (computers), etc.) have already achieved BS 5750; while in many other areas companies are in the process of achieving it. This includes the 'core business' in which the BS 5750 approach is being piloted within a large sewage works; while the 'spirit' and 'major components' of BS 5750 (quality plans and procedures) are being applied to the process of developing the industry 'Asset Management Plan' that is required for OFWAT.

The development of a quality strategy has been given a high profile within the WWG, with the formation of a 'Quality Group' drawing on senior managers from across the Group. The rationale of the Quality Group is premised upon a conceptualization of 'quality' that is central to WWG's corporate identity and image, and a fundamental strand of business planning. The approach to quality management at WWG was broken down into five stages:

1. *The Brief:* To Research and Report on the need to introduce a quality initiative across the organisation.
2. *Group Research:* Visits to organisations, management literature, and external consultant's input.

> *3. Building on Stated Objectives:* Vision and mission statements. Values, style and business strategy. Development of a quality strategy – viz . . . THAT QUALITY PERVADES THE ORGANISATION IN ALL RESPECTS. THE ACHIEVEMENT OF QUALITY IS TO BE SUPPORTED BY AN EVIDENT PERCEPTION BY EMPLOYEE AND CUSTOMER.
>
> *4. Strategy:* Build on our previous success story. Company-wide, low-key initiative. Introduce pilot schemes in selected areas to define the cost of quality. Review methodology. Promote throughout the organisation.
>
> *5. Support Needed:* Top management commitment. Pilot study champions. Input from Consultant.
>
> (internal WWG document)

The Quality Group came to the conclusion that there was a need for the development of a 'quality strategy' within the Group. The need for a 'strategy', rather than a 'policy', was a deliberate corporate-level decision. The Group was in a good position for the development of a quality strategy: 'quality' being a central and fundamental element in the Group's vision and mission statements. The WWG mission statement stated that the Group wishes to be seen as a market leader in the environmental quality field by 1995. The corporate and business values and style of the Group that derived from the vision and mission statements had been outlined to everyone in the organization in the form of a clear set of quality objectives. The objectives were disseminated through a 'Chief Executive's Roadshow' in which the Chief Executive toured the Group outlining WWG's key values and objectives. Everyone in the organization was aware of the quality process or strategy: 'to try to make sure that quality is achieved in every area of the Business by every employee wherever possible'.

The Quality Group attempted to established the extent to which the culture and values of WWG were conducive to the introduction of a quality strategy. Behind this lay the question of why WWG needed to develop a quality strategy at all. The Group Quality Manager's answer to this question was unequivocal and hinged on the *cost* of quality. Through a consideration of company information provided by the DTI, the Quality Group discovered that the 'cost of quality' could be between 15 and 40 per cent of turnover. The 'cost of quality' refers to the reduction in operating costs that can be achieved by companies following the introduction of TQM. Companies which fail to adopt the TQM strategy suffer 'costs' to efficiency and profitability and therefore become increasingly uncompetitive. The contribution that TQM would make to the reduction of costs was therefore the primary impetus to its development at WWG, and the immediate justification for reducing costs was related to the benefit this would have for customers. The Group Quality Manager outlined the feelings of senior executives prior to the decision to introduce TQM:

> We said there has to be something there that we can develop. Therefore, as an organization who eighteen months ago had a turnover of £200 million, we said that even if we achieve 1 per cent saving on turnover, then a £2 million saving, if nothing else, it would upgrade a sewerage works. We could use that money for the benefit of the customer.

The Quality Group were thus able to outline the two clear elements of the quality strategy: customer satisfaction and improving profitability. The strategy had to meet these key objectives and be quantifiable:

> We had to work through how we could reduce uncertainty and waste within the organization. How we could increase value for money in everything that we did. Bringing in the people aspect, it had to be something on a continuous basis, and whatever we did, we had to be able to measure the results. It was no use just reporting on general things. We had to see, in both financial terms but also in other ways, quality of service, etc., how we were squaring up to things!

The development of quality systems was considered in the context of commercial advantage, increased customer service, regulatory pressures, general business requirements and market sector requirements. The quality objectives were laid out in a formal quality structure which comprises three levels. Level One of the formal quality structure at WWG is constituted by the 'Quality Manual', a document that sets out and addresses every part of BS 5750. The Manual contains the 'quality policy' and 'objectives' of the Group, including how the senior management team will disseminate and develop the quality message throughout the organization and test for levels of understanding of the quality policy among staff. The key objective of the BSI is the development of a very clear operational and organizational structure. Section One of BS 5750 is focused on 'management responsibility'. The Manual reflects this through the way in which it sets out clear organizational structures which highlight not only key post-holders, but the impact of post-holders on the quality system. The Manual further defines the scope of work in the organization that is to be assessed. Level Two of the formal quality structure at WWG is constituted by a document that sets out operational procedures of the company in detail, including the managers or members of staff responsible for each procedure. Level Three of the structure is constituted by records and documentation that enable the quality system to be audited, including checklists, quality plans, guidelines and guidance notes. This is the quality systems model that WWG intends to use for quality initiatives throughout the Group; in particular, with regard to the development of wider quality initiatives in the form of TQM or a Continuous Improvement Programme (CIP). This quality approach is divided into two apparently complementary strategies: one strategy of striving for BS 5750 within subsidiary companies, and a second more ubiquitous strategy of developing TQM or CIP throughout the organization in departments and companies where BS 5750 is not required. As I will now demonstrate, the most important feature of the development of TQM at WWG has been the need to transform the corporate culture of the company.

TQM and the restructuring of corporate culture at WWG

The prior restructuring of WWG determined the way in which the quality initiative was introduced and developed. The Group decided against a 'big bang' TQM approach. Rather, the Group pursued an approach that attempted to build upon the 'human relations' developments that had occurred in the previous decade. The main elements of this 'staff development' were a programme of staff 'secondments' and 'team building' processes. The 'secondment process' encouraged managers, potential managers and supervisors to go on a series of 'secondments' throughout the organization. Lateral movement was thus a precondition of further promotion, and managers and potential managers were forced to 'go out and gain experience in the Business'. The 'Team Building Programme' had existed for the previous ten years and was a week-long intensive team-building exercise at one of the company's reservoir sites. The perceived success of the team-building programme influenced the Group's decision to develop a low-key approach to quality premised on a 'problem solving methodology' involving teamwork. The Group quality manager outlined the philosophy behind the quality initiative:

> [The programme] would involve people looking at various parts of the

> process, and not solving the problems, but analysing the problems. Seeing where the waste was, where the potential was for improvement. Coming up through the analytical and then problem-solving phase into a report-back to their manager, where they could actually demonstrate certain efficiencies or certain advantages or certain customer benefits. And it would then be the manager who would say: 'OK, we'll tackle this or that, or we may need more work in certain areas.'

The main concern of the Quality Group was that 'empowering' people within the organization would allow a refocusing of the way in which management information was transmitted, and particularly focus upon the role and function of middle management within the organization. The Group was particularly concerned by a growing body of management research which suggested that up to 60 per cent of quality initiatives 'fizzled out' before the start of their second year. The research highlighted the problems caused by a lack of resources and enthusiasm, and in particular, the problem of 'middle management mistrust' and the way TQM involves securing management commitment and control (Hill, 1991b). This problem was therefore addressed in the CIP methodology which was outlined by the Group Quality Manager:

> Inviting the manager of a department, with his team, to review how the department did their work. But importantly, whatever work the team came up with, to make it in a report back to management. So, it began and ended with the management. But the thick sandwich element of it was that the people in the problem-solving process were then allowed to get on with the enthusiastic side of developing things, to reduce the problems in their everyday life.

The process thus aimed at utilizing the expert knowledge of WWG staff in an attempt to solve the problems that they faced in their everyday working lives. This process yielded benefits for the company, for customers, and above all for the staff themselves:

> So the process was to reduce hassle in their everyday life, to get them involved with things, to look at the areas that they were experts in and experienced in, and to see if we could actually improve things for their benefit, and the knock-on effect is for the customer's benefit.

In order to test the 'quality process' methodology three areas of the company were selected to pilot the CIP, the basis of selection being areas with a high internal and external customer contact. The way the CIP was introduced at WWG was through an 'introductory seminar' in which the process was outlined to departmental staff by their senior manager and a member of the Quality Group. The average department contains 80–100 staff, and from these a 'pilot team' of eight to ten staff was selected at the seminar in order to address the 'key element' of the process – estimating the cost of quality. The groups were broken down into subgroups by function, and other staff with a particular area of expertise were invited to sit *ex officio* on the subgroups.

However, the definition of the concept 'cost of quality' developed into a serious obstacle to the development of the quality process in the pilot departments. Staff made the 'mistake' of equating the process with 'Taylorism'. The Group Quality Manager described this problem and how the Quality Group attempted to overcome it:

> Within our methodology what we found was that people viewed the 'cost of quality' with suspicion – . . . benefits or opportunities might have been better words to use – [because 'cost of quality'] had almost a works study connotation. People were a bit concerned . . . 'Is it works study by the back door?' In reality, what we meant by the 'cost of quality' was no more than: 'If you look at key areas of the business, how can you prioritize those into areas . . . [and ask whether] we could be misguidedly tackling one area only to find that it contributed only 1 per cent to the bottom line, whereas if they tackled another problem with the same level of involvement, it could have realised a better return?'

From the initial 'cost of quality' analysis, the 'pilot team' moved into the 'problem analysis' process. This was followed by the 'problem workshop' phase in which non-team members were drawn back into the process in order to explore what the team had done, and to contribute fresh ideas to the quality process. This was followed by a more detailed 'problem-solving' process in which the team made recommendations in a report to their manager. The manager had the power to accept or reject all or part of the proposals, or to suggest that the recommendations require more work. Indeed, it is a central feature of the CIPs philosophy that teams are able to 'flag up' an overview of the areas that require further research and problems which could be resolved. The methodology was given top-management approval and, in order to ensure that the programme was implemented in accordance with the methodology, external consultants were employed as facilitators and members of the Quality Group were appointed as process 'project managers'.

The Group Quality Manager argued that the pilot team process was a great success and that senior managers were considering the problem of how to proceed with the development of CIP throughout the Group. The process has to be flexible enough to meet the requirements of all parts of the group. The enterprise sector companies which require BS 5750 are able to fast-track the procedures and processes at a rapid rate through the parallel development of CIP. With the core business, where at present there is no pressure from OFWAT for companies to have BS 5750 or CIPs, the CIP process is being developed in a low-key way by local managers in order to increase efficiency. In the future, the Quality Manager projected that there will be teams covering every area of the Business, and an interchange and cross-fertilization between teams in different parts of the business. Managers will follow the 'learning curve of quality' in individual departments through which staff become more aware of their internal and external customers' requirements, and this will be expanded into a wider 'customer network' that will go beyond individual business areas. I will now explore the development of TQM within a subsidiary of WWG and at CITYWAT in order to show in more detail the way in which TQM impacts on management and labour processes within the water industry. This will seek to highlight the way in which there is an increasing divergence between the ideology and practice of TQM as one moves down the organizational hierarchy from senior managers through professional workers to manual workers. As we will see from the case studies below, TQM is not a postmodern management form that resolves the material contradictions of capitalist control, but a form of management ideology and practice which seeks to obscure the intensification of labour through an ideology of consumerism and empowerment.

BS 5750 accreditation at Western Engineering Consultants

Western Engineering Consultants (WEC), an engineering subsidiary of WWG, has recently been successful in attaining BS 5750. In order to illustrate more clearly the ways in which the development of quality management systems impact on the social and technical relations of an organization, I will examine in detail the processes, procedures and problems associated with the development of quality systems at WEC.

WEC was created from the engineering function of WWG following privatization. The company's business is concerned primarily with the design of large civil engineering projects (sewerage works, reservoirs, treatment works), and the company therefore employs a highly skilled and 'professional' workforce of designers and engineers. The case study is particularly interesting given the way in which civil engineering and civil engineers have traditionally dominated the water industry and also because these workers are engaged in the 'design process'. Thus an analysis of the restructuring of design engineering function at WWG is important as it stands at the intersection of a number of recent theoretical debates. First, it throws light on the way in which the 'professional managerial' or 'service' class has fundamentally transformed institutional and workplace politics (Lash and Urry, 1987) and is part of an emergent 'postmodern' economy concerned with the production of signs and culture rather than artefacts (Lash and Urry, 1994). Second, it addresses the debate concerning the extent to which the labour of professional workers has been subject to the same processes of deskilling and degradation as is outlined by Braverman (1974) in respect of manual and routine clerical workers (Glenn and Feldberg, 1979; Greenbaum, 1979; Kraft, 1977).

It is important that the 'design process' is not analysed in isolation but in relation to 'production in general' (Marx, 1971: 32). As Hales (1980) has argued, the labour of designers is part of an objective structure of apparatuses which link together a network of material labour processes. The design is not simply a scientific process but also embodies managerial and business concepts. A design has to work in a physical way *and* be manageable *and* allow a profit to be made. In other words, the concept or design produced by mental labour is *reproduced* in plans, computer programmes, plant and machinery and reservoirs in order to produce with one and only one end in mind – profit. The *preconceptualization* implied by the design process results, therefore, in the determination of the social relations underlying the labour processes of all the workers subordinate to design workers. In other words, design workers are implicated in the control of other workers. The key skills of a designer lie in thinking through capitalist relations of production in concrete terms. The way in which a process impacts upon the controllability of labour is a key consideration at the design stage and often this will take the form of attempts to automate living labour out of the production process. Within an organization the subjective will of one group of workers to conceptualize denies subjectivity to other groups of workers lower down the hierarchy.

As I mentioned above, the water industry has traditionally been dominated by the 'concretist' ideals of civil and sanitary engineering. The consent of engineers involved in both the design and implementation of civil engineering projects was secured by their attachment to technically defined notions of 'public service' – that reservoirs and sewerage works were designed in order to satisfy public needs and that the engineer was the servant of the public through his [*sic*] accountability to the local electorate. The Keynesian form of the state allowed local managers this discretion, and this was a major contributor to the eventual crisis and decomposition of the planner-state. The neo-liberal restructuring of the state has changed the 'rules' of the design 'game'. I will illustrate these points through a consideration of the introduction of TQM at the design subsidiary of WESTWAT Group. As we will see, the creation of WEC and the development of quality systems therein constitutes the *de facto* marginalization of the civil engineering function within WWG.

As I mentioned earlier, a primary function of TQM is to invade spaces created by workers under former workplace regimes. An important implication of quality management is the way in which the labour process becomes more *visible.* This can be illustrated through an exploration of the impact of BS 5750 accreditation. The accreditation process at WEC can be broken down into a series of stages:

1. Determination of functions and responsibility of design staff.
2. The transformation of responsibilities into 'quality' procedures.
3. The codification of procedures into a 'quality plan'.
4. The auditing of the procedures and the plan by the BSI.

I will explore each of the stages in turn. The first stage in the development of the quality system at WEC was the determination of the functions and responsibilities of design staff. This was achieved through the determination and decomposition of the design process. The Group Quality Manager describes how this was achieved and the problems it raised:

> We asked people to say to us what they thought the design process was, and not put it down in any formal way, but just through a half-day workshop we said to everyone 'You tell us what the design process is!' Now you might

> think that a designer would know when the process began and when the process ended, and to a large extent they did. Having said that, within the actual process there was disagreement. But essentially what we ended up with were nineteen points on what the design process was about.

An important element of a quality system is the development of a 'quality plan'. The establishment of what constituted the design process was an essential precondition of the development of the 'quality plan'. The WEC quality plan set out:

- who the client is
- who the designers are
- what the resource inputs would be
- what key documents would be included
- the programme
- regularity of consultation with client
- level of approval required from client
- form of design output, drawings, etc.
- verification and approval of designs

Within the 'quality plan' process there are a series of procedures concerning the development of the plan:

- use of codes and standards
- design controls to be included in the process
- how to review adequacy of documentation supplied by a client
- how documents are to be controlled
- control of design calculations (independently assessed).
- procedure for effecting changes in design
- reviewing design with client
- dealing with complaints from clients
- preparing tender documents
- awarding tender
- supplying records on completion

The first principle behind the development of the procedures was to keep them as short as possible. Each procedure was to be presented on one page, together with specifications concerning the purpose and scope of the procedure. The procedure was then broken down into a series of steps no longer than one or two lines, including the initials of the person responsible for the function described in that step. The latter point is very important, as procedures had to give both direction and ownership. Indeed, in developing the procedures there had been 'a subtle attempt to insert ownership on almost every line'. Secondly, the procedures had to be general: they concerned the activities of 'professional' workers, such as project managers, and therefore had to allow autonomy within a structure that gave general direction on process.

It is important that workers feel that they 'own' the quality systems. The procedures were, therefore, developed by the workers themselves. At WEC, the designers were invited to sit around a table and to talk through how they perceived the typical process of a design brief. The team initially laid out between twenty and thirty steps, which during a half-day workshop were reduced to seven or eight short steps. The remaining codes and procedures were developed by subgroups, and were presented to the designers for comments and recommendations and modified accordingly. This process took around four months, after which the final procedures were drafted and issued on a formal basis to everyone in the organization – which is a fundamental requirement of BS 5750. Following the drafting of the final procedures, WEC was assessed by the BSI and subsequently awarded BS 5750. The attainment of BS 5750 was important to WEC for reasons of commercial advantage. However, for the Group Quality Manager the important impact of BS 5750 has been on the behaviour and outlook of staff within the company:

> The real advantage of 5750 . . . was demonstrated on the day the recommendation came through. Everyone in the organization, in that design department, really their chests were two inches further out than they were that morning. And the group bonding after that was quite marked. Increasingly over the weeks and months ahead, just passing by people you could hear them on the telephone saying 'Oh yes, we've got 5750! First in the water industry!' Therefore, the ownership was quite terrific. The benefit, the spin-off, has been that the procedures have been reviewed once again. So that people involved in the quality system have actually said 'Hey, hang on a bit! We can fine-tune this even better. We can actually bring in things that have changed within the company organically within the last few months.' The ownership is very, very high. So although people may say that quality systems are very formal, they may stifle innovation, they're a bureaucratic nightmare, etc. etc., when they work well, and I've seen it work well, they really do touch on the total quality curve.

The introduction of TQM at WEC demonstrates the way in which TQM can be understood as a 'game' through which the designers actively consented to the intensified control of their activities. In practice, behind and through these games, the minimization of costs has become an increasingly important focus of the design process and this has involved a reconstitution of the ideological representation of design work – that design work benefits the abstract neo-liberal customer. TQM has played an important role in securing the consent of design workers to neo-liberal conceptions of public service through the way in which it has encouraged designers to develop a sense of 'ownership' to the bureaucratic procedures which impose a dynamic of constant efficiency improvement on the industry. In other words, rather than producing signs and symbols (Lash and Urry, 1994), designers are involved in the production of structures and working practices that will yield a profit for their employer. TQM in this sense obscures the intensification of both design and labour processes through a game in which commitment to customers shields the intensification of managerial control. While TQM has been successful in securing the consent of design workers, however, evidence of the introduction of TQM at CITYWAT suggests that it has been rather less successful among manual and routine clerical workers.

Right First Time and quasi-quality circles at CITYWAT

The demands of the OFWAT auditing systems and the increasing scrutiny of the City have given an important impetus to the development of TQM at CITYWAT. The company has appointed a 'Quality Assurance Manager' with the primary responsibility of overseeing the development and achievement of BS 5750 throughout the organization. The initial focus of the formal quality system was on the 'customer care' function, and particularly on the system that has been developed in order to monitor and audit the OFWAT performance measures. Following BSI accreditation it is intended that the BS 5750 approach be rolled out to the rest of the company. Developing systems in accordance with BS 5750 will ensure that all operations within the company, starting with the 'customer care' function and the OFWAT system, are repeatable: that is, it will ensure that all customers and customer information are treated identically in accordance with a manual to which staff are able continually to refer.

Alongside the formal BSI system, senior managers at CITYWAT decided to introduce an element of TQM into the organization. Following consultation with a series of management consultants, senior managers decided that TQM did not really 'fit' the 'company culture' at CITYWAT. TQM was perceived as being too 'flash' and 'clever'. Managers nevertheless perceived the need for an informal quality system to be developed in order to enhance the organizational culture of the company, and attempted to develop a form of TQM that was compatible with CITYWAT culture. The Customer Service Director explained the main features of the quality system, and noted the centrality of the new financial/regulatory framework to its inception and development:

> We have started running a programme called 'Right First Time', which partly explains to people what all the new regulatory framework looks like and why the company is now working in a different environment, and then goes on to say so, you know, we have a fixed income and we can't afford to waste money with mistakes. So we must increasingly try to get the job right first time. Which is TQM in so many words.

The definition of quality at CITYWAT is 'fit for purpose' or 'right', and this is reflected in the company's quality strategy – 'the right time, at the right price, at the right place'. The company has attempted to maintain the separation between 'levels of service' and 'quality'. The purpose of quality management, in other words, is not to ensure that service is constantly improved, but that the level of service which is currently provided is provided in an increasingly efficient way in order to reduce costs. Hence the Business and Customer Services Director argued:

> We've made great strides to separate levels of service from quality. Quality is what you do – you can then rack it up to all sorts of levels. You know, we've been through the classic argument that quality is not a Rolls Royce versus a Ford Sierra. It was a quality product, so the Ford Sierra is a quality product, and you must produce your Ford Sierra to the quality that you need. So I think we've tended to go straight down the 'fitness for purpose' route.

While the company does not have 'quality circles', it does make increasing use of 'working parties' in the 'problem-solving' process. Rather than a series of managers coming together to form the parties, the managers are themselves setting up working parties of employees to solve managerial problems. The same manager described how these groups work:

> [A manager] has a problem and he gets a working party of the workers together. You need a manager there to open a few doors and to give them a bit of clout, perhaps help them with processing. But the basic work is done by the people who've got to do it. They may need help with a bit of vision, they may need help with a bit of process. But I think using the sort of – not quite quality circle – but that sort of thing. [To say] 'Here we are lads, here's a problem, now you solve it for me!' You're beginning to get them on the ship. Now doing that certainly helps you break down the barrier . . . So a bit of inter-departmental working at the lowest level. It's a marvellous improvement.

Associated with the 'Right First Time' programme have been two key human resource developments: the introduction of 'internal customers' and the accreditation of all staff through the NVQ scheme. The introduction of the 'internal customer' involved everyone in the organization attending a two-day seminar. The sessions were structured around diagonal slices of the company in order to allow senior managers and directors to fulfil their role as cultural change-agents. The NVQ system is aimed at manual workers and lower-grade clerical staff, and aims to provide accreditation for staff carrying out functions for which no formal qualifications exist. The plan is to upgrade all manual and lower clerical staff to the appropriate NVQ level through a process which involves staff taking an exam and being awarded a certificate. The system is intended to benefit both the company and the individual employee: raising the self-esteem of workers within a system which enables the company to certify and accredit the quality of its 'human capital'.

The introduction of quality management at CITYWAT has not, however, been unproblematic. The Customer Services Director described how the word 'quality' has tended to create a mental block among employees who have tended to perceive it as an implied criticism of their current performance. In particular, the company found resentment among manual staff with the introduction of the NVQ scheme. Many workers failed to see the necessity of passing an exam and being given a piece of paper that certified that they were qualified to do a job that in many cases they had been doing for the past twenty or thirty years. In many ways the development of TQM has engendered distrust among manual employees. The rewards for the design workers at WEC for playing the TQM 'game' were the symbolic victory of being defined as a 'quality' organization and the material rewards attached to retaining a degree of creative autonomy and ensuring the profitability of an organization in which they had a relatively well-paid and prestigious position. The rewards for manual workers 'playing the game' are a little less obvious. The 'game' cannot go beyond the limits of profitability, and the behaviour of workers at CITYWAT illustrates the limits of the TQM game. Many workers have voiced the outrageous suggestion that an increase in the quality of their labour ought to be accompanied by an increase in its value. Further, many employees have voiced the fear that 'quality management' constitutes the entrance of 'Speedy Taylor' by the back door. The Customer Service Director outlined the ways in which employees have 'misunderstood' the new systems and have tended to see the new systems as:

> people coming in studying their job. 'Telling us how to do it! We think we should be paid more for doing this! If you're going to send me on a course, I want to be paid more! If you're going to ask me to get a qualification I want to be paid more!' So it's very difficult for a manual area, which in most companies has been sorely neglected for many years. And suddenly they say to them 'Good news, chaps! You're now going to be turned into quality workers!' For one, they probably thought they were anyway. Two, they know they've been studiously ignored for many years. And three, that's what they want paying for. We say: 'Yes, yes, and no!' So not an easy area to work through.

The term 'quality' has tended to 'jar' employees into a 'typical' response of 'We do a good quality job, don't we?', to which the company responds, 'Yes, but not in the right way!' The problem has thus been to make employees aware of the distinction between what they do and the way they do it. What they do (use-values) remains the same; the way they do it (the production of value, but ever quicker and more intensive) requires development. Quality assurance is seen by staff at CITYWAT as something related to the manufacture of washing machines; as having nothing to do with running a waterworks. The problem for CITYWAT is that it does not have anything specifically to do with managing a waterworks, but on the contrary, has everything to do with the production of value. There are, therefore, inherent risks to the TQM strategy and the involvement of workers in the process of management must be accompanied by the ideological commitment of workers to corporate objectives. As we have seen, this was a problem at CITYWAT and managers at WESTWAT have attempted to overcome this problem through an attempt to *sell* TQM through a discourse of consumerism.

Quality Management and the Problem of Abstraction

The introduction of quality management has had an important impact on the labour processes within water companies. The essence of quality management is the intensification of control within the labour process. In order to make the labour process more visible, the skill and knowledge of workers has to be incorporated into the organizational and bureaucratic structures of water companies. The intensification of control is legitimated through 'consumerist' discourse which emphasizes the way in which labourers own their position in the management hierarchy. Within WWG, quality has been 'sold' by stressing the way in which systems reduce the day-to-day problems of managers and staff. The Quality Manager described the way in which the Quality Group at WWG has attempted to 'sell' quality systems:

> We feel we have to sell it to people within the Group. To say 'Look, it will reduce your day-to-day hassle, if there are things within your job which you know are wrong or if you had the opportunity to put right'. We're just trying to build empowerment through the managers to the people to look at ways of reducing their hassle, and obviously then to reduce waste within their departments.

In other words, workers are invited to work more intensively in order to prevent call-backs (i.e. hassle) from internal and external customers, and thereby simultaneously deliver increased customer satisfaction and cost savings through more intense and attentive forms of working. Thus, the justification and legitimation of the processes are articulated through a discourse that stresses the way in which increased efficiency is passed directly to the customer. Public service is thus rearticulated in a neo-liberal form. The Quality Manager at WESTWAT described the way in which quality management benefits the customer:

> Our key requirements are to meet the requirements of the customer – whoever the customer is, whether it's internal or external. We could then save

> money, but obviously, that then has a direct knock-on to the bottom line. Saving 1 per cent means that we can either reduce the charge to customers or improve the service to customers by spending that saving.

The main impetus to the development of quality systems has been the valorization imperatives of the financial/regulatory regime introduced by the 1989 Water Act, and this illustrates the increasing alignment of state and capital within the institutional form of the water industry. The valorization imperatives imposed by global capital on the water industry have necessitated the development of a 'regime' of hegemonic despotism (Burawoy, 1986: 150–2) within the water industry and this has set the limits for and determined the content of the OFWAT 'regime'. Quality systems were introduced at WWG, for example, in the context of projected efficiency improvements of between £25 million and £80 million per annum. The new managerial systems have been legitimated through a 'consumerist' discourse that highlights the way in which improvements in efficiency benefit customers. But the customer is an essentially abstract being – a figment of the neo-liberal imagination. The contradictory form of both the organizational and the state 'regime' necessarily involves the substantive administration of real material interests and the depoliticization of both water companies and the regulator are necessarily partial and incomplete. TQM cannot solve the problem of control within the workplace and OFWAT cannot totally formalize the operational activity and the pressure of water customers through legal and monetary channels. In this sense the neo-liberal water industry remains riven with contradictions and these become increasingly apparent as we consider the way in which the ideology of consumerism is undermined by the perception of the water industry by its 'real' customers.

The meaning of the concept of 'quality' thus remains highly politicized and subject to ethical and material contestation (Walsh, 1995: 85–7). In responding to the crisis of the managerialist form of the industry, the neo-liberal restructuring has thus laid the basis for further crisis. Senior managers are concerned by the way in which the quality advances made by WESTWAT are not reflected in the public perception of either the company or the industry as a whole. The company is spending more on the customer following privatization and is committed to providing customers with adequate information about the company's activities in order to give them confidence that the company is acting in their interests. Perceptions of the company are, however, coloured by public perception of the water industry at the macro level:

> It's the public perception of the water industry in general, not just WESTWAT, that we're battling against. We have, for instance, still a long way to go in overcoming this privatization myth that now we're privatized everyone in the organization is on a fat salary. I'm not on a fat salary in terms of what I was on before privatization, but I still work as hard as I did before. Internally there are a lot of people actually saying 'Look, we are hard workers!' But it's very difficult to say that WESTWAT could influence the general public, when on *News at Ten* something indicates that, in macro terms, customers are paying more and there are water restrictions. Now, there are no water restrictions in WESTWAT [region]. But that colours the view and it's increasing.

Companies operating in the neo-liberal water industry have found it increasingly important to develop and maintain an image of themselves as 'quality' companies. It has been difficult to develop a public perception of water companies which would result in customers ranking their regional or local water undertaking alongside Marks & Spencer with respect to service and efficiency. The communication of quality improvement has been extremely problematic: senior managers feel they have faced an uphill struggle against an unfair media and an unsympathetic 'public'. The media often devotes 'unfair' and 'unwarranted' attention to the industry; feeding 'bad news' to a public among whom there is a predisposed appetite for 'bad news' about utility companies in general, and water companies in particular. Water companies are unable to resolve the contradiction between the development of abstract management (value) and the public perception of the use-values they produce. The fetishized appearance of the neo-liberal state as an embodiment of the 'common good' is constantly ruptured by the alienating and oppressive materiality of the substantive operations of state agencies and water companies.

In Chapter 7 I explore the alienating reality of the water industry in more detail through an assessment of the way in which neo-liberal regulation and management have transformed the position of labour within the water industry. I focus in particular on the way in which state and managerial restructuring has impacted on the personnel and health and safety policies of water companies. This highlights the contradictions of TQM, as a strategy which attempts simultaneously to maximize the subordination of labour within the labour process and to maximize the ideological commitment of workers to their own subordination. I will argue that this illustrates the enduring contradictions of public service in the neo-liberal social order.

7 The Contradictions of Quality Management

The restructuring and privatization of the water industry has been accompanied by the development of 'human resource management' (HRM). The resulting managerial restructuring has involved an attempt to release and develop the 'entrepreneurial' potential of managers and workers and has involved devolving managerial responsibility to increasingly low levels of the management hierarchy. It has also involved widening the responsibilities of managers and staff through attempts to develop more flexible working practices. The above initiatives have involved the creation of new appraisal and training mechanisms and new management information systems to monitor the development and performance of 'human resources'. These moves have been part of the wider 'quality' initiative outlined in the previous two chapters and have been suffused with a concern to develop a 'quality conscious' workforce committed to the 'total quality' process.

In this chapter I explore in more detail the new forms of management ideology and practice that have developed within the water industry as part of the increasing focus on 'quality'. I explore the way in which the neo-liberal restructuring of the water industry has involved a shift in the focus of management from the management of things towards the management of people. As I have argued in previous chapters, it is problematic to conceptualize the restructuring of management and labour process as principally an 'economic' phenomenon. The 'economic' content of the labour process is subject to the 'political' regulation of the 'internal' state and legitimated through materially-generated organizational ideologies (Burawoy, 1979: 109–20). In particular, the restructuring of the 'internal state' has involved an attempt to depoliticize the organizational structures of water companies. In the next chapter I will explore the way in which this process has impacted on patterns of collective bargaining. In this chapter I want to focus on the way in which the attempt to depoliticize the internal state has impacted upon management and management control systems.

The management of the water industry has traditionally been dominated by engineers. The restructuring of the public sector has resulted in the marginalization and displacement of engineers by management professionals and accountants (Armstrong, 1987: 434–6). In order to understand the importance of this development it is necessary to explore briefly the form and function of management in the capitalist enterprise. As I argued in Chapter 1, the development of the 'internal state' was the result of the shift from 'despotic' to 'hegemonic' regimes of domination, and resulted in the internalization of 'political' and 'ideological' state apparatuses within the workplace (Burawoy, 1979: 116–17). The politics of management is thus concerned with ensuring that the 'economic' activity of workers in the labour process is regulated through legal and monetary forms of regulation implied by the circuit of capital. Managers have to do this through bureaucratic and political modes of behaviour and, therefore, the contradiction between regulation and administration which marks the capitalist state has its origins in the contradictions of modern management within the sphere of production.

Modern management is concerned with the 'capital function' and management labour is thus unproductive and subject to processes of agency and trust rather than being constituted by a management labour process (Armstrong, 1987: 426–7, 1989: 307–12; Fox, 1985; cf. Braverman, 1974: 59–124). It is therefore possible to analyse the impact of HRM on the management structure of the water industry in terms of an attempt partially to avoid 'agency costs' through the tightening of management control systems. The 'relative autonomy' of management from the labour process allows managers to appear as a fetished embodiment of the 'common good' within the workplace (Nichols, 1969, 1980), and the increasing focus on costs has also allowed the function of finance and accountancy to capture the 'internal state' from the engineering function and to redefine the common good of water companies on the basis of 'cost reduction' and 'total customer satisfaction'. Management is not, however, simply about the realization of surplus value in the sphere of circulation but also involves co-ordinating the production of use-values in the sphere of production.

Management is thus itself a contradictory social form and, as Hyman (1987: 30) has argued, 'there is no one best way of managing these contradictions, only different routes to partial failure'. HRM and TQM do not constitute a panacea for the contradictions of Fabian state planning, and in this chapter I highlight some of the contradictions which are emerging from the introduction of these forms of management in the water industry.

The pressures of OFWAT and the City on water companies have resulted in costs becoming the principal concern of management. This has precipitated a struggle within management to demonstrate the ways in which different functions can contribute to the reduction of costs in general and to the reduction of management 'agency' costs in particular. In this battle the engineering function has been increasingly marginalized by 'professional' managers drawn principally from the accountancy function. The 'new' managers have been concerned to demonstrate the way in which costs could be reduced through the introduction of detailed management control systems alongside the latest panacea to emerge from the USA – HRM. These have been combined with a flattening of management hierarchies as managerial responsibility has been pushed further 'down the line'. Taken together, these developments have resulted in an attempt to overcome the contradictions of management through a movement towards the dissolution of functional boundaries within management. This has been manifested within the water industry through an attempt to create 'generalist' managers divorced from their functional specialism. There has been both a movement towards the intensification of management control and an attempt to reconstitute management on a more 'generic' or 'abstract' basis. I will now explore the development, limitations and contradictions of this process in the context of individual water companies.

Culling the Fat Cats: Management Restructuring at WESTWAT

During the 1980s, senior managers at WESTWAT pursued a conscious strategy that was designed to change the managerial culture of the company. The strategy was initiated by the Chief Executive and the Director of Human Resources. The genesis of the new culture could be traced back to 1979, when the newly-appointed Chief Executive declared that in future the company was to be operated as a 'well-run business'. In the words of the Senior Personnel Manager, the new Chief Executive's concerns were as follows:

> Get away from the fat cat, have as many people as you want, spend as much money as you want, it all goes on the water rate [mentality]. He wanted us to get rid of that, and he wanted us to be very efficient. He wanted us to be lean and mean basically.

The managerialist restructuring of the 1980s, and the regulatory/financial regime imposed by the 1989 Water Act, have constituted important dynamics with respect to levels of efficiency and profitability. These dynamics have had a fundamental impact on the human resource systems of water companies. The regulatory regime imposed by the state has been fundamental in determining the form of managerial control; although the form of the state emerged itself from the problem of imposing management control in the public sector. This has been particularly marked at WESTWAT, where the Senior Personnel Manager suggested that the pressures placed on the company by state regulation have played a major role in determining the shape of the new human resource structure:

> We had to face increasing regulation, which was a tremendous increase on what it had been previously and continues to be so. 'Customer care' came out of regulation . . . and new departments like 'customer care' sprung up. We embarked on a programme of 'customer care' with customers being internal as well as external. Basically, people were asked generally to do, not only their old job, but new additional things. We restructured on a much flatter structure, with less management tiers . . . So, the demands on people are clearly very much greater than they were before. Fewer and fewer specialists, and more and more generalists employing a wider range of skills.

In the higher levels of the company, the most important competence that the new environment has demanded has been that of staff 'having to learn to manage people'. The company has prioritized management skills over technical capacities and qualifications. The Senior Personnel Manager argued that while certain scientific positions will always require specific 'scientific' skills, many positions that had traditionally been filled by people drawn from particular disciplines in fact demanded man-management [*sic*] as their primary competence. The revenue department would traditionally have been headed by an accountant. Following restructuring, the Revenues Department is headed by a civil engineer, and perhaps inevitably the new Operations Director is an accountant. In contrast to the public sector industry, managers are appointed according to their ability to manage. The technical knowledge that is required for positions is supplied to managers through a specially developed 'Technical Support Group':

> Basically, if people are good managers, and the job has a good proportion of man-management skills involved, then that person is given the job, and away we go! And somehow or another, it's organized so that the technical support that may be lacking in his own background or qualifications is supplied by our Technical Support Group . . . or from other people around, by basic co-operation and collaboration, or by buying someone in from our enterprise companies.

The policy was operationalized through a strategy that attempted to create a new 'climate' within the company, which involved a thorough reassessment and reorientation of the role and function of management. The strategy was quite explicitly an attempt to replace the town hall/public service approach with a more dynamic and commercial type of management. The managerialization of the water industry produced large efficient entities capable of operating as units of capital. The successful valorization of capital, however, required the recomposition of the 'internal state' in order to direct the administrative and substantive activities of managers through the abstract forms of money and the law. This process of abstraction has pushed the focus of management away from 'solid line structures' occupied by a diverse range of functional managers, towards a concern to develop general skills *abstracted* from the substantive activity of supplying water and disposing of sewage. This process has been particularly evident with respect to the selection, training and appraisal of managers.

The process has been manifested at WESTWAT through the concern to develop abstract managerial skills. The tangible impact of this was felt through the way in which managers were appointed and promoted. In order to move away from the 'old solid line structures' that previously existed, the company decided not to allow upward promotion without an individual having first been moved or promoted sideways. This was facilitated by a series of secondments in which 'key people' in 'key jobs' moved around the organization in order to learn how the organization worked *in toto.* This 'cross-fertilization' allowed staff to develop skills from different parts of the organization. The secondments were accompanied by a series of initiatives that were aimed at increasing and developing managerial skills within the company. The company employed a team of human resource consultants in order to assess the skills that the company needed, and this led to the initiation of a series of management development programmes. One such programme encouraged staff to volunteer to be 'psychometrically tested', and they were given feedback on their 'management potential' by a qualified psychologist. Staff that were felt to have management potential were informed and directed down appropriate training and development routes; while those with less potential were told that they should not aspire to a management position, but were guided down other training and development routes that would enable them to 'manage their limitations'.

The company was concerned to break the domination of engineers. This involved restructuring the company in abstraction from its operational functions, and reconstituting the role and function of management within the company. The Senior Personnel Manager described the ideology behind the restructuring process as follows:

> We look at people very much in the round. We used to, before 1979, employ people basically according to their experience as engineers. If they were a good engineer then they ended up in a managerial job, and they might be lousy managers. And if the truth were known, 90 per cent of their new job might demand man-management skills.

The company's attitude to the appointment (and the recent reappointment) of managers is that technical and engineering qualifications are no longer preconditions for managerial positions. Rather, the approach is to examine carefully what the job really demanded, and to match individuals with the skills or potential skills demanded by the job. In the appointment and reappointment of 'key' managerial staff, the company employed 'manspecs' in order to determine an individual's 'fit'. Equally important to training and qualifications in this fit were 'managerial skills', namely, leadership skills, team membership and leadership skills, interpersonal skills, presentational skills, motivational skills and organizational skills. The company examined which of these skills a position required and then looked for these skills among individual staff. Where the skills were absent but the potential was there the company initiated training and development. The recomposition of management on a more abstract basis has thus been achieved through bureaucratic and administrative mechanisms which attempt to locate the 'abstract' potential in the 'concrete' attributes and activities of managers. This is essential because managers are concerned both with the realization of surplus value in the sphere of exchange and with its production in the murky world of the workplace. The production and realization of surplus value is dependent on the successful subordination of labour in the labour process and within the water industry this has been achieved through the political and ideological recomposition of the workplace regime through HRM. Maximizing the productivity of labour is dependent upon both the coercion implied by the wage-relation and the co-operation engendered by the ideological legitimacy of management (Fox, 1985: 50–2). HRM is thus an attempt to depoliticize the employment relation through the wage-form while simultaneously transforming the ideological legitimation of intensified control through the discourse of 'consumerism', rather than 'technical expertise'.

An important objective of managers in the water industry has been to increase the flexibility of staff and other resources. There is nothing particularly new about capital pursuing the flexibility of labour, as the 'inherent flexibility of human labour is the defining characteristic of labour power' (Pollert, 1988: 70–2). What is new are the ideological discourses which attempt to present the flexibility of labour within internal and external labour markets as the key to aligning the interests of capital and labour in a post-Fordist accumulation strategy of 'flexible accumulation'. The development of quality management within the water industry illustrates this ideological moment through the way in which the increasing flexibility of staff has been *sold* to workers through a consumerist discourse stressing ownership and empowerment. WESTWAT, for example, has pursued a conscious strategy of attempting to optimize the flexibility of staff. This has involved flexibility both between and within positions and locations in the company. The company has reached a flexibility agreement with its employees, and this 'allows people to swap and change jobs and locations almost at the drop of a hat'. The primary objective in developing the HRS at WESTWAT has been the creation of a highly skilled, flexible, polyvalent workforce. In 1991–2 the company invested over £1 million in a training programme which covered everything from skills training and development and further education courses to sponsoring staff on degrees, master's degrees and MBAs. According to the Senior Personnel Manager, these initiatives have not only resulted in the company becoming more responsive to its environment, but have served to enrich the working lives of employees within the company:

> Basically, we're looking for people to do everything that they can possibly do within their own job, and also to develop on to be promoted wherever possible. Even down to the clerks. We don't just hire clerks: they won't just be an admin clerk – they'll be a receptionist, they'll be a telephonist, they'll do photocopying, they'll do a whole range of things. They'll have what would be classed in other companies as three or four jobs . . . So as long as it's within their capability, and they can be trained for it, then they get trained. And that same approach goes for everyone throughout the company. We're very flexible, very quick on our feet . . . and we support that with a massive investment in training.

The restructuring of WESTWAT has also resulted in a marked reduction in managerial positions and a fundamental 'flattening' of managerial control structures. This new structure has heightened the importance of 'trust' and 'reliability', particularly in consideration of the way in which the operations of the water industry are constituted by geographically dispersed units. It has become increasingly important to ensure that staff are motivated, contented and trustworthy. At WESTWAT the period since 1979 has been one of constant 'change and improvement', in which the workforce of the company was reduced by 40 per cent in order to reduce costs and improve efficiency. The company's Senior Personnel Manager argued that 'trying to motivate people to do more was absolutely necessary as fewer people had more work to do in order to keep us going'. An important element in the restructuring of the HRS at WESTWAT has thus been the cultivation of a 'growth culture'. The main feature of this has been the introduction of a series of 'development programmes'.

The emphasis within WESTWAT is on training and development being 'employee-led'. Responsibility for training and career development is shared between the employee and the company. The company has attempted to create a climate in which employees who feel that they are capable of more challenging work, or feel that they want more responsibility, have the right to demand an interview with their supervisor or manager in order to discuss their career development. The interviews are not designed to assess aspects of the employee's day-to-day performance, but to address wider issues such as career development, and the extent to which the employee would like to take on more responsibility or be delegated more tasks. This often involves a consideration of 'job enlargement', 'job enrichment', 'job rotation', or various educational courses. The new culture that has been built steadily over the past decade is now fully developed and staff are fully conversant with the rules of the new game. They know instinctively what is required of them developmentally; they have to become 'rounded off as people' – which amounts to fulfilling their own potential through the development of abstract managerial 'skills', thus allowing them to do the best for both themselves and their company. The senior personnel manager argued that it was necessary to:

> get people in the round, to get them rounded off as people, to give them a third dimension, experience of man-management, experience of supervising people, moving them around the company. So we're basically trying to get them to develop in their own job to fulfil their potential, and we don't like wasting skills – if they've got skills and abilities that are innate to them we're looking to release them within their job, and if possible, if we recognize that they can do a bigger job and be promoted, then that's built into the progression as well and eventually they will be promoted.

In order to secure trustworthy and reliable workers WESTWAT has also developed a 'high reward' philosophy. The same manager pointed out that this involved more than paying good salaries. It contained a 'total employee package' comprising health and well-being, good offices, good vehicles, good depots, good working conditions out on site and a 'tremendous' record on health and safety. The relationship between this philosophy and employee relations is explicit:

> We do a whole host of things to make sure that our employees are well looked after. So that they'll want to come to work, they'll want to work for us, and they'll want to work hard. If you've got someone like that you don't have to worry too much about supervising them. So one of their skills or qualities would be self-supervision. A lot of our manual workers and craftsmen are 'off to the four winds' – you see them at 7.30 in the morning and don't see them again until 3.30 in the afternoon, apart from when a supervisor might visit a site. So there is a great deal of trust and reliability to be built in.

Indeed, trust and reliability have been key elements in the appointment and reappointment of staff:

> [Trust] is a particular thing that we look for in the interview. Someone might have all the skills and abilities, but can he be trusted to work 40 miles from the depot all day, every day on his own? Working out what needs to be done, doing it, doing it to standard, making sure it works, protecting the supply, protecting the customer, protecting the company.

The task of securing a trustworthy and reliable workforce through this process is seen as a 'moving target' which reflects the environment of 'continuous improvement' in which the company now operates. The management restructuring at WESTWAT illustrates the way in which the crisis of the capital relation within the state-owned water industry has resulted in the simultaneous economic, political and ideological restructuring of the social relations of production and the important linkages between the global and the factory regime. The changing ownership of the water industry is, however, a secondary factor in explaining the restructuring of management and labour processes. The principal factor is the form of regulation to which the industry is subjected. This can be demonstrated in two ways. First, the most intensive restructuring of the water industry took place while the industry was still in the public sector. Second, as I will now demonstrate, restructuring has been even more marked and intensive in those parts of the water industry that have always been in the private sector – the SWCs.

The transformation of human resource management has become even more rapid in respect of the former SWCs. At CITYWAT, the imperative to generate vast amounts of information for OFWAT has provided the major dynamic in the development of new information technology. The technology has facilitated both a reduction in the number of staff and the development of polyvalent skills among the remaining staff. The new framework has had an important impact on the types of skills that are important to the company; in particular a shift from a focus on engineering to a focus on accountancy. A senior executive at CITYWAT described the shift in the company culture and its impact on human resource management:

> Traditionally water companies were driven by the engineer. Very high quality stuff, very fine, but again almost endless resources to pay for it. We are now moving towards an area where you are customer driven. You get that right,

and you begin to appreciate that engineering operations are to support that direction. So don't tell the customer what he wants – find out what the customer wants, then engineer it.

The demands of the new environment have further focused the attention of the company on the process of management education and development. The company has traditionally focused management training and development on senior management. The new regulatory system is perceived to have had the most impact on supervisors; transforming them into managers, and transforming the skills they require from 'supervisory' to 'managerial'. The increasing focus on management 'accountability' is associated with a fundamental transformation of the company's payment and rewards system, with the development of 'appraisal' and 'performance-related pay'. The 'appraisal system' is currently applied to senior managers and has been designed in order that individual managers have elements of the 'Business Plan' inserted into their own individual contract of employment. Managers are rewarded in terms of the extent to which they achieve these objectives and thus in terms of the contribution they make to the success of the business. The appraisal system is currently being extended to supervisor level and below. The objective of the company is to introduce simply-defined targets at this level. For example, staff in the Accounts Department will be appraised in terms of the number of invoices they deal with. In order to maintain flexibility in the context of the bureaucratization associated with 'quality management', appraisal for more junior staff will also take into account the overall financial performance of the company:

It may be that the reward systems that you put in will have to reflect company performance as well as departmental performance. The prime focus is to get on to the person to do that properly, but you'd better understand that if someone comes along and wants a bit of help then you'd better do that because 20 per cent of your pay is going to be made up on how the company does. So I think it will want designing fairly carefully otherwise you might very well drive people further into boxes. 'I can't stop to help you! I've got a hundred invoices to shift today!'

Within two years the system will cover every employee in the organization, and in preparation for this the company has undertaken a comprehensive 'job evaluation programme' which has facilitated the development of a new grading system premised on 'single status' employees. The new systems are designed to increase the motivation of staff. They remove the rigid local government-type structure with its myriad of scales and increments and replace it with a structure that will provide incentives for staff to work harder and thus for the reward structure to differentiate between employees who perform well and those who perform badly. The former SWC sector has thus been subjected to the pressure of OFWAT and the City to subordinate operational activities to the valorization of capital. This is manifested in the intensification of management and labour control through the direct linking of the wage-form and profitability. This has also involved decollectivizing industrial citizenship and the development of organizational ideologies based on ownership and empowerment. In both the former RWAs and the former SWCs it has involved a struggle within management for control of the 'internal state' and the specific form taken by ideological representations of the 'common good'. This battle has been fought out in the processes through which managers are selected, appraised and, where appropriate, disposed of. The process of 'management appraisal' has thus played a central role in redefining and reconstituting the politics of public service, and I will now move to a more detailed assessment of how this process has operated within individual water companies.

Watching Us Watching You: The Problem of Managing Appraisal

Within water companies, managerial restructuring has involved an attempt to transform managers from bureaucrats into effective and trustworthy 'agents' of capital. Minimizing the costs of agency and ensuring that managers can be trusted to direct the activities of their company in the direction of maximum profitability is, however, highly problematic in an industry that has been traditionally dominated by the concretist attitudes of civil and sanitary engineering (see Chapter 6). This problem has been 'managed' through the introduction of new mechanisms of management appraisal which are premised on pinpointing, developing and rewarding 'abstract' management skill. What I mean by 'abstract' management skill is the capacity to recognize, albeit in a highly fetishistic and mystified way, that the substantive activities of water companies must necessarily be subordinated to the abstract power of money if the interests of the company, its customers and workforce are to be maximized. As I have mentioned earlier, however, this process is necessarily mediated by the substantive administrative procedures of the 'internal state' and in this sense merely recomposes the contradictions of capitalist management in a newer and more abstract form.

An example of the contradictions underlying the recomposition of management appraisal can be demonstrated through the way in which appraisal mechanisms have been developed at EASTWAT. The company made a conscious decision to limit the operation of the appraisal system to managers in recognition of their importance as cultural 'change agents'. The existing appraisal system was structured around an annual formal interview between a manager and her immediate superior, from which the latter was required to complete a multi-page questionnaire outlining the manager's performance against various measures. Senior managers at EASTWAT feel that the appraisal system has 'outlived its shelf-life'. The system did not fulfil the necessary criteria of setting quantifiable objectives within realistic time-frames or allow the effective identification of constraints. Thus the appraisal system did not provide an effective assessment of managerial performance, and in particular, failed to isolate managers who were performing badly.

The system was seen by senior managers to be a product of the 'old culture' of top–down bureaucratic inertia: an essential part of the transitional 'managerialist' form of management. It was necessary for the isolation of abstract management skills, but ineffective with respect to rewarding their successful application. The senior personnel director at EASTWAT outlined the way in which the system operated and the contradictions inherent in the administrative (concrete) quantification of abstract managerial performance:

> You don't pass down a multi-page questionnaire and say, 'See the individuals once a year, and fill in this form!' Even to the extent that they had a series of boxes and you drew a line in, and if you drew the line all the way over then that individual was fully OK on that particular aspect or question . . . Engineers – and we're an engineering business – would ring up and say 'Can you give us some clearer guidance on this line? What does 50 per cent mean in terms of the line? What does 25 per cent mean? What does 10 per cent

> mean? Can we draw in gradations so we can be absolutely precise about where the line is drawn?' Which wasn't the objective of the whole damn thing anyway! So the company culture wasn't ready for the appraisal system. I'd say 'Just give us an idea!' Had to be precise. But the appraisal system itself was old culture, down from the top, 'Fill in this form!'.

The perceived weaknesses of the appraisal system have resulted in senior managers being concerned to develop a 'sharper tool' for the assessment of managerial performance; a tool more relevant to the new empowering culture at EASTWAT. The plan is to develop a bottom-up appraisal system owned by managers themselves. The manager will meet with her team on a regular basis in order to discuss individual performance, company performance and the way in which the two are related. The process is designed to facilitate a more effective assessment of the contribution of a manager to the overall mission and objectives of the company, and to relate to this an element of the manager's pay. As I will show in the next section, which focuses on the management of health and safety, the new 'stakeholder' managers, empowered through the 'ownership' of their own responsibilities, are trusted only within the limits of their successfully contributing to the production of surplus value. Management appraisal is thus part of the administrative and political moment of the neo-liberal state within the water industry which complements the more generalized management information systems which have developed as part of the quality management initiative. The way in which health and safety has been restructured illustrates that what quality management aims at more than anything else is the total domination and control of living labour within the labour process. Behind the hegemonic manipulation of the political and ideological moments of the 'internal state' by HRM is the naked and unashamed despotism of capital.

Managing Safety and the Contradictions of Safety Management

The neo-liberal restructuring of the water industry has had a marked impact on the regulation and management of health and safety. There have been attempts to make health and safety more 'efficient' and 'effective' through the incorporation of the health and safety function within the new management information systems which have developed as part of HRM/TQM initiatives. These systems have forced managers to view health and safety as a *cost* to be minimized. The 'economics' of health and safety are subject to the political regulation of the internal state, which promotes the governance of health and safety on the basis of the individual responsibility of managers and workers and which legitimates this through a discourse of ownership and empowerment. This reconstitution of the internal state is mirrored by the neo-liberal form of health and safety regulation administered by the Health and Safety Executive (HSE). Prior to the restructuring of the water industry, the National Water Council had a co-ordinating and developmental role in respect of the water industry as a whole. The neo-liberal restructuring of the water industry transformed the relationship between the HSE and the water industry, and has resulted in the disaggregation of safety management and development. Companies face a diverse range of environmental, financial and cultural exigencies, and increasingly adopt different positions with regard to new legislation. The HSE, therefore, approaches companies individually for comments on draft proposals; and the responses to these are drafted either with exclusive reference to the environment of individual companies, or occasionally through informal contacts and liaison between two or more companies at safety officer level.

A key feature of the restructuring of safety management has been an attempt to shift the locus of responsibility for safety from 'expert' senior managers to line managers, supervisors and individual workers. The Safety Manager at WESTWAT argued that there had been a 'reliance on the centre' and that the new culture of the company, together with the demands of the new COSHH legislation (Control of Substances Hazardous to Health) which have important implications for the water industry, have made it important for safety to be managed 'out there' in the company rather than from the office of the health and safety manager. In particular, legislation pertaining to both COSHH and 'manual handling' places greater responsibility for safety on line managers and supervisors in the assessment of safe systems of work; and it is at this level that the HSE will increasingly focus following an incident. Legislation and the HSE have thus served an important role in redefining the relationship between senior and line managers, and this changing relationship has been mediated by the wider development of TQM within the industry. I will approach this through the elaboration of two case studies.

Safety first? Managing safety at EASTWAT

The management of health and safety at EASTWAT demonstrates the way in which the company has attempted to redefine and restructure the role, structure and culture of management. Management, including the management of safety, is now premised upon a 'culture of empowerment': a culture that is set out in the company's vision and mission statements and its 'Partnership Agreement'. The central feature of the new culture is that, through the dismantling of hierarchical and bureaucratic structures within the company, managers are 'empowered' and develop a sense of 'ownership' towards their responsibilities. Managers can then be 'trusted' to deliver to predetermined standards without there being a hierarchical structure with the functions of 'directing' and 'ensuring'. Hence, because managers have been empowered to deliver health and safety, and because they 'own' this responsibility, they can be trusted to deliver to the standards and procedure laid out in the company's safety procedures.

This ideal manager is, of course, abstracted from the contradictions which mark the capitalist mode of production, and exists only in management textbooks. The real manager has to live these contradictions and the trust and empowerment of managers is necessarily complemented by control. This is reflected at EASTWAT, where a computerized safety audit system is being developed alongside the new managerial culture – although the new system is legitimated through the 'consumerist' discourse of trust and empowerment. The new systems are premised upon the ideal manager, and it is clear that she is an abstraction:

> In a perfect world we'd almost be able to say 'We can forget health and safety now'. We've got a whole bunch of empowered health- and safety-conscious managers, who have got health and safety as a performance issue, and an accountable issue up there with all the rest – drinking water, sewage effluent, discharges and pollution, bathing beaches – all the major measures of performance, and up there with them is health and safety. That's fine, but we haven't got a perfect world, we don't have that scenario, and it's reflected in the fact that some of our indices, like accidents, vary. So we want to address that issue: the developmental scene is in effect to bring something in that will help managers understand and deliver on their health and safety performance.

The gap between abstract and real managers has resulted in the development of a new computerized health and safety audit system at EASTWAT. Given the managerial discourse of 'empowerment' and 'trust' within the company, the audit system is defined in terms of its supportive role in helping managers to understand and deliver their health and safety responsibilities. The 'tool' is manager-user-friendly and self-auditing, with the facility for building in support, analysis and control. An essential element of allowing managers to manage is that they manage themselves. Self-control and self-regulation have become key themes of the management approach at EASTWAT. This has been facilitated by the development of the new management information systems within the company. The Senior Personnel Manager outlined the relationship between control, trust and the development of the new IT systems within the company:

> I use control as the last word – it's not the word I would like to emphasize. We're looking for a system that will – given the culture of empowerment and ownership, and the awareness that goes with it – we want a system that will enhance that. But what we do think is needed is for managers to be able to have a tool, that they can use in a straightforward, easy way, that tells them how good they are doing on a particular performance index, which happens to be health and safety. Where they can see, by reviewing it themselves, that there are priority areas that are perhaps not being addressed as well as they could be, and they can put the remedial action into effect themselves, without there being recourse to some other support body like the safety function or the management function. I mean, these will ultimately exist, these facilities will be there – but as a support mode, to allow the manager himself to identify shortfalls in achievement and to do something about it.

The key objective of the new system is thus to facilitate self-assessment and self-control, which is mediated by the ultimate sanctions of the intervention of the managerial support function and thus the non-renewal of fixed-term contracts or a reduction in the performance-related element of salary. In order for the system to function as a mechanism of self-assessment and control, the design of the software incorporated and reflected the functions and responsibilities of managers from a diversity of levels and locations across the company. This is vital in order that managers develop a sense of 'ownership' towards the system. The system was tested in a large urban area covered by EASTWAT, and during the trial a series of 'tailor-fit' audit questions were developed appropriate to various levels within the water, sewage, support and stores functions. In order to engender 'ownership' it was important that managers could relate to the questions they were being asked. The overall objective is to develop a sense of managerial 'ownership' towards the system: to constrain the activities of managers within the new abstract management system with administrative and substantive control – although this is to be legitimated through the abstract logic of consumerist ideology. The Senior Safety Advisor at EASTWAT explained:

> There will be a series of tailor-fit audit questions for each audit area, and even a similar operational function may have a different series of questions. Because we want to make sure that managers own it, and say 'That's my system! It can help me!', and if they say that I think we can make it work. So the process is about identifying the audit questions with the managers, and then following up with agreeing with those managers the appropriate weighting, prioritizing – working them through.

The aim of the company is to integrate the health and safety auditing system into the company's main management information system. This will give senior managers access to performance information over a range of indices (DG performance indicators, DWI indicators, internal performance measures, cost performance measures and health and safety). Since the system has the facility for producing performance information at company, divisional and area levels, it will allow senior managers and directors to monitor divisional and area performance against the performance of the company as a whole. The integration of health and safety within the system is considered vital to raising the profile of safety within the company, as it will allow directors to receive a summary of health and safety performance alongside the other measures every three months. This will also have an important impact of further developing the managerial culture.

The management of health and safety at EASTWAT is to be structured around a computerized audit system 'owned' by managers. It is believed that the new system, and the new organizational culture of which it is part, obviate the need for a planned and structured system of safety inspections within the company. While planned inspections are only carried out following accidents and incidents, in the new managerial culture managers will be concerned with safety issues all the time and deal with issues and problems as they arise. This constitutes a significant move away from the old local government culture, in which the health and safety expert played a pivotal role: a culture in which, despite managers having health and safety procedures to follow, they invariably referred safety matters to the 'expert'. Managers are encouraged to manage health and safety themselves and to constantly implement and review procedures and deal with problems and risks as they arise. The Senior Safety Advisor contrasted the Fabian approach outlined above with the HRM approaches to health and safety:

> [The old culture] is the culture that doesn't empower, that pushes things to the specialist . . . Safety was a bit like that. Now we are saying, 'No!' There's a whole trend on the way that says that's not the scene any more 'That chap, that lady, works for you – not for a personnel officer, not for a safety officer. You are in charge of the whole of that person's working environment, and possibly a chunk of stuff that isn't their working environment' without being paternalistic of course, but by being supportive and interested. If there was an accident at home to one of your relatives, would you take an interest? Would you be concerned? Would you want to be seen to be doing all the right things? Answer, yes! Here's one of your employees, and he's had an accident; same rules, perhaps not the same amount of emotions, but still the same interest, action, concern has got to be there. Not passing the ball off, for the safety man to come in and do something about it. So we've seen a change. Some more quickly than others, but everybody is moving into that mode. If you're not then you're really *out of the game*! I like to think that we more than most have adopted that culture [my emphasis].

The management of health and safety can thus be understood as a 'game' in the same way that TQM was presented as a game in the previous chapter. The role of the safety function in the new organizational culture will be to help and support managers to manage safety themselves and enlist the active support of managers for the new system. The senior safety advisor at EASTWAT suggested that the new empowered managers will take great comfort from the knowledge that there is a safety man [*sic*] out there to help them; someone with an overall view who is able to highlight worrying trends that they may have overlooked. While the audit system does contain the facility for monitoring the performance of managers, it is there not to check up on them but to help and 'support' them. The Senior Personnel Manager at EASTWAT commented:

> We know they'll do it because they want to do it; because it's part of their

> accountability and responsibility and they've accepted this. We see it as a very positive step forward, and we've got the commitment of the company behind them doing it, as a tool, as a supportive tool to managers. Just like if I look on my screen there and I see an assets trend, or an overtime costs trend, or a payroll/manpower-related issue, I would feel quite happy about ringing the manager as low down as I could, to actually get hold of that individual supervisor and say: 'Any problem there? I don't know whether you've spotted it but it looks a little bit dodgy?' To me that's healthy, and that's the sort of environment we want to be in with health and safety. Right the way across, the 'doing' function and the 'support' function – that's the kind of relationship we're trying to develop.

Changes in the management of health and safety are part of a more fundamental reinterpretation and restructuring of the role and function of management at EASTWAT. Central to this has been the need to monitor and control costs. Accidents and injuries impose costs, and the new IT systems monitor the performance of managers *vis-à-vis* the minimization of health and safety costs. Managers and supervisors are trusted to deliver effective health and safety at the lowest cost within the context of the abstract control constituted by performance-related pay and fixed-term contracts. In other words, a principal consideration has been the *quantification* of safety management in order to drive down the costs of safety. This can be illustrated further by exploring the safety auditing system developed at WESTWAT.

Safety in numbers? Managing safety at WESTWAT

In order to monitor and audit safety management at WESTWAT, the company has introduced the International Safety Rating System (ISRS), a health and safety management audit system developed by the International Loss Control Institute of Loganville, Georgia, USA. An important factor in the development of the new system is the pressure from the HSE, which is considering the development of regulations requiring the adoption of formal management safety audits as a demonstration of compliance with the health and safety legislation in general and the forthcoming EC legislation in particular. The ISRS audit covers twenty elements and requires a total of 615 questions to be answered. It uses a weighted points scoring system in order to grade the audited operation up to five star awards in two award categories (standard and advanced). The 'Standard Programme' prioritizes five basic elements: leadership and administration, planned inspection, accident/incident investigation, organizational rules and personal protective equipment. In order to achieve a higher award on the standard programme, a higher weighted score must be achieved on all these elements, while advancement to the Advanced Programme requires achievement on increasing numbers of the optional elements (a Five Star Award on the Advanced Programme requiring a minimum score of 70 per cent on all twenty elements with a minimum average score of 90 per cent). When the system was initially introduced into WESTWAT, the company was unable to achieve even a One Star Award on the Standard Programme. The abstract from an internal report discusses this failure, together with the need for urgent remedial action:

> At this point in time WESTWAT is prevented from achieving a respectable base line award of three stars on the standard programme safety as a result of the lack of a planned programme of general safety inspection. The intention is to ensure that planned general safety inspections are conducted on a regular (at least every two months) basis with the primary responsibility being on the first line manager. Records of the inspections are to be maintained with a follow up system to ensure corrective actions are taken.
> (internal WESTWAT report, 28 October 1992)

The implementation of the system is at a relatively early stage. The failure of WESTWAT to carry out planned inspections either centrally or through supervision management resulted in the failure to achieve even the One Star Award on the Standard Programme. Despite this poor performance, the Senior Health and Safety Advisor at WESTWAT felt that the development of the system had been successful owing to the way in which it had provided an excellent impetus for the development of more efficient safety management in the future. The development of the ISRS system has highlighted a major weakness in the management of health and safety at EASTWAT: the failure of the company to monitor the extent to which procedures and safe systems of work are being effectively applied and adhered to by managers and employees. The shift in the locus of responsibility for safety towards line-managers and supervisors necessitated that monitoring at this level must itself be amenable to monitoring by senior managers. An important development has been the integration of planned inspections into the company's quality management approach. These are to be carried out according to a written procedure and to pre-set standards. In preparation for this all staff have taken part in a training programme dealing with the procedures and standards associated with planned inspections. Staff have been made aware of what is expected of them and have accepted that the inspection of safety systems is a routine aspect of their work to be undertaken on a weekly or monthly basis.

Legislation emanating from the HSE and the EC provided an important dynamic to the development of ISRS within WESTWAT, as many elements in ISRS (i.e. task analysis) are the subject of recent legislation. Indeed, the HSE has taken an increasing interest in systems such as ISRS which allow the development of a 'true' measure of safety performance rather than the measurement of failure through simple accident records. The neo-liberal state regulation of health and safety has thus become increasingly concerned with the *costs* of health and safety. The abstract premises of the ISRS system are illustrated by the origins of the system in the financial exigencies of the US insurance industry. As the Senior Safety Advisor explained, the ISRS

> effectively grew out of Frank Burn's experience within the American insurance industry. He was working for insurance companies carrying out studies in the companies they were covering. He looked at what was actually happening, and came up with conclusions that said 'Well, if we're going to insure that company it needs to change its approach altogether', and then said 'Well, we can devise a system that if they follow the insurers will be happy with, because they'll be able to see that there's a measure of improvement'.

The ultimate value of ISRS is thus the facility for measuring the costs and benefits of safety. The development of ISRS obviously imposes costs. The senior personnel manager at WESTWAT, however, envisaged that the costs will be minimal in comparison with anticipated benefits. The costs of safety staff are fixed and the costs of implementing ISRS are confined to the development of relevant procedures and documentation. The potential savings associated with ISRS are quite marked. An example given by the Senior Safety Advisor concerned 'lost time' incidents in the 1991–2 financial year. WESTWAT had 60 of these incidents in this time period, each one costing the company three working days and approximately £300 (an approximate total of £18,000). But the potential benefits are multiplied when the damage to plant and equipment from these incidents are considered. The Senior

Safety Advisor was, however, a little reticent in expressing his concern for dead labour (capital) in the health and safety equation:

> Now, when you start, and I'm saying when you do because we certainly don't, if you started to think in terms of the cost of damage to equipment that must ensue with such an accident performance, I'm sure then that the cost element must be very much more noticeable. And whilst you would need to put in procedures to measure that as well, it would fall out of the budget of a substantial company, anyway. You would be aware that the maintenance costs were being driven down by a greater margin than you would anticipate from the work being done by the maintenance group itself on the basis that they're not having to do it. So, yes, I can see that the benefits will show at some point in time. We will start to be looking at that, looking for it as a demonstration of the value of doing it.

The disaggregation of the water industry has resulted in a variety of managerial strategies and approaches to health and safety. Senior managers argue that the management of health and safety in the water industry has become more efficient and effective as accidents have been reduced and water companies take an increasingly proactive approach to the monitoring of health and safety policy. However, many of the potentially most dangerous functions within the water industry have been contracted out to other companies and to self-employed former employees (O'Connell Davidson, 1993: 110). The employees who remain in the water industry widely perceive that managers should devote more attention to health and safety issues: a survey of utility workers by Nichols and O'Connell Davidson (1993: 724–5) suggesting that 69 per cent of manual workers, 58 per cent of white-collar workers and 29 per cent of managers agreed with the proposition that management should attach more importance to the health and safety function. The restructuring of health and safety management is thus part of a generalized management strategy to reduce costs, and the gap between management rhetoric and reality is apparent to managerial and non-managerial workers within the industry.

As I will show in the next chapter, however, the changing form of health and safety management does demonstrate the way in which the neo-liberal restructuring of the capital relation has changed the 'political' and 'ideological' composition of the internal state within the water industry. The attempt to channel the substantive activities of the industry through the abstract forms of money and the law is manifested through the imposition of budgetary constraints on managers and the increasing use of contractors and semi-autonomous subsidiary companies. This has involved a fundamental individualization of industrial citizenship within the industry and the recomposition of rights and obligations on the basis of the impersonal and abstract citizen-consumer of neo-liberal social and economic theory. This has had a marked effect on the autonomous and collective organization and representation of labour through trade unions and on the constitutional arrangements which existed to mediate the relationship between managers and workers during the Keynesian form of the industry. As I will show in the next chapter, the 'political' form of public service trade unionism was an important factor in precipitating the crisis of the Keynesian 'planner-state', and the demobilization of this form of unionism has been the central focus of the neo-liberal restructuring of both the 'internal' and the 'global' state.

8 The Crisis of Public Service Trade Unionism

The neo-liberal state restructuring and privatization of the water industry have had a marked impact on patterns of industrial relations within the industry. The water industry emerged from local government, and the early development of collective bargaining was achieved through the establishment of 'Whitleyism' and the centralized joint-determination of local government pay and conditions. In the immediate post-war period the water industry was divorced from local government and a national joint council for the water industry was established. This body centrally determined pay and conditions for all water industry employees, with separate negotiating machinery for 'manual', 'craft' and 'staff' employees. The 1973 Water Act imposed a statutory industrial relations system on the industry and established the National Water Council (NWC) in order, *inter alia*, to co-ordinate industrial relations policy within the industry and to act as the employers' side during negotiations. Employees were represented through a 'closed shop' arrangement by a myriad of trade unions which sent representatives to the joint national councils: manual workers represented by GMBATU and NUPE, craft workers represented by EEPTU, AEU and UCATT and staff represented by NALGO, FUMPO and MATSA. The water industry has thus always been a highly unionized sector with highly centralized and bureaucratic collective bargaining arrangements.

The neo-liberal restructuring of the industry has fundamentally transformed this traditional pattern of industrial relations. The 1983 Water Act abolished the NWC, and the Water Authorities Association (WAA) which replaced the NWC had no statutory duties in respect of industrial relations. The statutory framework was thus replaced by a voluntary framework in 1983 and this allowed a greater amount of authority to be devolved to the RWAs. The voluntary framework was finally ruptured when Thames Water and Northumbrian Water left the arrangement, in 1988 and 1989 respectively, and they were followed by the remaining eight former RWAs in the 1990/91 pay round. The result has been the fragmentation of water industry collective bargaining and the development of company-level bargaining on pay and conditions. Water companies have gained the 'freedom' to pursue industrial relations strategies which are closely tailored to their own business needs. There are a number of general themes which emerge from the restructuring of industrial relations across the sector (see IRS Employment Trends 516).[1] First, the de-recognition of unions has been rare but some companies have rationalized bargaining arrangements by de-recognizing unions which only organize small numbers of workers. Second, pay bargaining has taken the form of long-term pay deals which in some cases reflect the demand for labour in the local economy and the level of profitability enjoyed by individual companies. Third, bargaining arrangements have been transformed through the introduction of single-table bargaining and the development of new consultative and representative forums, bringing managers and trade union representatives together on a company-wide basis. Finally, payment systems have been restructured in order to establish a closer link between pay and performance through the introduction of job-evaluation and performance-related pay. These developments highlight the way in which the regulation of labour through the wage-form has been intensified through the valorization imperatives that have been applied to the water industry by capital and the state.

There have been several attempts to explore the implications of neo-liberal restructuring for the organization of labour and patterns of collective bargaining. There is a divergence between analyses which stress the continued involvement of trade unions in stable collective bargaining arrangements (MacInnes, 1987) and those which stress the marginalization and exclusion of organized labour (Smith and Morton, 1993). Evidence from the water industry suggests that both of the above positions have a degree of validity. Water companies have mostly continued to maintain and expand consultative and bargaining arrangements, and have welcomed the involvement of trade unions in 'legitimate' areas of trade union concern such as pay and conditions, training and health and safety. The decentralization of collective bargaining and the narrowing of bargaining agendas has also resulted in the exclusion and marginalization of organized labour within the water industry. There are, however, important limitations to the industrial relations approach to these complex developments, because they cannot be analysed solely in terms of narrow 'economic indicators' concerning union recognition, the level of pay settlement, levels of industrial action and so on. These 'economic' developments have taken place in the context of a fundamental recomposition of the 'political' and 'ideological' form of labour regulation within the workplace (Holloway, 1987). It is only by exploring the 'political' and 'ideological' recomposition of the 'internal state that the full significance of the restructuring of industrial relations can be grasped' (Burawoy, 1979: 109–20).

The Keynesian planner-state socialized the law of value and this heightened the institutional autonomy of the workplace 'regime' within state agencies and enterprises. This allowed the development of a particular form of 'public service' trade unionism which claimed extensive 'industrial citizenship' rights for public service workers and legitimated these 'political' claims through an ideology stressing the commitment of public service unions to the 'public'. The autonomy of labour within the 'internal state' resulted in the marked politicization of the labour process within state enterprises and the involvement of trade unions in both day-to-day and strategic managerial decisions. The political autonomy of labour within the 'internal state' became an important determinant of the power and influence of labour within the nation state, with the result that the 'politics of production became inseparably linked to the fiscal crisis of the state' (Hyman, 1989b: 206). These developments marked a crisis of the 'capital relation' within the state and precipitated the neo-liberal restructuring which has attempted to reduce the 'political' autonomy of the state through a process in which state labour processes have been subjected to the valorization imperatives of capital. The 'economic' restructuring of the capital relation is, however, only one part of a more fundamental recomposition, involving the simultaneous economic, political and ideological restructuring of the capital relation. The 'political' restructuring has involved recomposing industrial citizenship on a more abstract and individualistic basis, while the ideological restructuring has involved an attempt to redefine the 'public good' on the basis of the impersonal 'customer' of neo-liberal social theory. The neo-liberal restructuring of the state has, therefore, fundamental implications for traditional forms of 'public service' trade unionism.

The ability of public service trade unions to conflate their own 'economic' interests within the labour process with wider 'political' and 'ideological' conceptions of the 'common good' played an important role in legitimating the process of neo-liberal restructuring. As the fiscal crisis of the state intensified, and the state became increasingly affected by the administrative paralysis which I explored in Chapter 3, the 'public service' trade unions remained ideologically committed to increasingly inefficient, ineffective and alienating public services. Indeed, the contradictions of 'public service' trade unionism resulted in the ideological construction of a discourse which presented the unions as *the* 'particular' interest which was operating against the 'general' or 'public' interest. This was manifested both at the level of the national state, in the hostility of the post-1979 Conservative administrations to organized labour in general and public sector trade unionism in particular, and within the internal state through the development of commercialized management styles which seek to marginalize and exclude trade unions.

In this chapter I explore the restructuring of industrial relations in the water industry in the context of an analysis which attempts to make explicit the institutional linkages between the state and the 'internal regime' within individual water companies (Hyman, 1989b: 202). I will show how the intensification of labour within the labour process has involved the recomposition of the 'internal state' and how this has been premised on the depoliticization and decollectivization of labour regulation by the state. As I will show in the second part of this chapter, public service trade unions have been forced to redefine themselves on the basis of the 'ideological' and 'political' regimes of individual water companies. As I will also argue, however, the administrative and micro-political mechanisms for integrating labour highlight the point that the subordination of labour to the abstract forms of money and the law can never be total and, while the terrain of struggle has shifted, organized labour within the water industry remains an important obstacle to the further subordination of water services by the abstract imperatives of capital accumulation.

Industrial Relations and the Recomposition of the 'Internal State'

The fragmentation of the water industry, and the demise of the NWC as a co-ordinating agency in respect of industrial relations, has resulted in a wide variety of industrial relations (IR) strategies across the water sector. In this section, I will contrast the exclusionary and incorporationary strategies pursued by WESTWAT and EASTWAT, with particular reference to the issue of health and safety. The divergence in these strategies highlights that there is not a 'pure' form of neo-liberal management, premised on the total exclusion of organized labour and the total individualization of social relations. The generation of 'consent' within water companies to increasingly intense management control within the labour process necessarily requires the 'political' orchestration of workers within the 'internal state' as 'industrial citizens'. What has occurred has been that this 'citizenship' has become increasingly abstract as the autonomy of the 'internal state' from the production of surplus value in the labour process has been reduced. In other words, the contradictions of the 'internal state' as manifested in the contradiction between administration and regulation have been reconstituted rather than transcended, and these IR strategies remain 'different routes to partial failure' (Hyman, 1987: 30).

Company unionism and the micro-politics of exclusion at WESTWAT

WESTWAT has pursued an exclusionary strategy with respect to the trade unions organizing within the company. Indeed, the company has replaced the trade-union-based system of consultative committees and shop steward representation with a 'company council' system. The unions retain a role in disciplinary matters and on the safety committee, and a full-time representative of the 'confederation of trade unions' (made up of the eight unions that organize in the company) is allowed to sit on the 'company council' in an 'advisory' capacity. The new structure comprises a main 'company council' that deals with company-wide issues, the members of which are drawn from the seven 'employee councils' that are situated around the company. The councillors that sit on the councils are all employees of the company, and the councillors have exclusive rights with respect to the negotiation of terms and conditions, the interpretation of agreements, and the representation of staff in grievances and disciplinary matters.

The main impetus to the development of the new IR system was the refusal of the trade unions to co-operate with the company in the development of single-table negotiations and the harmonization of terms and conditions. The company was eager to move away from the Whitley system, which involved dealing with eight trade unions on three negotiating bodies, for staff, craft and manual workers. The company decided that it would deal with only one trade union and deal directly with employees – rather than dealing with staff indirectly through a 'third party'. The Senior Personnel Manager alluded to the way in which this was related to the new managerial ethos:

> We decided that we only wanted one trade union, and we wanted, as well, not to talk through trade unions. There were wrong, biased messages getting filtered through when we did that. Staff were tending to look to trade unions rather than to their supervisors with problems. We believed supervisors needed to do their jobs properly and they needed support for that. So we didn't want to deal with a third party.

The development of the new IR system carried a risk. The water industry is highly unionized, and while WESTWAT had faced no industrial action since the national strike of 1983, there was a risk of both local and even national action following their decision. The risks were felt to be justified in the pursuit of a labour relations framework that was not based on potential conflict. In addition to the potential conflict in dealing with trade unions, a further problem for WESTWAT was the extent to which the unions organizing in the company were indelibly tarnished with a public sector/town hall image. In the run-up to privatization, for example, WESTWAT had initially opposed privatization. The company was then forced into 'conceding the inevitable' and attempted to 'make the best of the situation'. Senior managers suggest that the continued opposition of the trade unions to privatization did not reflect the concerns of WESTWAT staff but the 'self-interest' of the trade unions. The Senior Personnel Manager argued that the unions

> were coming on very strong from all angles, and not least of all because of self-interest. Does National And Local Government Officers have a place in a privatized company? National Union of Public Employees in a private com-

> pany? It doesn't fit at all! Some of them started to get very worried because of self-interest. We think that we have a good relationship with our employees. So although the unions were worried, the employees were not. The employees knew that the same team of managers, who had built up a good reputation and a good relationship, were going to be there after privatization as well. I think they took a lot of comfort from that.

A primary consideration of managers at WESTWAT has thus been the establishment of more 'direct' communications with employees through the marginalization of 'third party' involvement by trade unions. Through a consideration of health and safety I will show how this reflects the recomposition of the political 'regime' within the company and the way in which this has impacted on and been facilitated by the restructuring of health and safety regulation at the macro level of the state. The trade unions have been excluded from the development of health and safety at a macro level since the abolition of the NWC in the early 1980s. The new safety manager at WESTWAT was recently brought in from the chemical industry, and he argued that the new systems for managing health and safety at company level will not necessarily hinder the development of codes and standards; rather, it would change the form in which these are determined, leading to the development of a more 'private sector' way of working. The new company council system has allowed the company to heighten the awareness of workplace representatives about the issue of health and safety, and to define the 'problem' of safety and establish internal regulatory mechanisms which attempt to subordinate health and safety to the effective production of surplus value. Paradoxically, this has been achieved by increasing the involvement of staff in health and safety issues. The Senior Safety Manager highlighted these developments:

> I think we are getting more involvement, simply because we have raised the profile of safety within the company. The [staff] who used to be the trade union safety representatives and shop stewards, who are now the area councillors sitting on the company council, are more aware themselves of safety. Because we have been proactive, and gone to them and said 'This is what we're doing, and this is what we think is of interest to you and your role'. And we're directly involved in the training of company councillors, which was put on and organized with a local university.

The exclusion of organized labour at WESTWAT is thus part of the neo-liberal recomposition of the 'internal state' within the company. The company council arrangement represents an attempt to reconstitute 'industrial citizenship' in a way that limits the autonomy of labour to pursue its interests independently of capital and the capital relation. Senior managers at WESTWAT present the 'company council' system as very 'democratic' and analogous to Parliament. The company councillors range from mainlayers to senior managers and represent all the staff in their geographical/operational area. The exclusion of trade unions at WESTWAT has, therefore, been legitimated on the basis of neo-liberal 'citizenship' rights, and the specificity of WESTWAT is derived from the way in which citizenship rights and obligations are mediated by the 'company council'. In other water companies, trade unions have not been excluded but the recomposition of the 'internal state' has resulted in a similar reconstitution of 'industrial citizenship'. I will illustrate this through a discussion of the introduction of the new co-operative consultation framework at EASTWAT.

Co-operative consultation and the micro-politics of incorporation at EASTWAT

The restructuring of the 'internal state' at EASTWAT has involved an attempt to elicit the active co-operation of trade union representatives in a limited number of functions such as health and safety. As I will show below, there has been an attempt to limit trade union involvement to areas and issues which either do not threaten or which contribute to the generation of surplus value within the company. As I have already highlighted, management is a contradictory process and this is particularly evident in the way in which the imperative to reduce costs has undermined the effectiveness of health and safety management within the water industry. This contradiction is becoming increasingly evident to managers with responsibility for health and safety. The Senior Personnel Manager at EASTWAT, who has special responsibility for the management of health and safety, argues that the absence of a national water industry co-ordinating body for health and safety 'works against the efficiency of the function'. There is a 'logic' for companies to co-operate and pool expertise in this area. An industry speaking with one voice obviously has more weight and influence in dealing with the HSE than a fragmented industry. Why, then, are water companies pursuing the seemingly illogical strategy of developing health and safety policy as isolated individual companies? The answer to this question is to be found at the macro 'frontier of control': labour has been totally excluded and marginalized at this level, and the development of a national co-ordinating body for health and safety would threaten this continued exclusion. Companies are afraid of losing an element of their 'individual decision-making process':

> It's the thin end of the wedge scenario. You start off with health and safety – the next thing you know, the trade unions will only talk to a water industry health and safety forum, and they're very anxious to set up something like that. Then what else creeps into the agenda – does training creep in? There's health and safety training – does it extend itself? The next thing we're back to pay and conditions, and so on and so forth. The sensitivity at the moment, which is very, very high, would say that at all accounts don't even open the potential for us to be seen to be acting, not as an individual PLC.

The HRM strategy of the company has attempted to achieve the increasing marginalization of trade unions. The company has developed a pay and conditions package and formula that, according to the senior personnel manager, practically 'puts the unions out of business'. Senior managers also argue that trade unions have been marginalized as the quality of management has improved. Hence:

> Inevitably part of the process of managers becoming damn good managers is that the people who work for them have more confidence in going to them and getting something sorted out. Now in that sense, yes, there is a marginalization process, but we make no apologies for that. Managers are going to get better, and are getting better. There's probably an inverse relationship – influence of trade union, influence of managers – and as they get better one goes up while the other goes down.

The marginalization of trade unions at EASTWAT has resulted in an increasing emphasis by the unions on health and safety and the related issue of occupational health. This constitutes what the Senior Personnel Manager termed a 'struggle for role definition'. Senior managers argue that the unions have been marginalized by the company on the quantitative issue of pay and conditions and are attempting to redefine their role around providing qualitative support for their members. Trade unions have attempted to increase their involvement in an area which they perceive to be low on the managerial scale of priorities. However, this can have beneficial consequences for the company:

> We talk about managers owning health and safety – individual staff do as well. The safety representatives, who tend to be the trade union shop stewards, or opinion leaders almost, they're talking health and safety as well – it can only enhance what we're trying to do. So I think there is mutuality, with the approach to health and safety as an issue. There's less and less to do in some respects, and I suppose that complacency can be something that can creep in.

Senior managers at EASTWAT have thus been happy to preserve trade union involvement in the management of health and safety within the company. This has included a commitment to maintaining the involvement of union representatives in the jealously guarded role of safety representative. Indeed, the safety representative role, 'properly done', is perceived by senior managers to be a very supportive method of developing the issue of health and safety in the workplace. The involvement of the trade unions in health and safety can provide an important counterweight to the management complacency that inevitably develops in a low-risk area such as the water industry. The Senior Safety Manager highlighted the importance of having trade unions involved in health and safety management:

> There is a tendency for managers to stand away from that as a priority. Because let's face it, if we have dirty water in an area it's in all the newspapers. If someone twists an ankle or has a spinal injury it doesn't get into the press, and it's a rare event where there is a serious injury that does get in the press. Now, that's a cynical business way at looking at it. So, you're keeping things in place, and you're making sure that things are updated, but you address the business issues, and the priorities as they are, and health and safety is not the top. Trade unions have seen that. They know that, the trade union safety reps know that.

In contrast to the micro-exclusion of trade unions in the management of health and safety at WESTWAT, EASTWAT has followed a strategy of micro-incorporation. The price of incorporation for the unions has been the requirement that they 'buy into' the new organizational culture at EASTWAT, and this has been reflected in the structure and operation of health and safety representation and consultation within the company. The company has retained the company-level and divisional-level formal safety committees, but the committees have been fundamentally restructured in line with the company's new organizational culture. The committees were relics of the managerialist form of the company, in which senior managers and safety experts were confronted by trade union representatives with a catalogue of health and safety issues and problems to which the managers were expected to respond. The new 'forums' constitute a 'qualitative change' *vis-à-vis* the old committees. The committees have been transformed from adversarial two-sided committees into 'round table' forums for co-operation and development. The shift in the locus of managerial responsibility for health and safety from senior specialist managers to line-managers and supervisors has driven down the management–union frontier of control in safety management to the supervisor–safety representative level. The committees have consequently been transformed into co-operative forums that are increasingly concerned with developmental issues, such as awareness and health issues, that transcend the traditional health and safety agenda. The Senior Safety Manager described the approach of the newly constituted forums as follows:

> The issues are not in the model they were before. 'Can we develop?' is the sort of question, 'Can we move on?', and quite often the answer is 'Yes we can, and we should!'. And it's sort of more of a coming together – there isn't two sides of the table. There's a group of people with a declared interest in health and safety trying to move a thing forward in a sensible way. That reflects human resource development across the business.

The 'internal state' within EASTWAT has thus been reconstituted on a neo-liberal basis which attempts to realign the regulatory activities of the 'internal state' with the valorization imperatives operating within the labour process. This has involved a transformation of the role and function of trade unions within the company. The weakness of labour within the labour process has allowed the demolition of the 'political' and 'ideological' structures which constituted the strength and the organizational form of public service trade unionism. The result has been not only that trade unions within EASTWAT have been forced into a defensive strategy of accommodation to a neo-liberal accumulation strategy but, more importantly, that the process of restructuring has created a crisis of identity and a struggle for 'role-definition' for trade unions within the neo-liberal EASTWAT regime. I will now explore this crisis and the attempt by the unions to resolve the crisis, through a consideration of the way in which trade unions operating within the water industry have responded to the crisis and restructuring of the public service state.

Public Service Trade Unionism and the Crisis of the State

The culture and practice of public service trade unionism need to be examined in the context of the logical and historical development of the capitalist state. The corporatist and Keynesian policies of the post-war period undermined the illusion of state autonomy as the rapid growth of state employment and state expenditure produced an increasingly serious fiscal crisis of the state. The growth in state functions and state labour increasingly resulted in the politicization of the labour process and a growth in workplace-based trade union activity in the public services (Fryer *et al.*, 1978: Hyman, 1989b: 202–23; Kessler, 1986, 1989; Terry, 1982; Winchester, 1983). The neo-liberal restructuring of the 1980s was an attempt to re-establish the autonomy of state and economy, and to resolve the crisis of the state through the depoliticization of social relations within and between public service agencies. The public service trade unions were a central obstacle to neo-liberal restructuring and the struggle between state and labour has been central to redefining the material and discursive meaning of public service as a state ideology and practice.

The neo-liberal restructuring of public services has been bitterly resisted by public service trade unions (Foster, 1993; Foster and Taylor, 1994). The particular form of resistance was determined by the location of public service trade unions between the 'twin forces of public policy of the state on the one hand and public consumption and reaction on the other' (Fryer, 1989: 39).[2] The contradictory position of state workers has allowed union activity to combine 'political' issues around the nature of public services with the 'economic' concerns of employees, and thereby conflate what are usually seen as the distinctive 'economic' and 'political' objectives of trade unions (Flanders, 1968; Hyman, 1989b: 44–5). In his examination of the fiscal crisis of the state, O'Connor (1973) predicted that a 'commonality of interests' with client groups would emerge among public sector employees, as they would begin to see them as political equivalents in their struggle to maintain services. This in turn would lead to demands from members that the unions should involve themselves in wider social issues. The 'commonality of interests' may be said to be determined through the objective contradictory position of state workers within a contradictory state formation. State workers sell their labour for wages while the immediate purpose of their labour is the direct provision of use-values (Fairbrother, 1989). In other words, for state workers there is a direct, visible link between the politics of production and the 'politics of politics'.

The restructuring and privatization of the water industry provoked a sustained campaign of opposition from the trade unions organizing within the industry. The focus of the opposition was the extent to which privatization threatened the 'public service' orientation of the industry and therefore the levels of service provided to consumers. In an attempt to reunify the concerns of trade unionists and the wider public, the central rallying point for the campaigns opposing restructuring and privatization thus became the notion of 'public service' and the delivery of services by public servants who, in alliance with users of services, could confront the neo-liberal attack. The problem faced by the water unions is that they were forced into defending a notion of 'public service' and the 'common good' which had been fundamentally discredited by the oppressive and alienating form of the planner-state. This contradiction was inherent in trade union campaigns against privatization and also in the internal restructuring of trade unions following the restructuring process.

Privatization and the politics of 'public service'

The national trade union campaign against water privatization has been presented as a unique example of a unified campaign which overcame both sectionalism and economism (Ogden, 1991). While the campaigns did partially overcome the traditional economism of public service trade unions, the self-representation of the unions as guardians of the 'public interest' needs to be assessed in the context of the contradictory position of state labour. The principal ideological focus of the campaigns was the way in which the public sector water industry embodied the ethical and moral principles of 'public service'. The water industry 'worked' in its present form and should, therefore, remain 'public' – a central slogan of the campaign being 'Water Works Keep it Public!'. The defects of the water industry were presented as resulting from the way in which the Conservative Party had failed to provide the industry with adequate levels of investment. The struggle between the state and organized labour with respect to the water industry during the 1980s took the form of a struggle over the form of 'public service'. The unions were defending an essentially 'Fabian' model of public service, premised on the democratic control and accountability of services directly administered by the state. The neo-liberal project of restructuring was an attempt to redefine public service and the 'common good' on the basis of the maximum utility of individual marginal-maximizing consumers in the market. The neo-liberal water industry emerged from the struggle of these contradictory pressures and internalized them within its administrative and regulatory form. As I will also demonstrate the partial defeat of the unions in this process precipitated the crisis and restructuring of public service trade unionism.

The trade union campaign brought together an array of pressure groups concerned with the operational activities of water companies: environmental groups concerned with the pollution of rivers and beaches, consumer groups concerned with the quality of drinking water and the price of water services and amenity groups concerned with access to the land of water undertakers for activities such as angling, walking and water sports. The campaign played a fundamental role in the determination of the administrative and regulatory regime associated with the 1989 Water Act. NALGO[3] was a 'public service' union and for union officers it was an intrinsic part of union's 'culture' to take an interest in environmental and consumer issues. These concerns were heightened during the anti-privatization campaign. During the 1980s NALGO ran a series of campaigns, at both national and regional levels, against plans to privatize the water industry. At the national level, the 'Water Industry Liaison Committee' was established, and both this committee and the regional committees involved both trade unions and environmental and consumer groups.

During the anti-privatization campaign the unions organizing within the water industry built up relationships and sophisticated channels of communication with environmental and consumer organizations. During the campaign NALGO was in daily contact with organizations such as Friends of the Earth (FoE), and representatives of these groups were invited to sit upon trade union committees. The effectiveness of the campaign was dependent upon the large amount of operational information that the unions received from their members. The unions 'manipulated' this information and passed it on to other relevant groups in the campaign. In the West Midlands region these concerns led to the formation of a joint trade-union-led regional campaign which also involved consumer and environmental groups. The involvement of such groups reflected a conscious decision taken by the unions. The regional officer for NALGO, who was also secretary of the campaign, recalls its founding philosophy and the Fabian discourse through which the campaign was articulated:

> There is no doubt that [as] part of our campaign against privatization we very consciously said: 'This is not just an issue that applies to us as trade unionists and employees, but something that is a matter of major public concern from the angle of the public as consumers, but also from an environmental angle as well.' Therefore, the whole nature of the anti-privatization campaign was very much a public campaign designed to reach out to and involve consumers' groups and so on.

NALGO perceived the privatization of the water industry as against the 'public interest' and ultimately against the national interest. The struggle between the state and organized labour was, moreover, central in redefining the 'common good' and 'public service' in its neo-liberal form. The success of the anti-privatization campaign in which NALGO played such a prominent part played a major role in defining the shape of the post-privatized neo-liberal industry. Senior NALGO officers argued that the campaigns had a major impact on service and environmental issues. In particular they see the pressure exerted by the union campaigns as fundamental with respect to the establishment of the NRA as a separate regulatory agency, and the heightened public awareness on the issues of water standards which led to the tight regulatory framework administered by OFWAT and the DWI. The pressure exerted by the campaigns was also manifested with respect to the so-called Green Dowry given to the water companies to clean up water supplies. The National Officer for water argued:

> The fact that they felt obliged to put money into the Water Industry was testimony to the fact that we and others had been raising the importance of the issue on the political agenda – the fact that the water industry is suffering from under-investment, that it was not meeting European Quality Standards, that sewerage works were not meeting their consent conditions. I think our campaign, along with the others, was part of bringing that in.

The way in which water companies are devoting an increasing level of resources to 'customer care' is also presented as a result of the trade union campaign by NALGO officers. The realization that the water industry was unpopular led companies to devote more time and resources to 'communicating' with a public among whom a heightened perception and awareness had been created *vis-à-vis* the need for improved levels of service. While NALGO officers accept that the industry is indeed trying to improve its service, they continue to articulate Fabian notions of public service. A regional officer argued that true 'customer care' was incompatible with the private ownership of the water industry. However, despite his 'obvious' support for water remaining in the public sector he had no 'starry-eyed' illusions that the water industry was, in anything but the most tenuous way, publicly responsive.

The role of the unions in the anti-privatization campaign has resulted in serious organizational difficulties for the trade unions following privatization. Senior managers in the water industry perceive NALGO as being too 'political': a town hall union exuding political dogma. Despite the claim that 'public service' trade unionism is not incompatible with private sector industry, NALGO's concern with operational issues has been pushed into the background following privatization. This reflects a conscious concern to develop a working relationship with the newly-privatized companies in order to protect members' interests in the traditional areas of pay and conditions. The national officer responsible for the water industry argued that NALGO would only return to campaigning on the subject of water as a product with the election of a Labour Government. Concerns with water as a product had, he said,

> slipped into the background a bit . . . I don't think it plays a major part in our thinking at the moment anyway. It may do again say if a Labour Government got back into power. What we'd do is, we'd go and dig out all the things we were saying – we do keep them all on file, close at hand. We do talk to the Labour Party. If an election was announced, we'd then go out and dig out all these statements we've made, and all these policy documents. And we probably would then start using that sort of approach, playing more on the nature of water as product.

The main problem faced by NALGO is a reluctance by managers to involve trade unions in operational matters. Despite the rhetoric of

NALGO representatives, a working relationship with water company managers requires an acceptance of the total commodification of water. In practice, this has meant the increasing marginalization of NALGO. Despite moves towards employee involvement by many water companies, approaches made by NALGO on the issue of employee involvement have not been welcomed. Many of the objections to involving NALGO in service issues arise from the acrimony developed by the anti-privatization campaign and, indeed, many activists reciprocate the distrust and oppose the idea of NALGO involvement in operational matters. A senior regional officer argued:

> Our wish to be more involved, not just in straight terms and conditions issues, but wider issues of service and so on – to comment on that – have not generally met with a good response. They've felt that this is really trade unions being political again – getting a bit too big for their boots, and threatening management's right to manage. Although on the other hand, you do find them saying that they would welcome their employees' involvement. But I don't really think they would involve their employees through a trade union route – they'd welcome it through a management route. [But] it seems to me to be a hallmark of whether you truly want to involve people, as to whether you're prepared to give them independence in their way of putting forward issues – or at least autonomy – and it's only really through the trade union route that they can have that.

The neo-liberal recomposition of the water industry thus resulted in a serious 'identity crisis' and a crisis of 'role definition' for NALGO within the water industry. The abolition of centralized bargaining and the recomposition of 'industrial citizenship' within the internal 'regimes' of individual water companies on a more individualistic and abstract basis have precluded the involvement of autonomous labour organizations in the operational and strategic managerial decisions of the industry. The weakness of the union within the industry is highlighted by the shift in its 'political' aspirations to the macro level and the vague notion among union officials that the return of a Labour government will restore the union's power base within the institutional structure of the industry. As a result, NALGO has subsequently attempted to adopt strategies and procedures which it feels are appropriate to the private sector water industry. As I will illustrate below, this has involved attempting to depoliticize the organizational culture and structure of the union in relation to the water industry.

The reinvention of public service trade unionism: shedding the 'town hall' image

The restructuring and privatization of the water industry has forced NALGO to consider a radical 'cultural change'. The privatization of gas and transport in the early 1980s resulted in a severe 'culture shock' and the union received many complaints from members that the image and form of organization of NALGO was no longer 'relevant'. The entry of electricity and water industries into the private sector has resulted in nearly a third of NALGO membership being in the private sector. NALGO has been concerned to restructure its operations in order to make the union more relevant to private sector members. 'Promoting NALGO in the water industry' was a campaign which involved employing MORI to ascertain the views of ordinary members with respect to their opinion of NALGO, their perception of the industry following privatization and the level of morale in the union. The national officer in charge of the campaign argued that its major objective has been to adapt NALGO to the new private sector environment in which it now operates in order to resolve the 'culture shock' suffered by the union following privatization and to reconstitute the image of the union on a 'private sector' basis.

The major cultural challenge facing NALGO in the water industry is the perception among both managers and members that NALGO is a 'town hall union'. The campaign is responding to this through the promotion of the water identity of NALGO. The national officer for water observed:

> All the minority services complain like mad about the local government image, so what we're doing now is – and this appeared in the MORI survey as well as in the complaints – is to try and create a brand image. It's using a lot of advertising jargon and marketing techniques and this kind of thing, to actually try to make water members feel that [NALGO] is a water union, and take out any references to local government wherever possible.

The 'tailoring' of services to individual industries has been facilitated by the development of new technology. The monthly newspaper *Public Service* was redesigned in order to tailor the front and back pages to individual industries – in the past the union previously published only one edition, which was widely perceived to be dominated by local government issues. The recruitment and publicity material of the union with respect to the water industry was similarly cleared of any mention of local government. In respect of NALGO literature the national officer argued:

> When people get it, at least they might think, you know, NALGO is a water industry union . . . [It] will have no reference on it to local government, it will all be about water, the water industry, and the whole process is about tailoring and getting rid of the local government image . . . If there is an important local government story, or an issue, we would obviously expect them to be aware of it, or tell our members in the water industry about it. But there is a feeling that this gets rammed down their throat a bit, and we're using all these modern techniques to get away from that.

The concern to make NALGO more relevant to the new private sector industry has been reflected in the West Midlands region by attempts to adapt the 'public service' background and traditions of the union to the new private sector industry. The 'political' campaigning of NALGO in the 1980s led senior managers within Severn Trent to question its relevance to the newly privatized industry. Senior managers perceived NALGO as too political: a reflection of both its involvement in the anti-privatization campaign and its enduring image as a 'town hall union'. The result has been that NALGO has stopped campaigning on operational and environmental issues. In an attempt to display the relevance of NALGO to the neo-liberal water industry, the union has attempted to frame the annual pay negotiations in the context of the valorization imperatives of the companies. NALGO has developed an understanding of the pressures on private sector companies. The senior regional officer argued:

> One of the things that has been significant about our approach to pay negotiations, and has been applauded by some of the more enlightened managers but I think has been rather resented by some of the others, is the fact that we have not just said we want lots more money, but we have presented for two years running very carefully researched pay claims, that looks at the commercial situation of the company, that examines that and analyses it, and sets the pay claim in that context. Now, they have this prejudice that public sector, or public service, means town hall, means just excessive political dogma. It doesn't meet with the facts!

As we have seen, the 'political' autonomy of public service managers and trade unions within the planner-state directly linked the 'politics of production' with the fiscal crisis of the state. The resulting crisis destroyed the material basis of public service trade unionism as strategic and operational management were subordinated to the market and politically-mediated market proxies. The resultant restructuring of the water industry has forced trade union officers and activists to confine their activities to 'economic' struggles around the 'wage form'. The demobilization of the trade unions within the water industry was, however, only partially achieved. Trade unions still have an autonomous presence in most water companies and are becoming increasingly proficient in the decentralized bargaining arena. There is also evidence that a majority of both manual and clerical staff believe that the unions now have too little power (Nichols and O'Connell Davidson, 1993: 722) and these two factors could provide the material context for the development of a revitalized workplace unionism in the industry. There is, moreover, a residual resistance among staff to the commodification of an essential service such as water (*ibid.*: 714). The quantitative data survey alluded to above is supported by the comments of NALGO activists working within the industry, who continue to feel that they have an obligation to protect the consumer and to place the interests of the consumer before the interests of their company.

Safe in Their Hands? The New Politics of Public Service

NALGO activists argue that the commitment of waterworkers and their unions to 'public service' has endured through privatization. Despite the fact that the industry may now be investing more on capital goods projects and appears to be operating more efficiently, this is not felt to justify the privatization of the industry. While investment in capital infrastructure may be rising, and while the companies may be devoting more time and resources to the development of 'customer care' systems, there remains a feeling among many rank and file NALGO members that the company by which they are employed is less interested in the service provided to *real* consumers. This view is premised upon the perceived attempts of senior managers to get away from Fabian notions of 'public service' and to replace them with abstract neoliberal conceptions of 'public service':

> All of a sudden they're no longer consumers, they're customers. I've been brought up in a public service for 30-odd years, and I think I'm a public

servant. But they're trying to get out of this public service image now. They are a private company, who provide a service. Rather than provide a service to the consumer, [they] provide a service that the customer buys. And in a monopoly situation, the customer has no option but to buy it. I try to treat people in my work the same way that I've always treated them. But that is not the message now.

The politicized form of traditional 'public service' trade unionism resulted in many activists perceiving that they had an obligation to get involved in service and operational issues. The legitimacy for NALGO's involvement in service issues is presented as the dual role of NALGO members as both employees and consumers of an essential product. Prior to privatization, NALGO shop stewards in the West Midlands regularly attended the divisional 'Consumer Consultative Committee' (CCCs) meetings. In the context of the managerialist restructuring of the 1980s, the combining of trade union and consumer roles was very much frowned upon by senior managers. The neo-liberal restructuring and the subsequent depoliticization of the water industry has made the dual role of NALGO members as producers and consumers problematic. However, the extent to which traditional notions of 'public service' attitudes prevail among union activists is illustrated by the following assessment of the limits of trade union involvement and activity in the neo-liberal water industry by a senior shop steward:

I don't think personally that there should be any limits. After all, every member of the union is at the end of the day . . . a consumer. The service that they get is the service that any other consumer gets, and as such, if they're not pushing the service aspect, they're not only letting other consumers down, they're letting themselves down. Any suggestion that we can make to better the service, they should certainly be listening, if not as an employee then as a consumer.

Despite the depoliticization of the water industry, NALGO activists continue to make many suggestions about service to the consumer at branch level. NALGO members include supervisors and managers, and this clearly enhances the scope for involvement on operational issues. Following privatization, managers have expressed a greater willingness to listen to the suggestions of the union, and have actually taken several NALGO ideas on board. There remains an unwillingness among managers, however, to acknowledge the source of the suggestions. A shop steward commented:

> [While] a lot of the suggestions have been taken on board, OK then they come out as [company] proposals, and it's not known in meetings that the union has suggested them. Certainly, they are listening more to us than they would three or four years ago. Three or four years ago it was 'Oh no, not them again!' And I think they eventually realized that some of our ideas were not as bloody crazy as they thought, and they realized eventually that we had put a lot of thought into what we were saying. So yes, but it's not in an open way. If we had to publicize it, we'd have to do it through the branch newsletter, because management wouldn't actually say, 'This has been amended because of the union!'

The primary concern of NALGO activists and officers is thus with the 'monopoly' nature of water as a product, and the extent to which essential products such as water are not 'safe' in the care of private monopolists. NALGO continues to advocate the policy of returning the water industry to the public sector despite the fact that such a policy could alienate many of its members on higher grades who have benefited financially from the commercialization and privatization of the industry. A senior shop steward commented, with reference to his own branch:

> Now, OK, it may not please a lot of the members, because a lot of the members are making a lot of money out of privatization. Some of them are on 25 per cent bonus, and they're the people who are on £32,000 in any case. [But] I'm a firm believer that, under whatever guise, I am a public servant. Because there is no other place that they can go to get water.

While there have been important changes in the regulation of industrial relations, the above illustrates important continuities in respect of an enduring commitment of waterworkers to traditional notions of public service. While the restructuring of the labour process within the industry has shifted the 'frontier of control' away from labour, trade unions continue to enjoy an autonomous 'political' existence within the 'internal state', and are, therefore, able to challenge the ideological discourse of 'quality' and 'consumerism' on which the neo-liberal ideology of public service is premised. Indeed, the vociferous opposition of the trade unions to privatization, and the in many ways successful anti-privatization campaign co-ordinated by the trade unions, were fundamental in the determination of the regulatory regime associated with the 1989 Water Act. While OFWAT was established as a market proxy, it has an autonomous political form and this provides the space for a renewed politics of public service by the trade unions. Similarly, the opposition of the trade unions to privatization was instrumental in the creation of the NRA (now part of the Environment Agency) as an independent state regulator to monitor the environmental activities of water companies. There are signs that the autonomous 'political' form of these agencies can provide the basis for a reinvigorated public service trade unionism.

An important example of the above point is a recent series of campaigns initiated by GMBATU. Following privatization the union has attempted to maintain 'political' campaigning while attempting to distance these activities from the 'economic' collective bargaining role of the union. The main 'political' concern of GMBATU has been the way in which privatization involved a loss of public and democratic accountability. In the immediate aftermath of privatization the union launched an initiative on 'public accountability in the water industry'. This was organized around the strategy of GMBATU acquiring nominal shareholdings in the ten privatized water companies and then using environmental information supplied by FoE to raise issues of drinking water quality and pollution control at the AGMs of water companies. The campaign was designed to be a bottom–up campaign through which local activists liaised locally with FoE and attended the AGMs as GMBATU proxies. The campaign was premised on the 'political' interests of 930,000 GMBATU members as citizens rather than the 'economic' interests of GMBATU members working within the water industry. The co-ordinator of the GMBATU campaign argued that the primary motivation for the campaign was the desire to maintain the water industry as a public service accountable to the public and to defend the basic necessities of life from 'Thatcherism'.

GMBATU stressed the important distinction and separation of the 'political' campaign on the water industry and the 'economic' role of the union within the collective bargaining machinery of the industry. The campaign co-ordinator argued that the campaign involved the union acting as a 'corporate citizen' exercising its political rights to make its views known: a role which was totally discrete from the role the union played in collective bargaining machinery, which was an objective need for both employees and the water companies. The distinction, however, was not recognized by senior managers within the water industry. The campaign failed to develop at the workplace level owing to the introduction of 'confidentiality clauses' into contracts of employment and the 'intimidation' of shop stewards organizing the campaign. While this particular campaign was unsuccessful, therefore, it demonstrates the contradictions inherent to the neo-liberal form of the water industry and the way in which the struggle over the public service state is an enduring feature of the neo-liberal water industry. In the final chapter I will explore more fully the contradictions of neo-liberalism and the way it offers the potential for new forms of struggle and resistance 'in and against' the neo-liberal state.

Notes

1. This report disaggregates the trends briefly highlighted in this section and explores the important divergences between companies operating in the sector.
2. As was noted in Chapter 2, the origins and potency of public service trade unionism in the 1890s lay in the way the activities of public service workers unite the 'economic' and 'political' spheres (Hobsbawm, 1968: 158–78). This highlights the centrally important position of state workers in the development and crisis of the planner-state and the importance for capital in marginalizing and transforming public sector trade unionism.
3. The fieldwork on which this book is based took place before the amalgamation of NALGO with the National Union of Public Employees (NUPE) and the Confederation of Health Service Employees (COHSE) to form UNISON.

9 The Politics of Public Service

In this book, I have argued that in order to develop a clear understanding of the development and crisis of public service as a state ideology and practice it is necessary to analyse the development of institutional forms of public service administration and regulation in the context of the logical and historical contradictions of capital accumulation. I have argued that it is only through an understanding of the highly contradictory nature of state administration that the recent commercialization and privatization of state services can be understood. I have argued that it is necessary to see the development and crisis of public service as a manifestation of *class struggle.* The forms of public administration which I have explored in this book were historical manifestations of class struggle, and their changing institutional forms of public service provision reflect the balance of class forces at particular historical moments. In this final chapter I want to conclude by emphasizing the contradictory nature of public service and the way in which a 'value theoretical' analysis of the type presented in this book can uncover these contradictions and highlight the potential for new forms of political struggle over the form and content of public service.

In Britain, public service emerged as a state ideology and practice during the nineteenth century. During that century the contradictions of capital accumulation appeared as the physical destruction of living labour power. The intensification of the labour of the working class in the labour process depressed the 'effective demand' of the working class for privately produced utility services, and this resulted in the newly industrialized cities being plagued by disease, squalor and insanitary living conditions. As I argued in Chapter 1, the capitalist state is logically and historically premised on the maintenance of capitalist commodity relations, and the maintenance of the state as an embodiment of the 'common good' is dependent on the formal equivalence of capital and labour in the sphere of exchange. In order to maintain the formal equivalence between capital and labour in the sphere of exchange the state became increasingly involved in the regulation of public services. Throughout the nineteenth century legislation attempted to 'regulate' the production of water services through the 'legal form' of contract. Legislation was passed which attempted to force water companies to supply water services on demand and determined maximum levels of price and minimum levels of service. The legislation was resisted by water capitals as it posed a direct threat to the valorization of capital, and as a consequence the state became increasingly involved in the direct administration of water services through forms of municipal enterprise and *ad hoc* bodies and commissions.

As I argued in Chapter 1, the capitalist state is a contradictory social form and the 'political' contradictions of the state appear as the contradiction between administration and regulation. The state was a logical and historical precondition for and a historical result of the generalization of capitalist commodity relations, but was determined in a 'political' form which was not directly subordinate to capital. Municipal enterprise constituted an attempt to socialize the costs of reproducing labour without rupturing the liberal form of the state. The municipal state was a distinctive political administrative form but the weakness of labour as a class power allowed the mediation of the administrative activities of the state through the abstract forms of law and money. This was manifested in the subordination of waterworkers to the wage form and by the provision of services on the basis of fiscal probity and contractual relations of exchange. While the initial development of municipal enterprise was contradictory, therefore, it did not rupture the liberal form of the state, and the production and reproduction of labour was successfully contained within the abstract order.

The increasing resistance of labour to the commodity form and the political organization of labour towards the end of the nineteenth century did, however, rupture the liberal state form. The politics of public service increasingly became a struggle over the form of public service: an attempt by workers to capture the administrative institutions of the state and pursue their own material interests as an autonomous social movement. The direct representation of labour within the municipal state and the discretionary powers of municipal state administration resulted in a serious 'fiscal crisis' of the municipal state. The crisis of the municipal state occurred in the context of a more generalized crisis of capital accumulation and resulted in the recomposition of capital and the state on the basis of the accumulation of relative surplus value. As I mentioned in Chapter 3, this was a form of 'class compromise' which involved the recomposition of the state in a Keynesian form, and resulted in the incorporation of the autonomous movement of labour within the administrative moment of the state. This development fundamentally transformed the politics of public service.

As Burawoy (1986: 122–55) has argued, the shift from capital accumulation based on absolute surplus value to capital accumulation based on relative surplus value resulted in a shift in the form of control within the workplace. The shift from 'despotic' to 'hegemonic' regimes involved the composition of an 'internal state' within the workplace. In order to secure the consent of workers to the intensified control of the labour process, workers were incorporated as 'industrial citizens' with political rights and duties within the workplace and these arrangements were given legitimacy through the development of materially-generated ideological discourses which developed around the game-like nature of both the labour process and the institutional mechanisms of collective bargaining. In the public services these arrangements took on a particular potency. The development of centralized bargaining through the Whitely system related the pay and conditions of public servants directly to the fiscal crisis of the nation state. The socialization of capital accumulation through the KWS, moreover, allowed public service managers and workers a great deal of autonomy over the way in which services were organized and delivered. The direct employment of public servants by the state allowed the development of highly politicized forms of 'industrial citizenship' and provided the material grounding for the ideologies of public service which developed around public service management and trade unionism.

The Keynesian planner-state thus developed through class struggle and resulted in the incorporation of labour within the state in a highly contradictory way. The development of 'public service' bureaucracy allowed the demands of the labour movement as both producers and consumers to be 'planned' in the context of the valorization imperatives of an increasingly 'socialized' and 'centralized' capital. In the UK the development of the 'public service' state was legitimated through 'Fabian Socialism' which highlighted the 'democratic' and progressive nature of centralized state planning. The attempt to 'plan' water resources came up against the problem that the administrative activities of the state are necessarily realized through the regulatory forms of law and money. The resulting 'fiscal crisis' rendered the water industry increasingly ineffective and resulted in an increasingly serious institutional paralysis within the industry. Among important state actors the crisis was seen as a 'technical' problem: a problem which could be overcome through the rationalization of the state and the application of science and technology in an attempt to overcome the dysfunctions of state planning. Within the administrative moment of the nation state, hydrological and engineering 'experts' sitting on bodies such as the CAWC and the WRB attempted to tackle the emerging contradictions of the state through technocratic and managerial restructuring. The result of this was the rationalization of the water industry through *de facto* nationalization of the water industry by the 1973 Water Act.

The managerialization of the water industry was an attempt to solve the fiscal crisis of the state through technocratic and scientific rationalization. The problem was that this process of rationalization created a crisis of rationality within the industry. The Fabian social democratic ideals which underpinned the public service ethos of the industry were sacrificed in order to subject the industry to commercial and technocratic operating criteria. The enduring isolation of the industry from the dynamics of capital accumulation, however, resulted in there being no rational basis for the development of operational and strategic management decisions by state bureaucrats and managers. As a result the water industry in its post-1979 form became increasingly ineffective. The operation of the industry resulted in fiscal inflation and the constraints imposed by the state in response resulted in further cuts in investment and levels of service. The Fabian/Keynesian form of state and management *decomposed from within*, and the recomposition of the state in a form more functional for capital was legitimated through a neo-liberal discourse which highlighted the ineffectiveness which resulted from the institutional paralysis of 'managerialism'. Neo-liberalism was more than a discourse, however, and the last two decades have seen the material restructuring of the state and capital in an attempt to resolve the fiscal crisis of the planner-state water industry.

The crisis of the planner-state developed because Keynesianism involved incorporating the autonomy of labour within the administrative moment of the state. The attempt to manage capital at the macro level allowed the organization of production and distribution within individual services to be based on highly bureaucratic criteria which were underpinned by essentially social democratic ideologies. These ideologies included the notion that 'public need' should come before profit and that 'equity' was a more important value than 'efficiency'. These ideologies were underpinned by the power of labour within the labour process – not just in the public services but a generalized strength which was the main dynamic for the initial development of Keynesianism. The power of labour within the public services was, however, linked directly to the fiscal crisis of the state, and for this reason, reducing the autonomy of public service workers has been a principal focus of neo-liberal restructuring. In respect of the water industry, the above objective was initially achieved by the imposition of performance aims and finance limits in order to intensify public service labour processes. But this was only the 'economic' moment in a far more fundamental restructuring of the capital relation. Public service workers had extensive 'political' rights and duties within the workplace which, as I argued above, were underpinned by a social democratic conception of public service and the 'public interest'. The neo-liberal restructuring of public services has attempted to destroy this regime and create a form of 'hegemonic despotism' (Burawoy, 1986: 148–52) within the water industry. This has become increasingly manifest with the development of HRM/TQM within the industry. As part of an emerging 'hegemonic despotic' regime these forms of management involve an attempt to intensify the exploitation of labour within the labour process while simultaneously achieving the active consent of workers to this intensification. HRM and TQM are able to do this owing to the way in which these forms of management involve the imposition of legal and monetary forms on to the regulation of labour and the way in which this generates the mystified appearance of empowerment among public service workers.

In order to understand this it is necessary to reiterate the material contradictions underlying money and the law. Marx (1976: 711–24; 943–1084) highlighted the way in which the unity of capitalist production as a labour process and a valorization process subordinated the production and reproduction of labour-power to the abstract power of money capital. In this book I have also highlighted the importance of law in regulating the reproduction of capitalist commodity relations. Law and money are not 'things' or 'discourses' but material processes which secure the subordination of labour by capital. The importance of HRM/TQM in the water industry lies in the way it attempts to restructure the 'economic', 'political' and ideological moments of the capital relation on the basis of the abstract regulatory forms of law and money. The 'totality' of TQM is constituted by the way in which this form of management simultaneously addresses and attempts to intensify all facets of the capital relation in a systematic way. TQM implies the simultaneous decollectivization, individuation and contractualization of the labour process, the development of new individualized modes of interest mediation and 'industrial citizenship' and the imposition of a discourse which articulates ideologies of enterprise and consumerism in an attempt to legitimate this form of restructuring.

The above restructuring of the capital relation is part of a wider process of state restructuring. During the 1980s the state was recomposed in order to make the administration of water services more functional for capital. This restructuring created large, efficient entities in the form of the RWAs capable of operating as capital. This restructuring occurred in the context of a global crisis of capital over-accumulation, and the ultimate privatization of the industry is thus part of a neo-liberal accumulation strategy premised on mobilizing counter-tendencies to the over-accumulation of capital. The privatization of the water industry is thus part of a wider 'monetarist' project of imposing the 'disinterested' law of money onto the institutional forms of state and society (Clarke, 1988: 356). TQM should, then, be understood as the manifestation at the level of the labour process of the attempt to resolve the crisis and contradictions of Keynesianism through an increasing alignment of state and capital on the basis of the valorization imperatives of a globalized neo-liberal capitalism. In the case of the water sector, the state has been recomposed in the form of OFWAT whose administrative function is to safeguard the interests of water industry 'customers' while simultaneously ensuring the efficient valorization of water industry capital.

The past two decades have thus seen a transformation in the form of public service and the kinds of citizenship rights enjoyed by the users of services. In order to overcome the fiscal crisis of the planner-state there has been a recomposition of public services in an attempt to subordinate the production and distribution of services to the regulatory forms of law and money. This has resulted in the recomposition of citizenship rights on an abstract, individuated basis: an attempt to limit citizenship rights to the rights enjoyed by individual commodity owners and purchases in the market. The vitality of this new form of citizenship has been celebrated by the Conservative Party through such initiatives as the Citizen's Charter, by the Labour Party through its support for the strengthening of consumer rights and by neo-liberal state agencies and academics from a variety of perspectives who stress the empowering nature of citizenship of this type (Featherstone, 1991; Harrison, 1991; Mort, 1989). This is also the type of citizenship which the water companies and other firms have attempted to develop as part of the neo-liberal recomposition of the workplace regime. The important point that I have demonstrated in this book is that this form of citizenship does not resolve the contradictions of the public service state. Neo-liberal citizenship rights are still administered by state institutions that exist in a 'political' form which is not directly subordinate to the dynamics of neo-liberal capital accumulation. While the demobilization of organized labour has resulted in the 'emptying out' of the substantive and democratic modes of interest mediation within the state, this process cannot be total owing to the contradictory form of the capitalist state. There is, therefore, still room within the administrative moment of the state for a renewed politics of public service. There is also a sense in which the collapse of the KWS, and the fetished social democratic appearance of the 'common good' it articulated, has made the alienating and oppressive content of the state more visible. The oppressive content of neo-liberal public service can be illuminated further by emphasizing the contribution that a 'form-theoretical' analysis can make to uncovering the contradictory determination of capitalist social forms.

In this book I have developed a 'form-theoretical' analysis of the development, crisis and restructuring of the public service water industry. I have explored this process through an exploration of the social forms of existence through which this area of social life has developed historically and the logical contradictions underlying these social forms of existence. I have argued that these contradictions emanate from the capitalist 'value form' and the crises and social struggles which result from the value relations of capitalist society. The overall conclusion of this book is that the historical materialist approach developed by Marx has an enduring importance in allowing a critical insight into the fetished appearance of capitalist social forms. The concept of *value* is thus the key which enables the secrets of public service to be unlocked. In capitalist society social relations inevitably take the form of things, and this 'real mystification' has been reproduced in the analyses of public service and the state that have dominated social science over recent years. The challenge for an actual understanding of public service is to reveal the material relations underlying the mystical shell of public service. The enduring importance of Marx's labour theory of value is that it highlights the oppressive relations underlying the fetished categories of capitalist development (Clarke, 1980) and the way in which these fetished categories can be overcome through struggle (Elson, 1979: 171–4).

The value theory of labour is important in that it allows capitalism to be grasped as a contradictory, crisis-ridden process, subject to continual change. In my analysis I have attempted to demonstrate the contradictions which underpin the reconstituted neo-liberal form of the water industry. The recomposition of the water industry has not resolved the crisis of public service but has merely laid the seeds for further crisis. The second implication of value form analysis is the way in which it can contribute to overcoming the fragmentation by which capitalist exploitation is experienced. The history of public service is marked by the subordination of the interests of public servants to consumers, and this has been intensified through the development of HRM/TQM. Marx, however, demonstrated the way in which production and consumption were 'distinctions within a unity' (Marx, 1973a: 99). It is important to recognize, therefore, that neo-liberal citizenship rights are premised on the subordination of labour within the labour process. This highlights the importance of attempting to unite producers and consumers in opposition to the alienating contradictions of neo-liberal public service. A revitalized politics of public service must overcome both the traditional economism of the labour movement and the celebration of fragmentation which is currently fashionable among postmodern social movements and academics.

The politics of public service must therefore begin with the autonomous organization and struggle of public service workers against the 'economic' and 'political' forms through which their labour is subordinated to the abstract power of capital. This must be related to the creation and strengthening of networks and alliances between public service workers and social groups concerned with consumption and the environmental impact of public service provision. The focus of struggle has to be against the subordination of public service provision to the abstract power of money and the law, and a recognition that these are the processes through which human needs are subordinated to the valorization of capital. We must rediscover the totality of capitalist oppression and alienation and develop forms of political mobilization which celebrate the autonomy of social movements while moving beyond forms of fragmented struggle which are themselves manifestations of the fetished nature of political and social struggle within the capitalist order. These are the vital components for a revitalized process of struggle in and against the public service state.

Appendix

The operational performance of water companies is measured by OFWAT through the following sets of indicators.

1. 'Condition J' levels of service indicators

DG1. Raw water availability – number of customers whose water resource availability is below reference standard.
DG2. Pressure of water mains – number of customers with water main pressure below reference standard.
DG3. Interruptions to water supplies – number of customers that have had interruptions to supply without warning for longer than the reference period.
DG4. Hosepipe restriction – number of customers notified of hosepipe restrictions.
DG5. Flooding incidents from sewers – number of customers' properties where flooding from sewers has occurred more frequently than the reference period.
DG6. Response to billing queries – number and banded response times for meaningful responses to customer queries.
DG7. Response to written complaints – number and banded response time for meaningful response.
DG8. Response to development control consultations.
With regard to DG2, DG3 and DG5 companies have to demonstrate both short- and medium-term improvements and the way in which they relate to investment programmes. The reference standards for DG 1, 2, 3, 5 have where possible been set by consensus with the industry, or where this was not possible by the Director General of OFWAT after consideration of appropriate measures and definitions.

2. Other performance indicators

These relate to the water and environmental quality aspects regulated by the DWI and the NRA. OFWAT is developing mechanisms by which information on performance and projected improvements in quality can be made available for monitoring company performance.

3. Levels of activity

This is a long-term measure that is intended to provide a cross-check between level of service indicators, other performance indicators and investment in underground assets. It takes the form of an indicator of the length of water mains/sewer renewed.

4. Asset condition indicators

Standard classifications for structural and hydraulic capacity.

(*OFWAT Annual Report 1989*, London: HMSO)

Bibliography

Aglietta, M. (1979) *A Theory of Capitalist Regulation: The US Approach*, London: Verso.

Altvarter, E. (1973) 'Some problems of state interventionism', *Kapitalistate*, No. 1.

Armstrong, P. (1987) 'Engineers, management and trust', *Work, Employment and Society*, Vol. 1, No. 4, pp. 421–40.

Armstrong, P. (1989) 'Management, labour process and agency', *Work, Employment and Society*, Vol. 3, No. 3, pp. 307–22.

Auster, R. D. and Silver, M. (1979) *The State As a Firm: Economic Forces in Political Development*, The Hague: Martinus Nijhoff.

Baker, W. (1984) 'The social structure of a securities market', *American Journal of Sociology*, Vol. 89, pp. 775–811.

Baker, W. (1990) 'Market networks and corporate behaviour', *American Journal of Sociology*, Vol. 96, pp. 589– 625.

Barry, E. E. (1965) *Nationalisation in British Politics: The Historical Background*, London: Cape.

Barry, N. P. (1987a) *The New Right*, London: Croom Helm.

Barry, N. P. (1987b) 'Understanding the market', in M. Loney (ed.) *The State of the Market: Politics and Welfare in Contemporary Britain*, London: Sage.

Batstone, E., Ferner, A. and Terry, M. (1984) *Consent and Efficiency: Labour Relations and Management Strategy in the State Enterprises*, Oxford: Basil Blackwell.

Baudrillard, J. (1968) *Le system des objects*, Paris: Denoël Gonthier.

Baudrillard, J. (1970) *La société de consommation*, Paris: Gallimard.

Baudrillard, J. (1981) *For a Critique of the Political Economy of the Sign*, St Louis: Telos Press.

Baudrillard, J. (1988) *Selected Writings*, ed. M. Poster, Cambridge: Polity.

Bell, D. (1961) *The End of Ideology*, New York: Collier-Macmillan.

Bell, D. (1976) *The Cultural Contradictions of Capitalism*, New York: Basic Books.

Beynon, H. and McMylor, P. (1985) 'Decisive power: the new Tory state against the miners', in H. Beynon (ed.) *Digging Deeper: Issues in the Miners' Strike*, London: Verso.

Binns, P. (1980) 'Law and Marxism: a critique of "The general theory of law and marxism" ', *Capital and Class*, No. 10.

Birch, A. (1964) *Representative and Responsible Government*, London: Allen and Unwin.

Blanke, B. Jürgens, U. and Kastendiek, H. (1974) 'Zur neueren marxistischen Diskussion über die Analyse von Form und Funktion des bürgerlichen Staates', *Prokla*, Vol. 14, No. 5, pp. 51–102.

Bonefeld, W. (1991) 'The reformulation of state theory', in W. Bonefield and J. Holloway (eds) *Post-Fordism and Social Form: A Marxist Debate on the Post-Fordist State*, London: Macmillan.

Bonefeld, W. (1992) 'Social constitution and the form of the capitalist state', in W. Bonefeld, R. Gunn and K. Psychopedis (eds) *Open Marxism: Volume One. Dialectics and History*, London: Pluto Press.

Bonefeld, W. and Holloway, W. (1991) *Post-Fordism and Social Form: A Marxist Debate on the Post-Fordist State*, London: Macmillan.

Bowman, J. C. (1992) 'Improving the quality of our water: the role of regulation by the National Rivers Authority', *Public Administration*, Vol. 70, Winter, pp. 565–76.

Bradley, K. and Hill, S. (1983) 'After Japan: the quality circle transplant and productive efficiency', *British Journal of Industrial Relations*, Vol. 21, November, pp. 291–311.

Bradley, K. and Hill, S. (1987) 'Quality circles and managerial interests', *Industrial Relations*, Vol. 26, pp. 68–82.

Braverman, H. (1974) *Labor and Monopoly Capitalism*, New York: Monthly Review Press.

Brennan, M. (1991) 'Mismanagement and quality circles: how middle managers influence direct participation', *Employee Relations*, Vol. 13, No. 3.

Briggs, A. (1968) *Victorian Cities*, London: Pelican.

Buchanan, A. and Clapham, S. (1988) *Utilities: Preview of the Privatisation of the Water and Electricity Industries*, London: Hoare and Govett Investment Research Ltd.

Buchanan, J. and Tullock, G. (1962) *The Calculus of Consent*, Michigan: Ann Arbor.

Bullock, P. and Yaffe, D. (1975) 'Inflation, the crisis and the post-war boom', *Revolutionary Communist*, Vol. 4, No. 5.

Bullpitt, J. (1986) 'The discipline of the new democracy: Mrs Thatcher's domestic statecraft', *Political Studies*, Vol. 34, pp. 19–39.

Burawoy, M. (1979) *Manufacturing Consent: Changes in the Labour Process Under Monopoly Capitalism*, Chicago: University of Chicago Press.

Burawoy, M. (1986) *The Politics of Production*, London: Verso.

Burnham, J. (1945) *The Managerial Revolution*, Harmondsworth: Penguin.
Callaghan, B., Coote, A., Hulme, G. and Stewart, J. (1990) *Meeting Needs in the 1990s: The Future of Public Service and the Challenge for Trade Unions*, Social Policy Paper No. 2, London: Institute for Public Policy Research.
Clarke, J., Cochrane, A. and Smart, C. (1987) *Ideologies of Welfare: From Dreams to Disillusion*, London: Hutchinson.
Clarke, S. (1980) 'The value of value', *Capital and Class*, No. 10, pp. 1–17.
Clarke, S. (1988) *Keynesianism, Monetarism and the Crisis of the State*, Aldershot: Edward Elgar.
Clarke, S. (1991a) 'Marxism, sociology and Poulantzas's theory of the state', in S. Clarke (ed.) *The State Debate*, London: CSE/Macmillan.
Clarke, S. (1991b) *Marx, Marginalism and Modern Sociology: From Adam Smith to Max Weber*, 2nd edn, London: Macmillan.
Cleaver, H. (1979) *Reading Capital Politically*, Brighton: Harvester Press.
Cleaver, H. (1992) 'The inversion of class perspective in Marxian theory: from valorisation to self-valorisation', in W. Bonefeld, R. Gunn and K. Psychopedis (eds) *Open Marxism: Volume Two: Theory and Practice*, London: Pluto Press.
Clegg, S. (1989) *Frameworks of Power*, London: Sage.
Clegg, S. (1990) *Modern Organizations: Organization Studies in a Postmodern World*, London: Sage.
Coates, K. and Topham, T. (1994) *The Making of the Labour Movement: The Formation of the Transport and General Workers' Union 1870–1922*, Nottingham: Spokesman.
Cole, G. D. H. (1920) *Social Theory*, London: Methuen.
Cole, G. D. H. (1943) *Fabian Socialism*, London: Frank Cass.
Cole, G. D. H. (1950) *Socialist Economics*, London: Victor Gollancz.
Cole, G. D. H. (1972) *Self-Government in Industry*, London: Hutchinson.
Cole, G. D. H. (1973) 'Introduction', in Rousseau, J.-J., *The Social Contract and Discourses*, (ed. J. H. Brumfitt and J. C. Hall), London: Dent.
Cole, G. D. H. (1980) *Guild Socialism Restated*, London: Transaction Books.
Cousins, C. (1988) 'The restructuring of welfare work: the introduction of general management and the contracting out of ancillary services in the NHS', *Work, Employment and Society*, Vol. 2, pp. 210–28.
Coyle, A. (1985) 'Going private: the implications of privatization for women's work', *Feminist Review*, Vol. 21, pp. 5–24.
Crosland, C. A. R. (1952) 'The transition from capitalism', in R. H. S. Crossman (ed.) *New Fabian Essays*, London: Turnstile Press.
Crossman, R. H. S. (1956) *Planning for Freedom*, London: Hamish Hamilton.
Crozier, M., Huntington, S. P. and Watanuki, S. (1975) *The Crisis of Democracy: Report to the Trilateral Commission on the Governability of Liberal Democracies*, New York: New York University Press.

Dahl, R. (1956) *A Preface to Democratic Theory*, Chicago: University of Chicago Press.

Dahl, R. (1961) *Who Governs? Democracy and Power in an American City*, New Haven: Yale University Press.

Dahl, R. (1982) *Dilemmas of Pluralist Democracy: Autonomy Versus Control*, New Haven: Yale University Press.

Dahl, R. (1985) *A Preface to an Economic Theory of Democracy*, London: Polity Press.

Delbridge, R., Turnbull, P. and Wilkinson, B. (1992) 'Pushing back the frontiers: management control and work intensification under JIT/TQM factory regimes', *New Technology, Work and Employment*, Vol. 7, pp. 97–106.

Department of the Environment (1971) *The Future Management of Water in England and Wales: A Report by the Central Advisory Water Committee*, London: HMSO.

Department of the Environment (1973) *A Background to Water Reorganization in England and Wales*, London: HMSO.

Dix, B. and Williams, S. (1987) *Serving the Public, Building the Union: The History of NUPE*, London: Lawrence & Wishart.

Douglas, J. (1976) 'The overloaded crown', *British Journal of Political Science*, Vol. 6.

Du Gay, P. (1996) *Consumption and Identity at Work*, London: Sage.

Du Gay, P. and Salaman, G. (1992) 'The [cult]ure of the customer', *Journal of Management Studies*, Vol. 29, No. 5, pp. 615–33.

Dunleavy, P. (1981) 'Professions and policy change: notes towards a model of ideological corporatism', *Public Administration Bulletin*, Vol. 36, pp. 3–16.

Dunleavy, P. (1982) 'Quasi-governmental sector professionalism', in A. Barker (ed.) *Quangos in Britain*, London: Macmillan.

Dunleavy, P. and O'Leary, B. (1987) *Theories of the State: The Politics of Liberal Democracy*. London: Macmillan.

Edwards, R. (1979) *Contested Terrain: The Transformation of the Workplace in the Twentieth Century*, New York: Basic Books.

Elson, D. (1979) *Value: The Representation of Labour in Capitalism*, London: CSE Books.

Engels, F. (1987) *The Condition of the Working Class in England*, Harmondsworth: Penguin.

Fairbrother, P. (1989) 'State workers: class position and collective action', in G. Duncan (ed.) *Democracy and the State*, Cambridge: Cambridge University Press.

Fairbrother, P. (1994) *Politics and the State as Employer*, London: Mansell.

Falkus, M. E. (1967) 'The British gas industry before 1850', *Economic History Review*, Vol. 20, pp. 494–508.

Falkus, M. E. (1977) 'The development of municipal trading in the nineteenth century', *Business History*, Vol. 19, No. 2, pp. 134–61.

Featherstone, M. (1991) *Consumer Culture and Postmodernism*, London: Sage.
Ferner, A. (1985) 'Political constraints and managerial strategies: the case of working practices in British Rail', *British Journal of Industrial Relations*, No. 23, pp. 47–70.
Ferner, A. (1987) 'Public enterprises and the politics of commercialism: changing industrial relations in British and Spanish railways', *Work, Employment and Society*, Vol. 1, No. 2, pp. 179–204.
Ferner, A. (1989) *Ten Years of Thatcherism: Changing Industrial Relations in British Public Enterprises*, Warwick Papers in Industrial Relations, No. 27, Coventry: Industrial Relations Research Units, School of Industrial and Business Studies, University of Warwick.
Fevre, R. (1986) 'Contract work in the recession', in K. Purcell, S. Allen, A. Watson and S. Wood (eds) *The Changing Experience of Employment*, London: Macmillan.
Fine, B. and O'Donnell, K. (1981) 'The nationalized industries', in *Socialist Economic Review 1981*, London: Merlin.
Flanders, A. (1968) 'Trade unions in the 60s', in A. Flanders, *Management and Trade Unions*, London: Hutchinson.
Flegstein, N. (1987) 'The interorganizational power struggle: the rise of finance presidents in large corporations', *American Sociological Review*, Vol. 52, pp. 44–58.
Foster, D. (1993) 'Industrial relations in the public sector: the impact of privatisation', *Political Quarterly*, Vol. 64, No. 1, pp. 49–59.
Foster, D. and Taylor, G. (1994) *Privatization and Public Service Trade Unionism*, UWE Occasional Papers in Sociology, No. 11, Bristol: University of the West of England.
Foucault, M. (1967) *Madness and Civilization*, London: Tavistock.
Foucault, M. (1977) *Discipline and Punish: The Birth of the Prison*, Harmondsworth: Penguin.
Foucault, M. (1981) *The History of Sexuality: An Introduction*, Harmondsworth: Penguin.
Fox, A. (1985) *Man Mismanagement*, 2nd edn, London: Hutchinson.
Fredman, S. and Morris, G. (1989) *The State As Employer: Labour Law in the Public Services*, London: Mansell.
Friedman, M. (1968) 'The role of monetary policy', *American Economic Review*, Vol. 58, No. 1, pp. 1–17.
Friedman, M. (1982) *Capitalism and Freedom*, Chicago, IL: Chicago University Press.
Friedman, M. and Friedman, R. (1980) *Free to Choose*, Harmondsworth: Penguin.
Fryer, B., Manson, T. and Fairclough, A. (1978) 'Employment and trade unionism in the public services', *Capital and Class*, No. 4, Spring, pp. 70–7.
Fryer, R. H. (1989) 'Public service trade unionism in the twentieth century', in

R. Mailly, S. Dimmock and A. Sethi (eds) *Industrial Relations in the Public Services*, London: Routledge.

Fuller, L. and Smith, V. (1991) 'Consumers' reports: management by customers in a changing economy', *Work, Employment and Society*, Vol. 5, No. 1, pp. 1–16.

Galbraith, J. K. (1953) *American Capitalism and the Concept of Countervailing Power*, Boston: Houghton Mifflin.

Galbraith, J. K. (1969) *The New Industrial State*, Harmondsworth: Penguin.

Gamble, A. (1979) 'The free economy and the strong state', in R. Miliband and J. Saville (eds) *The Socialist Register 1979*, London: Merlin.

Gamble, A. (1988) *The Free Economy and the Strong State: The Politics of Thatcherism*, London: Macmillan.

George, V. and Wilding, P. (1985) *Ideology and Social Welfare*, London: RKP.

Gerstenberger, H. (1990) *Die subjektlose Gewalt. Theorie der Entstehung bürgerlicher Staatsgewalt*, Münster westfälisches: Dampfboot.

Gerstenberger, H. (1992) 'The bourgeois state form revisited', in W. Bonefeld, R. Gunn and K. Psychopedis (eds) *Open Marxism: Volume One: Dialectics and History*, London: Pluto.

Gibbon, G. and Bell, R. W. (1939) *History of the London County Council 1889–1939*, London: Macmillan.

Giddens, A. (1990) *The Consequences of Modernity*, Cambridge: Polity Press.

Glenn, E. K. and Feldberg R. L. (1979) 'Proletarianising office work', in A. Zimbalist (ed.) *Case Studies in the Labour Process*, London: Monthly Review Press.

Gorz, A. (1982) *Farewell to the Working Class: An Essay on Post-Industrial Socialism*, London: Pluto Press.

Greenbaum, J. M. (1979) *In the Name of Efficiency: Management Theory and Shopfloor Practice*, Philadelphia: Temple University Press.

Gough, I. (1975) 'State expenditure in advanced capitalism', *New Left Review*, No. 92, pp. 53–92.

Gough, I. (1979) *The Political Economy of the Welfare State*, London: Macmillan.

Grey, C. (1994) 'Career as a project of the self and labour process discipline', *Sociology*, Vol. 28, No. 2, pp. 479–97.

Habermas, J. (1987) *The Theory of Communicative Action Volume Two: Lifeworld and System: A Critique of Functionalist Reason*, Cambridge: Polity Press.

Habermas, J. (1988) *Legitimation Crisis*, Cambridge: Polity Press.

Hales, M. (1980) *Living Thinkwork: Where Do Labour Processes Come From?*, London: CSE Books.

Hall, S. (1983) 'The great moving right show', in S. Hall and M. Jacques (eds) *The Politics of Thatcherism*, London: Lawrence & Wishart.

Hall, S. (1988) *The Hard Road to Renewal: Thatcherism and the Crisis of the Left*, London: Verso.

Hall, S. (1989) 'The meaning of new times', in S. Hall and M. Jacques (eds)

New Times: The Changing Face of Politics in the 1990s, London: Lawrence & Wishart.

Hall, S. and Jacques, M. (eds) (1989) *New Times: The Changing Face of Politics in the 1990s*, London: Lawrence & Wishart.

Halperin, M. H. (1974) *Bureaucratic Politics and Foreign Policy*, Washington, DC: Brookings Institution.

Harrison, M. L. (1991) 'Citizenship, consumption and rights: a comment on B. S. Turner's theory of citizenship', *Sociology*, Vol. 25, No. 2, pp. 204–14.

Harvey, D. (1989) *The Condition of Postmodernity*, Oxford: Basil Blackwell.

Harvey, L. (1990) *Critical Social Research*, London: Unwin Hyman.

Hayek, F. A. (1944) *The Road to Serfdom*, London: Routledge & Kegan Paul.

Hayek, F. A. (1960) *The Constitution of Liberty*, London: Routledge & Kegan Paul.

Heller, A. (1974) *The Theory of Need in Marx*, London: Allison & Busby.

Heydebrand, W. (1989) 'New organizational forms', *Work and Occupations*, Vol. 16, No. 3, 323–57.

Hill, S. (1991a) 'How do you manage a flexible firm? The total quality model', *Work, Employment and Society*, Vol. 5, No. 3, pp. 397–416.

Hill, S. (1991b) 'Why quality circles failed but Total Quality Management might succeed', *British Journal of Industrial Relations*, Vol. 24, No. 4, pp. 397–413.

Hill, S. (1995) 'From quality circles to Total Quality Management', in A. Wilkinson and H. Willmott (eds) *Making Quality Critical: New Perspectives on Organizational Change*, London: Routledge.

Hinton, J. (1983) *Labour and Socialism: A History of the British Labour Movement 1867–1974*, Sussex: Wheatsheaf.

Hirsch, J. (1991a) 'Fordism and post-Fordism: the present crisis and its consequences', in W. Bonefeld and J. Holloway (eds) *Post-Fordism and Social Form: A Marxist Debate on the Post-Fordist State*, London: Macmillan.

Hirsch, J. (1991b) 'The Fordist security state and the new social movements', in S. Clarke (ed.) *The State Debate*, London: Macmillan.

HMSO (1944) *A National Water Policy*, London: HMSO, Cmnd 6515.

HMSO (1986) *Privatisation of the Water Authorities in England and Wales*, London: HMSO, Cmnd 9734.

Hobsbawm, E. J. (1968) *Labouring Men: Studies in the History of Labour*, London: Weidenfeld & Nicolson.

Hobsbawm, E. (1984) *Worlds of Labour: Further Studies in the History of Labour*, London: Weidenfeld & Nicholson.

Hodgson, G. (1984) *The Democratic Economy*, Harmondsworth: Penguin.

Hoggett, P. (1991) 'A new managerialism in the public sector', *Policy and Politics*, Vol. 19, No. 4, pp. 243–56.

Hoggett, P. (1996) 'New modes of control in the public service', *Public Administration*, Vol. 74, Spring, pp. 9–32.

Holloway, J. (1987) 'The red nose of Nissan', *Capital and Class*, No. 32, pp. 42–64.

Holloway, J. (1991) 'The Great Bear: post-Fordism and social form: a comment on Bonefeld and Jessop', in W. Bonefeld and J. Holloway (eds) *Post-Fordism and Social Form: A Marxist Debate on the Post-Fordist State*, London: Macmillan.

Holloway, J. and Picciotto, S. (1978) *State and Capital: A Marxist Debate*, London: Edward Arnold.

Holloway, J. and Picciotto, S. (1991) 'Capital, crisis and the state', in S. Clarke (ed.) *The State Debate*, London: Macmillan.

Hyman, R. (1975) *Industrial Relations: A Marxist Introduction*, London: Macmillan.

Hyman, R. (1987) 'Strategy or structure? Capital, labour and control', *Work, Employment and Society*, Vol. 1, No. 1, pp. 25–65.

Hyman, R. (1989a) *Strikes*, 4th edn, London: Macmillan.

Hyman, R. (1989b) *The Political Economy of Industrial Relations: Theory and Practice in a Cold Climate*, London: Macmillan.

IDS (1989) *Company Councils*, Study 437. London: Income Data Services Ltd.

IDS (1990) *Total Quality Management*, Study 457. London: Income Data Services Ltd.

IDS (1994) *Company Councils*, Study 561. London: Income Data Services Ltd.

IDS (1995) *Customer Care*, Study 582. London: Income Data Services Ltd.

IRS (1992) *IRS Employment Trends 516*, July.

Jenkins, A. (1994) 'Just-in-time, "regimes" and reductionism', *Sociology*, Vol. 28, No. 1, pp. 21– 30.

Jessop, B. (1990) *State Theory: Putting Capitalist States in their Place*, Cambridge: Polity Press.

Jessop, B. (1991) 'Regulation theory, post-Fordism and the state: more than a reply to Werner Bonefeld', in W. Bonefeld and J. Holloway (eds) *Post-Fordism and Social Form: A Marxist Debate on the Post-Fordist State*, London: Macmillan.

Jessop, B. (1994) 'Post-Fordism and the state', in A. Amin (ed.) *Post-Fordism: A Reader*, Oxford: Blackwell.

Jessop, B., Bonnett, K. and Bromley, S. (1990) 'Farewell to Thatcherism? Neoliberalism and "new times" ', *New Left Review*, No. 179, pp. 81–102.

Jessop, B., Bonnett, K., Bromley, S. and Ling, T. (1988) *Thatcherism: A Tale of Two Nations*, Oxford: Basil Blackwell/Polity Press.

Jordon, A. G., Richardson, J. J. and Kimber, R. H. (1977) 'The origins of the Water Act 1973', *Public Administration*, Vol. 55, No. 3, pp. 317–34.

Kay, G. and Mott, J. (1982) *Political Order and the Law of Labour*, London: Macmillan.

Keat, R. and Abercrombie, N. (1991) *Enterprise Culture*, London: Routledge.

Kessler, I. (1986) 'Shop stewards in local government revisited', *British Journal of Industrial Relations*, Vol. 24, No. 3, pp. 419–41.

Kessler, I. (1989) 'Bargaining strategies in local government', in R. Maillly, S. Dimmock and A. Sethi (eds) *Industrial Relations in the Public Services*, London: Routledge.

King, A. (1975) 'Overload: problems of governing in the 1970s', *Political Studies*, Vol. 23.

Kraft, P. (1977) *Programmes and Managers: The Routinization of Computer Programming in the United States*, New York: Springer-Verlag.

Labour Party (1989) *Meet the Challenge: Make the Change*, London: The Labour Party.

Laclau, E. (1987) 'Class war and after', *Marxism Today*, Vol. 31, No. 4.

Lash, S. and Urry, J. (1987) *The End of Organized Capitalism*, Cambridge: Polity Press.

Lash, S. and Urry, J. (1994) *Economies of Signs and Space*, London: Sage.

Legge, K. (1989) 'Human resource management: a critical analysis', in J. Storey (ed.) *New Perspectives on Human Resource Management*, London: Routledge.

Legge, K. (1995) 'HRM: rhetoric, reality and hidden agendas', in J. Storey (ed.) *Human Resource Management: A Critical Text*, London: Routledge.

Lipietz, A. (1982) 'Towards global Fordism', *New Left Review*, No. 132.

Lipietz, A. (1987) *Mirages and Miracles: The Crisis of Global Fordism*, London: Verso.

Littlechild, S. C. (1986) *Privatisation of the Water Authorities in England and Wales*, London: HMSO.

London Edinburgh Weekend Return Group (1979) *In and Against the State*, London: Pluto Press.

Luhmann, N. (1979) *Trust and Power*, New York: Wiley.

Lukes, S. (1973) *Individualism*, Oxford: Basil Blackwell.

MacInnes, J. (1987) 'Why nothing much has changed: recession, restructuring and industrial relations since 1979', in *Employee Relations*, Vol. 9, No. 1.

Mackenzie, N. (ed.) (1978) *The Letters of Sidney and Beatrice Webb*, London: Cambridge University Press.

Marx, K. (1954) *Capital, Vol. I: Capitalist Production*, London: Lawrence & Wishart.

Marx, K. (1959) *Capital, Vol. III: Capitalist Production As a Whole*, London: Lawrence & Wishart.

Marx, K. (1969) *Theories of Surplus Value, Volume Two: Ricardo, and Theories of Rent and Profit*, London: Lawrence & Wishart.

Marx, K. (1971) *A Contribution to the Critique of Political Economy*, London: Lawrence & Wishart.

Marx, K. (1973a) *Grundrisse: Foundations of the Critique of Political Economy*, London: Allen Lane.

Marx, K. (1973b) 'The Eighteenth Brumaire of Louis Bonaparte', in *Surveys from Exile. Political Writings, Volume 2*, Harmondsworth: Penguin.

Marx, K. (1974) 'The civil war in France', in *The First International and After. Political Writings, Volume 3,* Harmondsworth: Penguin.

Marx, K. (1975) 'Economic and philosophical manuscripts', in *Early Writings,* Harmondsworth: Penguin.

Marx, K. (1976) *Capital: A Critique of Political Economy, Vol. I,* Harmondsworth: Penguin.

Marx, K. and Engels, F. (1965) *The Manifesto of the Communist Party,* Peking: Foreign Language Press.

Marx, K. and Engels, F. (1970) *The German Ideology,* London: Lawrence & Wishart.

Mattick, P. (1971) *Marx and Keynes: The Limits of the Mixed Economy,* London: Merlin.

Mazier, J. (1982) 'Growth and crisis – A Marxist interpretation', in A. Boltho (ed.) *The European Economy: Growth and Crisis,* Oxford: Oxford University Press.

Melitz, J. (1959) 'The trade unions and Fabian Socialism', *Industrial and Labor Review,* Vol. 12, July.

Miliband, R. (1969) *The State in Capitalist Society,* London: Weidenfeld & Nicolson.

Miliband, R. (1970) 'The capitalist state', *New Left Review,* No. 59.

Mill, J. S. (1991) *On Liberty and Other Essays,* Oxford: Oxford University Press.

Millward, B. (1991) 'Emergence of gas and water monopolies in nineteenth century Britain: contested markets and public control', in J. Foreman-Peck (ed.) *New Perspectives in Late Victorian Economy: Essays in Quantitative Economic History 1860–1914,* London: Cambridge University Press.

Minford, P. (1987) 'The role of the social services: a view from the New Right', in M. Loney (ed.) *The State of the Market: Politics and Welfare in Contemporary Britain,* London: Sage.

Mort, F. (1989) 'The politics of consumption', in S. Hall and M. Jacques (eds) *New Times: The Changing Face of Politics in the 1990s,* London: Lawrence & Wishart.

Müller, W. and Neusüss, C. (1978) 'The "welfare state illusion" and the contradiction between wage labour and capital', in J. Holloway and S. Picciotto (eds) *State and Capital: A Marxist Debate,* London: Edward Arnold.

Murray, R. (1989) 'Fordism and post-Fordism', in S. Hall and M. Jacques (eds) *New Times: The Changing Face of Politics in the 1990s,* London: Lawrence & Wishart.

Nabb, H. (1987) *The Bristol Gas Industry 1815–1949,* Bristol: The Historical Society.

Nairn, T. (1965) 'The nature of the Labour Party', *New Left Review,* No. 27.

Nairn, T. (1972) 'The English working class', in R. Blackburn (ed.) *Ideology and Social Science,* London: Fontana.

Nairn, T. (1981) 'The crisis of the British state', *New Left Review,* No. 130.

National Consumer Council (1989) *In the Absence of Competition: A Consumer View of Public Utilities Regulation*, London: HMSO.

National Water Council (1983) *Annual Report and Accounts 1982/3*, London: HMSO.

Negri, T. (1978/9) 'Capitalist domination and working class sabotage', in *Working Class Autonomy and the Crisis*, London: CSE/Red Notes.

Negri, T. (1988) *Revolution Retrieved: Selected Writings on Marx, Keynes, Capitalist Crisis and New Social Subjects 1967–83*, London: Red Notes.

Nichols, T. (1969) *Ownership, Control and Ideology*, London: Allen & Unwin.

Nichols, T. (1980) 'Management, ideology and practice', in G. Esland and G. Salaman (eds) *Politics of Work and Organisation*, Buckingham: Open University Press.

Nichols, T. and Beynon, H. (1977) *Living With Capitalism: Class Relations in the Modern Factory*, London: Routledge & Kegan Paul.

Nichols, T. and O'Connell Davidson, J. (1993) 'Privatization and economism: an investigation amongst "Producers" in two privatized public utilities in Britain', *Sociological Review*, Vol. 41, No. 4, pp. 707–30.

Niskanen, W. (1971) *Bureaucracy and Representative Government*, New York: Aldine-Atherton.

Niskanen, W. (1973) *Bureaucracy: Servant or Master?*, London: Institute of Economic Affairs.

Nove, A. (1983) *The Economics of Feasible Socialism*, London: Allen & Unwin.

Oakland, J. S. (1989) *Total Quality Management*, London: Heinmann.

O'Connell Davidson, J. (1993) *Privatization and Employment Relations: The Case of the Water Industry*, London: Mansell.

O'Connell Davidson, J., Nichols, T. and Sun, W. (1991) *Privatization and Change: Employee Attitudes to Privatized Utilities*, Working Paper, University of Leicester.

O'Connor, J. (1973) *The Fiscal Crisis of the State*, New York: St Martin's Press.

Offe, C. (1984) *Contradictions of the Welfare State*, London: Hutchinson.

Offe, C. (1985) 'New social movements: challenging the boundaries of institutional politics', *Social Research*, Vol. 52, No. 4.

OFWAT (1990a) *Annual Report 1989*, London: HMSO.

OFWAT (1990b) *Paying for Water: A Time for Decisions*, Birmingham: OFWAT.

OFWAT (1991) *Annual Report 1990*, London: HMSO.

Ogden, S. (1991) 'The trade union campaign against water privatisation', *Industrial Relations Journal*, Vol. 22, No. 2, pp. 20–35.

Ogden, S. (1992) 'Decline and fall: national bargaining in British Water', *Industrial Relations Journal*, Vol. 24, No. 1, pp. 1–21.

Olson, M. (1965) *The Logic of Collective Action*, New Haven, CT: Yale University Press.

Olson, M. (1982) *The Rise and Decline of Nations*, New Haven, CT: Yale University Press.

Pashukanis, E.B. (1989) *Law and Marxism: A General Theory*, London: Pluto Press.

Pearson, R. (1986) 'Female workers in the First and Third Worlds: the "Greening" of women's labour', in K. Purcell, S. Allen, A. Watson and S. Wood (eds) *The Changing Experience of Employment: Restructuring and Recession*, London: Macmillan.

Pease, E. R. (1916) *The History of the Fabian Society*, London: Firfield.

Pelling, H. (1968) *Popular Politics and Society in Late Victorian Society*, London: Macmillan.

Pendleton, A. and Winterton, J. (1993) 'Public enterprise industrial relations in context', in A. Pendleton and J. Winterton (eds) *Public Enterprise in Transition: Industrial Relations in State and Privatized Corporations*, London: Routledge.

Pfeffer, N. and Coote, A. (1991) *Is Quality Good for You? A Critical Review of Quality Assurance in Welfare Services*, Social Policy Paper No. 5, London: Institute for Public Policy Research.

Pollert, A. (1988) 'Dismantling flexibility', *Capital and Class*, No. 34, Spring, pp. 42–75.

Poulantzas, N. (1973) *Political Power and Social Classes*, London: New Left Books.

Poulantzas, N. (1978) *State, Power, Socialism*, London: New Left Books.

Robson, W. A. (1935) 'The public utility services', in H. J. Laski, W. I. Jennings and W. A. Robson (eds) *A Century of Municipal Progress 1835–1935*, London: George Allen & Unwin.

Rosdolsky, R. (1974) 'Comments on the method of Marx's *Capital*', *New German Critique*, Vol. 1, No. 3.

Rosdolsky, R. (1977) *The Making of Marx's Capital*, London: Pluto.

Rose, N. (1989) *Governing the Soul: The Shaping of the Private Self*, London: Routledge.

Rose, R. (1984) *Big Government: The Programme Approach*, London: Sage.

Rose, R., Page, E., Parry, R., Guy Peters, B., Pignatelli, A. and Schmidt, K. D. (1985) *Public Employment in Western Nations*, Cambridge: Cambridge University Press.

Rubin, I. I. (1973) *Essays on Marx's Theory of Value*, Montreal: Black Rose.

Sanderson, I. (1992) 'Introduction: the context of quality in local government', in I. Sanderson (ed.) *Management of Quality in Local Government*, Harlow: Longman.

Saunders, P. (1984) ' "We can't afford democracy too much": findings from a study of regional state institutions in South East England', in *Urban and Regional Studies Working Papers*, No. 43, University of Sussex.

Saunders, P. (1985a) 'Corporatism and urban service provision', in W. Grant (ed.) *The Political Economy of Corporatism*, London: Macmillan.

Saunders, P. (1985b) 'The New Right is half right', in A. Seldon (ed.) *The Right Enlightenment*, Sevenoaks: Economic and Literary Books.

Saunders, P. (1991) *What Difference Has Water Privatisation Made?: Consumers, Shareholders and Voters*, Working Paper 80, Centre for Urban and Regional Research, University of Sussex.

Saunders, P. and Harris, C. (1990) 'Privatization and the consumer', *Sociology* Vol. 24, No. 1, pp. 57–75.

Saunders, P. and Harris, C. (1994) *Privatization and Popular Capitalism*, Buckingham: Open University Press.

Saville, J. (1973) 'The ideology of Labourism', in R. Benwick, R. N. Berki and B. Parekhi (eds) *Knowledge and Belief in Politics*, London: Allen & Unwin.

Saville, J. (1988) *The Labour Movement in Britain*, London: Faber & Faber.

Schumpeter, J. (1944) *Capitalism, Socialism and Democracy*, London: Allen & Unwin.

Schwartz, P. (1966) 'John Stuart Mill and laissez-faire: London Water', *Economica*, Vol. 33.

Scott, A. (1994) *Willing Slaves? British Workers Under Human Resource Management*, Cambridge: Cambridge University Press.

Sewell, G. (1990) 'Management information systems for JIT production', *Omega*, Vol. 18, No. 2, pp. 490–503.

Sewell, G. and Wilkinson, B. (1992) ' "Someone to watch over Me": surveillance, discipline and the just-in-time labour process', *Sociology*, Vol. 26, No. 2, pp. 271–89.

Sheldrake, J. (1991) *Industrial Relations and Politics in Britain 1880–1989*, London: Pinter.

Simon, H. (1957) *Administrative Behaviour*, 2nd edn, New York: Free Press.

Smellie, K. B. (1957) *A History of Local Government*, London: Allen & Unwin.

Smith, M. (1986) *The Consumer Case for Socialism*, Fabian Tract 513, London: Fabian Society.

Smith, P. and Morton, G. (1993) 'Union exclusion and the decollectivisation of industrial relations in contemporary Britain', *British Journal of Industrial Relations*, Vol. 31, No. 1, pp. 97–114.

Stoker, G. (1989) 'Creating a local government for a post-Fordist society: the Thatcherite project?', in J. Stewart and G. Stoker (eds) *The Future of Local Government*, London: Macmillan.

Storey, J. (1992) *Developments in the Management of Human Resources*, Oxford: Basil Blackwell.

Storey, J. and Sisson, K. (1990) 'Limits to transformation: human resource management in the British context', *Industrial Relations Journal*, Vol. 21, pp. 60–5.

Taylor, A. J. (1972) *Laissez-Faire and State Intervention in 19th Century Britain*, London: Macmillan.

Taylor, G. (1996) 'OFWAT and the regulation of change', in D. Braddon and

D. Foster (eds) *Privatization: Social Science Themes and Perspectives*, Aldershot: Dartmouth.

Terry, M. (1982) 'Organizing a fragmented workforce: shop stewards in local government', *British Journal of Industrial Relations*, Vol. 20, No. 1, pp. 97–114.

Thompson, E. P. (1978) *The Poverty of Theory and Other Essays*, London: Merlin.

Thornley, C. (1995) *The 'Model Employer' Myth: The Need for Theoretical Renewal in Public Sector Industrial Relations*, 13th Annual International Labour Process Conference, University of Central Lancashire, 5–7 April.

Vernon, R. (1980) 'Introduction', in G. D. H. Cole, *Guild Socialism Restored*, London: Transaction Books.

Wagner, A. (1962) 'Three abstracts on public finance', in R. A. Musgrave and A. Peacock (eds) *Classics on the Theory of Public Finance*, London: Macmillan.

Walsh, K. (1995) 'Quality through markets: the new public service management', in A. Wilkinson and H. Willmott (eds) *Making Quality Critical: New Perspectives on Organizational Change*, London: Routledge.

Water Resources Board (1973a) *Water Resources in England and Wales*, London: HMSO.

Water Resources Board (1973b) *The Trent Research Programme*, London: HMSO.

Webb, S. (1962) 'History (the basis of Socialism)', in *Fabian Essays*, London: George Allen & Unwin.

Webb, S. and Webb, B. (1923) *The Decay of Capitalist Civilisation*, London: George Allen & Unwin.

Webb, S. and Webb, B. (1937) *Soviet Communism: A New Civilisation*, 2nd edn, London: Victor Gollancz.

Webb, S. and Webb, B. (1963) *English Local Government, Volume Four: Statutory Authorities for Special Purposes with a Summary of the Development of Local Government Structures*, London: Frank Cass.

Webb, S. and Webb, B. (1965) *The History of Trade Unionism*, New York: Augustus M. Kelly.

Weber, M. (1968) *Economy and Society*, Berkeley: University of California Press.

Webster, F. and Robbins, K. (1993) ' "I'll be watching you": a comment on Sewell & Wilkinson', *Sociology*, Vol. 27, No. 2, pp. 243–52.

White, H. (1981) 'Where do markets come from?', *American Journal of Sociology*, Vol. 87, pp. 517–47.

Wilkinson, A., Marchington, M., Goodman, J. and Ackers, P. (1993) 'Total Quality Management and employee involvement', *Human Resource Management Journal*, Vol. 2, No. 4, pp. 1–20.

Williams, T. I. (1981) *A History of the British Gas Industry*, Oxford: Oxford University Press.

Williamson, O. E. (1975) *Market and Hierarchies: Analysis and Anti-Trust Implications,* New York: Free Press.

Williamson, O. E. (1985) *The Economic Institutions of Capitalism,* New York: Free Press.

Williamson, O. E. (1994) 'Transaction cost economics and organization theory', in N. J. Smelser and R. Swedberg (eds) *The Handbook of Economic Sociology,* Princeton, NJ: Princeton University Press.

Winchester, D. (1983) 'Industrial relations in the public sector', in G. Bain (ed.) *Industrial Relations in Britain,* Oxford: Basil Blackwell.

Wood, E. M. (1991) *The Pristine Culture of Capitalism: A Historical Essay on Old Regimes and Modern States,* London: Verso.

Wright, A. W. (1976) 'From Fabianism to Guild Socialism: the early political thought of G. D. H. Cole', *Society for the Study of Labour History,* No. 32, Spring.

INDEX